MODERN ITALIAN POETS.

MODERN
ITALIAN POETS

ESSAYS AND VERSIONS

BY

W. D. HOWELLS

WITH PORTRAITS

Essay Index Reprint Series

BOOKS FOR LIBRARIES PRESS
FREEPORT, NEW YORK

First Published 1887
Reprinted 1972

Library of Congress Cataloging in Publication Data

Howells, William Dean, 1837-1920.
  Modern Italian poets; essays and versions.

  (Essay index reprint series)
  Reprint of the 1887 ed.
  Bibliography: p.
  1. Italian poetry--18th century--History and criticism. 2. Italian poetry--19th century--History and criticism. 3. Poets, Italian.
  PQ4109.H7 1972   851'.009   72-6857
  ISBN 0-8369-7246-5

PRINTED IN THE UNITED STATES OF AMERICA

CONTENTS.

	PAGE.
INTRODUCTION	1
ARCADIAN SHEPHERDS	11
GIUSEPPE PARINI	25
VITTORIO ALFIERI	51
VINCENZO MONTI	102
UGO FOSCOLO	116
ALESSANDRO MANZONI	126
SILVIO PELLICO	175
TOMMASO GROSSI	178
LUIGI CARRER	184
GIOVANNI BERCHET	188
GIAMBATTISTA NICCOLINI	196
GIACOMO LEOPARDI	244
GIUSEPPE GIUSTI	275
FRANCESCO DALL' ONGARO	300
GIOVANNI PRATI	323
ALEARDO ALEARDI	333
GIULIO CARCANO	360
ARNALDO FUSINATO	362
LUIGI MERCANTINI	366
CONCLUSION	369

PORTRAITS.

	Page
Vittorio Alfieri	56
Vincenzo Monti	106
Ugo Foscolo	124
Alessandro Manzoni	136
Tommaso Grossi	178
Giambattista Niccolini	208
Giacomo Leopardi	248
Giuseppe Giusti	280
Francesco Dall' Ongaro	308
Giovanni Prati	326
Aleardo Aleardi	336

INTRODUCTION

This book has grown out of studies begun twenty years ago in Italy, and continued fitfully, as I found the mood and time for them, long after their original circumstance had become a pleasant memory. If any one were to say that it did not fully represent the Italian poetry of the period which it covers chronologically, I should applaud his discernment; and perhaps I should not contend that it did much more than indicate the general character of that poetry. At the same time, I think that it does not ignore any principal name among the Italian poets of the great movement which resulted in the national freedom and unity, and it does form a sketch, however slight and desultory, of the history of Italian poetry during the hundred years ending in 1870.

Since that time, literature has found in Italy the scientific and realistic development which has marked it in all other countries. The romantic school came distinctly to a close there with the close of the long period of patriotic aspiration and endeavor; but I do not know the more recent work, except in some of the novels, and I have not attempted to speak of the newer poetry represented by Carducci. The translations here are my own; I have tried to make them faithful; I am sure they are careful.

Possibly I should not offer my book to the public at all if I knew of another work in English studying even with my incoherence the Italian poetry of the time mentioned, or giving a due impression of its extraordinary solidarity. It forms part of the great intellectual movement of which the most unmistakable signs were the French revolution, and its numerous brood of revolutions, of the first, second, and third generations, throughout Europe; but this poetry is unique in the history of literature for the unswerving singleness of its tendency.

The boundaries of epochs are very obscure, and of course the poetry of the century closing in 1870 has much in common with earlier Italian poetry. Parini did not begin it, nor Alfieri; it began them, and its spirit must have been felt in the perfumed air of the soft Lorrainese despotism at Florence when Filicaja breathed over his native land the sigh which makes him immortal. Yet finally, every age is individual; it has a moment of its own when its character has ceased to be general, and has not yet begun to be general, and it is one of these moments which is eternized in the poetry before us. It was, perhaps, more than any other poetry in the world, an incident and an instrument of the political redemption of the people among whom it arose. "In free and tranquil countries," said the novelist Guerrazzi in conversation with M. Monnier, the sprightly Swiss critic, recently dead, who wrote so much and so well about modern Italian literature, "men have the happiness and the right to be artists for art's sake: with us, this would be weakness and apathy. When I write it is because I have something *to do;* my books are not productions, but deeds. Before all, here in Italy we must be men. When we have not the sword, we must take the pen. We heap together materials for building batteries and fortresses, and it is our misfortune if these structures are not works of art. To write slowly, coldly, of our times and of our country, with the set purpose of creating a *chef-d'œuvre,* would be almost an impiety. When I compose a book, I think only of freeing my soul, of imparting my idea or my belief. As vehicle, I choose the form of romance, since it is popular and best liked at this day; my picture is my thoughts, my doubts, or my dreams. I begin a story to draw the crowd; when I feel that I have caught its ear, I say what I have to say; when I think the lesson is growing tiresome, I take up the anecdote again; and whenever I can leave it, I go back to my moralizing. Detestable æsthetics, I grant you; my works of siege will be destroyed after the war, I don't doubt; but what does it matter?"

II

THE political purpose of literature in Italy had become conscious long before Guerrazzi's time; but it was the motive of poetry long before it became conscious. When Alfieri, for example, began to write, in the last quarter of the eighteenth century, there was no reason to suppose that the future of Italy was ever to differ very much from its past. Italian civilization had long worn a fixed character, and Italian literature had reflected its traits; it was soft, unambitious, elegant, and trivial. At that time Piedmont had a king whom she loved, but not that free constitution which she has since shared with the whole peninsula. Lombardy had lapsed from Spanish to Austrian despotism; the Republic of Venice still retained a feeble hold upon her wide territories of the main-land, and had little trouble in drugging any intellectual aspiration among her subjects with the sensual pleasures of her capital. Tuscany was quiet under the Lorrainese dukes who had succeeded the Medici; the little states of Modena and Parma enjoyed each its little court and its little Bourbon prince, apparently without a dream of liberty; the Holy Father ruled over Bologna, Ferrara, Ancona, and all the great cities and towns of the Romagna; and Naples was equally divided between the Bourbons and the bandits. There seemed no reason, for anything that priests or princes of that day could foresee, why this state of things should not continue indefinitely; and it would be a

INTRODUCTION.

long story to say just why it did not continue. What every one knows is that the French revolution took place, that armies of French democrats overran all these languid lordships and drowsy despotisms, and awakened their subjects, more or less willingly or unwillingly, to a sense of the rights of man, as Frenchmen understood them, and to the approach of the nineteenth century. The whole of Italy fell, directly or indirectly, under French sway; the Piedmontese and Neapolitan kings were driven away, as were the smaller princes of the other states; the Republic of Venice ceased to be, and the Pope became very much less a prince, if not more a priest, than he had been for a great many ages. In due time French democracy passed into French imperialism, and then French imperialism passed altogether away; and so after 1815 came the Holy Alliance with its consecrated contrivances for fettering mankind. Lombardy, with all Venetia, was given to Austria; the dukes of Parma, of Modena, and Tuscany were brought back and propped up on their thrones again. The Bourbons returned to Naples, and the Pope's temporal glory and power were restored to him. This condition of affairs endured, with more or less disturbance from the plots of the Carbonari and many other ineffectual aspirants and conspirators, until 1848, when, as we know, the Austrians were driven out, as well as the Pope and the various princes small and great, except the King of Sardinia, who not only gave a constitution to his people, but singularly kept the oath he swore to support it. The Pope and the other princes, even the Austrians, had given constitutions and sworn oaths, but their memories were bad, and their repute for veracity was so poor that they were not believed or trusted. The Italians had then the idea of freedom and independence, but not of unity, and their enemies easily broke, one at a time, the power of states which, even if bound together, could hardly have resisted their attack. In a little while the Austrians were once more in Milan and Venice, the dukes and grand-dukes in their different places, the Pope in Rome, the Bourbons in Naples, and all was as if nothing had been, or worse than nothing, except in Sardinia, where the constitution was still maintained, and the foundations of the present kingdom of Italy were laid. Carlo Alberto had abdicated on that battle-field where an Austrian victory over the Sardinians sealed the fate of the Italian states allied with him, and his son, Victor Emmanuel, succeeded him. As to what took place ten years later, when the Austrians were finally expelled from Lombardy, and the transitory sovereigns of the duchies and of Naples flitted for good, and the Pope's dominion was reduced to the meager size it kept till 1871, and the Italian states were united under one constitutional king — I need not speak.

In this way the governments of Italy had been four times wholly changed, and each of these changes was attended by the most marked variations in the intellectual life of the people; yet its general tendency always continued the same.

III

The longing for freedom is the instinct of self-preservation in literature; and, consciously or unconsciously, the Italian poets of the last hundred years constantly inspired the Italian people with ideas of liberty and independence. Of course the popular movements affected literature in turn; and I should by no means attempt to say which had been the greater agency of progress. It is not to be supposed that a man like Alfieri, with all his tragical eloquence against tyrants, arose singly out of a perfectly servile society. His time was, no doubt, ready for him, though it did not seem so; but, on the other hand, there is no doubt that he gave not only an utterance but a mighty impulse to contemporary thought and feeling. He was in literature what the revolution was in politics, and if hardly any principle that either sought immediately to establish now stands, it is none the less certain that the time had come to destroy what they overthrew, and that what they overthrew was hopelessly vicious.

In Alfieri the great literary movement came from the north, and by far the larger number of the writers of whom I shall have to speak were northern Italians. Alfieri may represent for us the period of time covered by the French democratic conquests. The principal poets under the Italian governments of Napoleon during the first twelve years of this century were Vincenzo Monti and Ugo Foscolo — the former a Ferrarese by birth and the latter a Greco-Venetian. The literary as well as the political center was then Milan, and it continued to be so for many years after the return of the Austrians, when the so-called School of Resignation flourished there. This epoch may be most intelligibly represented by the names of Manzoni, Silvio Pellico, and Tommaso Grossi — all Lombards. About 1830 a new literary life began to be felt in Florence under the indifferentism or toleration of the grand-dukes. The chiefs of this school were Giacomo Leopardi; Giambattista Niccolini, the author of certain famous tragedies of political complexion; Guerrazzi, the writer of a great number of revolutionary romances; and Giuseppe Giusti, a poet of very marked and peculiar powers, and perhaps the greatest political satirist of the century. The chief poets of a later time were Aleardo Aleardi, a Veronese; Giovanni Prati, who was born in the Trentino, near the Tyrol; and Francesco Dall Ongaro, a native of Trieste. I shall mention all these and others particularly hereafter, and I have now only named them to show how almost entirely the literary life of militant Italy sprang from the north. There were one or two Neapolitan poets of less note, among whom was Gabriele Rosetti, the father of the English Rosettis, now so well known in art and literature.

IV

In dealing with this poetry, I naturally seek to give its universal and æsthetic flavor wherever it is separable from its political quality; for I should not hope to interest any one else in what I had myself often found very tiresome. I suspect, indeed, that political satire and invective are not relished best in free countries. No danger attends their exercise; there is none of the charm of secrecy or the pleasure of transgression in their production; there is no special poignancy to free administrations in any one of ten thousand assaults upon them; the poets leave this sort of thing mostly to the newspapers. Besides, we have not, so to speak, the grounds that such a long-struggling people as the Italians had for the enjoyment of patriotic poetry. As an average American, I have found myself very greatly embarrassed when required, by Count Alfieri, for example, to hate tyrants. Of course I do hate them in a general sort of way; but having never seen one, how is it possible for me to feel any personal fury toward them? When the later Italian poets ask me to loathe spies and priests I am equally at a loss. I can hardly form the idea of a spy, of an agent of the police, paid to haunt the steps of honest men, to overhear their speech, and, if possible, entrap them into a political offense. As to priests — well, yes, I suppose they are bad, though I do not know this from experience; and I find them generally upon acquaintance very amiable. But

1*

all this was different with the Italians: they had known, seen, and felt tyrants, both foreign and domestic, of every kind; spies and informers had helped to make their restricted lives anxious and insecure; and priests had leagued themselves with the police and the oppressors until the Church, which should have been kept a sacred refuge from all the sorrows and wrongs of the world, became the most dreadful of its prisons. It is no wonder that the literature of these people should have been so filled with the patriotic passion of their life; and I am not sure that literature is not as nobly employed in exciting men to heroism and martyrdom for a great cause as in the purveyance of mere intellectual delights. What it was in Italy when it made this its chief business we may best learn from an inquiry that I have at last found somewhat amusing. It will lead us over vast meadows of green baize enameled with artificial flowers, among streams that do nothing but purl. In this region the shadows are mostly brown, and the mountains are invariably horrid; there are tumbling floods and sighing groves; there are naturally nymphs and swains; and the chief business of life is to be in love and not to be in love; to burn and to freeze without regard to the mercury. Need I say that this region is Arcady?

ARCADIAN SHEPHERDS

ONE day, near the close of the seventeenth century, a number of ladies and gentlemen — mostly poets and poetesses according to their thinking — were assembled on a pleasant hill in the neighborhood of Rome. As they lounged upon the grass, in attitudes as graceful and picturesque as they could contrive, and listened to a sonnet or an ode with the sweet patience of their race, — for they were all Italians, — it occurred to the most conscious man among them that here was something uncommonly like the Golden Age, unless that epoch had been flattered. There had been reading and praising of odes and sonnets the whole blessed afternoon, and now he cried out to the complaisant, canorous company, "Behold Arcadia revived in us!"

This struck everybody at once by its truth. It struck, most of all, a certain Giovan Maria Crescimbeni, honored in his day and despised in ours as a poet and critic. He was of a cold, dull temperament; "a mind half lead, half wood," as one Italian writer calls him; but he was an inveterate maker of verses, and he was wise in his own generation. He straightway proposed to the tuneful *abbés, cavalieri serventi,* and *précieuses,* who went singing and love-making up and down Italy in those times, the foundation of a new academy, to be called the Academy of the Arcadians.

Literary academies were then the fashion in Italy, and every part of the peninsula abounded in them. They bore names fanciful or grotesque, such as The Ardent, The Illuminated, The Unconquered, The Intrepid, or The Dissonant, The Sterile, The Insipid, The Obtuse, The Astray, The Stunned, and they were all devoted to one purpose, namely, the production and the perpetuation of twaddle. It is prodigious to think of the incessant wash of slip-slop which they poured out in verse; of the grave disputations they held upon the most trivial questions; of the inane formalities of their sessions. At the meetings of a famous academy in Milan, they placed in the chair a child just able to talk; a question was proposed, and the answer of the child, whatever it was, was held by one side to solve the problem, and the debates, *pro* and *con,* followed upon this point. Other academies in other cities had other follies; but whatever the absurdity, it was encouraged alike by Church and State, and honored by all the great world. The governments of Italy in that day, whether lay or clerical, liked nothing so well as to have the intellectual life of the nation squandered in the trivialities of the academies — in their debates about nothing, their odes and madrigals and masks and sonnets; and the greatest politeness you could show a stranger was to invite him to a sitting of your academy;

to be furnished with a letter to the academy in the next city was the highest favor you could ask for yourself.

In literature, the humorous Bernesque school had passed; Tasso had long been dead; and the Neapolitan Marini, called the Corrupter of Italian poetry, ruled from his grave the taste of the time. This taste was so bad as to require a very desperate remedy, and it was professedly to counteract it that the Academy of the Arcadians had arisen.

The epoch was favorable, and, as Emiliani-Giudici (whom we shall follow for the present) teaches, in his History of Italian Literature, the idea of Crescimbeni spread electrically throughout Italy. The gayest of the finest ladies and gentlemen the world ever saw, the *illustrissimi* of that polite age, united with monks, priests, cardinals, and scientific thinkers in establishing the Arcadia; and even popes and kings were proud to enlist in the crusade for the true poetic faith. In all the chief cities Arcadian colonies were formed, "dependent upon the Roman Arcadia, as upon the supreme Arch-Flock," and in three years the Academy numbered thirteen hundred members, every one of whom had first been obliged to give proof that he was a good poet. They prettily called themselves by the names of shepherds and shepherdesses out of Theocritus, and, being a republic, they refused to own any earthly prince or ruler, but declared the Baby Jesus to be the Protector of Arcadia. Their code of laws was written in elegant Latin by a grave and learned man, and inscribed upon tablets of marble.

According to one of the articles, the Academicians must study to reproduce the customs of the ancient Arcadians and the character of their poetry; and straightway "Italy was filled on every hand with Thyrses, Menalches, and Melibœuses, who made their harmonious songs resound the names of their Chlorises, their Phyllises, their Niceas; and there was poured out a deluge of pastoral compositions," some of them by "earnest thinkers and philosophical writers, who were not ashamed to assist in sustaining that miserable literary vanity which, in the history of human thought, will remain a lamentable witness to the moral depression of the Italian nation."

As a pattern of perfect poetizing, these artless nymphs and swains chose Constanzo, a very fair poet of the sixteenth century. They collected his verse, and printed it at the expense of the Academy; and it was established without dissent that each Arcadian in turn, at the hut of some conspicuous shepherd, in the presence of the keeper (such was the jargon of those most amusing unrealities), should deliver a commentary upon some sonnet of Constanzo. As for Crescimbeni, who declared that Arcadia was instituted " strictly for the purpose of exterminating bad taste and of guarding against its revival, pursuing it continually, wherever it should pause or lurk, even to the most remote and unconsidered villages and hamlets "— Crescimbeni could not do less than write four dialogues, as he did, in which he evolved from four of Constanzo's sonnets all that was necessary for Tuscan lyric poetry.

"Thus," says Emiliani-Giudici, referring to the crusading intent of Crescimbeni, "the Arcadians were a sect of poetical Sanfedists, who, taking for example the zeal and performance of San Domingo de Guzman, proposed to renew in literature the scenes of the Holy Office among the Albigenses. Happily, the fire of Arcadian verse did not really burn! The institution was at first derided, then it triumphed and prevailed in such fame and greatness that, shining forth like a new sun, it consumed the splendor of the lesser lights of heaven, eclipsing the glitter of all those academies — the Thunderstruck, the Extravagant, the Humid, the Tipsy, the Imbeciles, and the like — which had hitherto formed the glory of the Peninsula."

I

GIUSEPPE TORELLI, a charming modern Italian writer, in a volume called *Paessaggi e Profili* (Landscapes and Profiles), makes a study of Carlo Innocenzo Frugoni, one of the most famous of the famous Arcadian shepherds; and from this we may learn something of the age and society in which such a folly could not only be possible but illustrious. The patriotic Italian critics and historians are apt to give at least a full share of blame to foreign rulers for the corruption of their nation, and Signor Torelli finds the Spanish domination over a vast part of Italy responsible for the degradation of Italian mind and manners in the seventeenth century. He declares that, because of the Spaniards, the Italian theater was then silent, "or filled with the noise of insipid allegories"; there was little or no education among the common people; the slender literature that survived existed solely for the amusement and distinction of the great; the army and the Church were the only avenues of escape from obscurity and poverty; all classes were sunk in indolence.

The social customs were mostly copied from France, except that purely Italian invention, the *cavaliere servente*, who was in great vogue. But there were everywhere in the cities coteries of fine ladies, called *preziose*, who were formed upon the French *précieuses* ridiculed by Molière, and were, I suppose, something like what is called in Boston demi-semi-literary ladies — ladies who cultivated alike the muses and the modes. The preziose held weekly receptions at their houses, and assembled poets and cavaliers from all quarters, who entertained the ladies with their lampoons and gallantries, their madrigals and gossip, their sonnets and their repartees. "Little by little the poets had the better of the cavaliers: a felicitous rhyme was valued more than an elaborately constructed compliment." And this easy form of literature became the highest fashion. People hastened to call themselves by the sentimental pastoral names of the Arcadians, and almost forgot their love-intrigues so much were they absorbed in the production and applause of "toasts, epitaphs for dogs, verses on wagers, epigrams on fruits, on Echo, on the Marchioness's canaries, on the Saints. These were read here and repeated there, declaimed in the public resorts and on the promenades," and gravely studied and commented on. A strange and surprising jargon arose, the utterance of the feeblest and emptiest affectation. " In those days eyes were not eyes, but pupils; not pupils, but orbs; not orbs, but the Devil knows what," says Signor Torelli, losing patience. It was the golden age of pretty words; and as to the sense of a composition, good society troubled itself very little about that. Good society expressed itself in a sort of poetical gibberish, " and whoever had said, for example, Muses instead of Castalian Divinities, would have passed for a low-bred person dropped from some mountain village. Men of fine mind, rich gentlemen of leisure, brilliant and accomplished ladies, had resolved that the time was come to lose their wits academically."

II

In such a world Arcadia flourished; into such a world that illustrious shepherd, Carlo Innocenzo Frugoni, was born. He was the younger son of a noble family of Genoa, and in youth was sent into a cloister as a genteel means of existence rather than from regard to his own wishes or fitness. He was, in fact, of a very gay and mundane temper, and escaped from his monastery as soon as ever he could, and spent his long life thereafter at the comfortable court of Parma, where he sang with great constancy the fortunes of varying dynasties and celebrated in his verse all the polite events of society. Of course, even a life so pleasant as this had its little pains and mortifications; and it is history that when, in 1731, the last duke of the Farnese family died, leaving a widow, "Frugoni predicted and maintained in twenty-five sonnets that she would yet give an heir to the duke; but in spite of the twenty-five sonnets the affair turned out otherwise, and the extinction of the house of Farnese was written."

Frugoni, however, was taken into favor by the Spanish Bourbon who succeeded, and after he had got himself unfrocked with infinite difficulty (and only upon the intercession of divers princes and prelates), he was as happy as any man of real talent could be who devoted his gifts to the merest intellectual trifling. Not long before his death he was addressed by one that wished to write his life. He made answer that he had been a versifier and nothing more, epigrammatically recounted the chief facts of his career, and ended by saying, "of what I have written it is not worth while to speak"; and posterity has upon the whole agreed with him, though, of course, no edition of the Italian classics would be perfect without him. We know this from the classics of our own tongue, which abound in marvels of insipidity and emptiness.

But all this does not make him less interesting as a figure in that amusing literarified society; and we may be glad to see him in Parma with Signor Torelli's eyes, as he " issues smug, ornate, with his well-fitting, polished shoe, his handsome leg in its neat stocking, his whole immaculate person, and his demure visage, and, gently sauntering from Casa Caprara, takes his way toward Casa Landi."

I do not know Casa Landi; I have never seen it; and yet I think I can tell you of it: a gloomy-fronted pile of Romanesque architecture, the lower story remarkable for its weather-stained, vermiculated stone, and the ornamental iron gratings at the windows. The *porte-cochère* stands wide open and shows the leaf and blossom of a lovely garden inside, with a tinkling fountain in the midst. The marble nymphs and naiads inhabiting the shrubbery and the water are already somewhat time-worn, and have here and there a touch of envious mildew; but as yet their noses are unbroken, and they have all the legs and arms that the sculptor designed them with; and the fountain, which after disasters must choke, plays prettily enough over their nude loveliness; for it is now the first half of the eighteenth century, and Casa Landi is the uninvaded sanctuary of Illustrissimi and Illustrissime. The resplendent porter who admits our melodious Abbate Carlo, and the gay lackey who runs before his smiling face to open the door of the *sala* where the company is assembled, may have had nothing to speak of for breakfast, but they are full of zeal for the grandeur they serve, and would not know what the rights of man were if you told them. They, too, have their idleness and their intrigues and their life of pleasure; but, poor souls! they fade pitiably in the magnificence of that noble assembly in the sala. What coats of silk and waistcoats of satin, what trig rapiers and flowing wigs and laces and ruffles; and, ah me! what hoops and brocades, what paint and patches! Behind the chair of every lady stands her cavaliere servente, or bows before her with a cup of chocolate, or, sweet abasement! stoops to adjust the foot-stool better to her satin shoe. There is a buzz of satirical expectation, no doubt, till the abbate arrives, "and then, after the first compliments and obeisances," says Signor Torelli, "he throws his hat upon the great arm-chair, recounts the chronicle of the gay world," and prepares for the special entertainment of the occasion.

"'What is there new on Parnassus?' he is probably asked.

"'Nothing', he replies, 'save the bleating of a lambkin lost upon the lonely heights of the sacred hill.'

"'I'll wager,' cries one of the ladies, 'that the shepherd who has lost this lambkin is our Abbate Carlo!'

"'And what can escape the penetrating eye of Aglauro Cidonia?' retorts Frugoni, softly, with a modest air.

"'Let us hear its bleating!' cries the lady of the house.

"'Let us hear it!' echo her husband and her cavaliere servente.

"'Let us hear it!' cry one, two, three, a half-dozen, visitors.

"Frugoni reads his new production; ten exclamations receive the first strophe; the second awakens twenty *evvivas;* and when the reading is ended the noise of the plaudits is so great that they cannot be counted. His new production has cost Frugoni half an hour's work; it is possibly the answer to some Macænas who has invited him to his country-seat, or the funeral eulogy of some well-known cat. Is fame bought at so cheap a rate? He is a fool who would buy it dearer; and with this reasoning, which certainly is not without foundation, Frugoni remained Frugoni when he might have been something very much better. . .
If a bird sang, or a cat sneezed, or a dinner was given, or the talk turned upon anything no matter how remote from poetry, it was still for Frugoni an invitation to some impromptu effusion. If he pricked his finger in mending a pen, he called from on high the god of Lemnos and all the iron-workers of Olympus, not excepting Mars, whom it was not reasonable to disturb for so little, and launched innumerable reproaches at them, since without their invention of arms a penknife would never have been made. If the heavens cleared up after a long rain, all the signs of the zodiac were laid under contribution and charged to give an account of their performance. If somebody died, he instantly poured forth rivers of tears in company with the nymphs of Eridanus and Heliades; he upbraided Phæthon, Themis, the Shades of Erebus,

and the Parcæ. . . The Amaryllises, the Dryads, the Fauns, the woolly lambs, the shepherds, the groves, the demigods, the Castalian Virgins, the loose-haired nymphs, the leafy boughs, the goat-footed gods, the Graces, the pastoral pipes, and all the other sylvan rubbish were the prime materials of every poetic composition."

III

Signor Torelli is less severe than Emiliani-Giudici upon the founders of the Arcadia, and thinks they may have had intentions quite different from the academical follies that resulted; while Leigh Hunt, who has some account of the Arcadia in his charming essay on the Sonnet, feels none of the national shame of the Italian critics, and is able to write of it with perfect gayety. He finds a reason for its amazing success in the child-like traits of Italian character; and, reminding his readers that the Arcadia was established in 1690, declares that what the Englishmen of William and Mary's reign would have received with shouts of laughter, and the French under Louis XIV. would have corrupted and made perilous to decency, "was so mixed up with better things in these imaginative and, strange as it may seem, most unaffected people, the Italians,— for such they are,—

that, far from disgusting a nation accustomed to romantic impulses and to the singing of poetry in their streets and gondolas, their gravest and most distinguished men and, in many instances, women, too, ran childlike into the delusion. The best of their poets," the sweet-tongued Filicaja among others, "accepted farms in Arcadia forthwith; . . . and so little transitory did the fashion turn out to be, that not only was Crescimbeni its active officer for eight-and-thirty years, but the society, to whatever state of insignificance it may have been reduced, exists at the present moment."

Leigh Hunt names among Englishmen who were made Shepherds of Arcadia, Malthias, author of the " Pursuits of Literature," and Joseph Cowper, "who wrote the Memoirs of Tassoni and an historical memoir of Italian tragedy," Haly, and Mrs. Thrale, as well as those poor Della Cruscans whom bloody-minded Gifford champed between his tusked jaws in his now forgotten satires.

Pope Pius VII. gave the Arcadians a suite of apartments in the Vatican; but I dare say the wicked tyranny now existing at Rome has deprived the harmless swains of this shelter, if indeed they had not been turned out before Victor Emmanuel came.

In the chapter on the Arcadia, with which Vernon Lee opens her admirable Studies of the Eighteenth Century in Italy, she tells us of several visits which she recently paid to the Bosco Parrasio, long the chief fold of the Academy. She found it with difficulty on the road to the

Villa Pamphili, in a neighborhood wholly ignorant of Arcadia and of the relation of Bosco Parrasio to it. "The house, once the summer resort of Arcadian sonneteers, was now abandoned to a family of market-gardeners, who hung their hats and jackets on the marble heads of improvvisatori and crowned poetesses, and threw their beans, maize, and garden-tools into the corners of the desolate reception-rooms, from whose mildewed walls looked down a host of celebrities — brocaded doges, powdered princesses, and scarlet-robed cardinals, simpering drearily in their desolation," and "sad, haggard poetesses in sea-green and sky-blue draperies, with lank, powdered locks and meager arms, holding lyres; fat, ill-shaven priests in white bands and mop-wigs; sonneteering ladies, sweet and vapid in dove-colored stomachers and embroidered sleeves; jolly extemporary poets, flaunting in many-colored waistcoats and gorgeous shawls."

But whatever the material adversity of Arcadia, it still continues to reward ascertained merit by grants of pasturage out of its ideal domains. Indeed, it is but a few years since our own Longfellow, on a visit to Rome, was waited upon by the secretary of the Arch-Flock, and presented, after due ceremonies and the reading of a floral and herbaceous sonnet, with a parchment bestowing upon him some very magnificent possessions in that extraordinary dreamland. In telling me of this he tried to recall his Arcadian name, but could only remember that it was "Olympico something."

GIUSEPPE PARINI

I

IN 1748 began for Italy a peace of nearly fifty years, when the Wars of the Succession, with which the contesting strangers had ravaged her soil, absolutely ceased. In Lombardy the Austrian rulers who had succeeded the Spaniards did and suffered to be done many things for the material improvement of a province which they were content to hold, while leaving the administration mainly to the Lombards; the Spanish Bourbon at Naples also did as little harm and as much good to his realm as a Bourbon could; Pier Leopoldo of Tuscany, Don Filippo I. of Parma, Francis III. of Modena, and the Popes Benedict XIV., Clement XIV., and Pius VI. were all disposed to be paternally beneficent to their peoples, who at least had repose under them, and in this period gave such names to science as those of Galvani and Volta, to humanity that of Beccaria, to letters those of Alfieri, Filicaja, Goldoni, Parini, and many others.

But in spite of the literary and scientific activity of the period, Italian society was never quite so fantastically immoral as in this long peace, which was broken only by the invasions of the French republic. A wide-spread sentimentality, curiously mixed of love and letters, enveloped the peninsula. Commerce, politics, all the business of life, went on as usual under the roseate veil which gives its hue to the social history of the time; but the idea which remains in the mind is one of a tranquillity in which every person of breeding devoted himself to the cult of some muse or other, and established himself as the conventional admirer of his neighbor's wife. The great Academy of Arcadia, founded to restore good taste in poetry, prescribed conditions by which everybody, of whatever age or sex, could become a poetaster, and good society expected every gentleman and lady to be in love. The Arcadia still exists, but that gallant society hardly survived the eighteenth century. Perhaps the greatest wonder about it is that it could have lasted so long as it did. Its end was certainly not delayed for want of satirists who perceived its folly and pursued it with scorn. But this again only brings one doubt, often felt, whether satire ever accomplished anything beyond a lively portraiture of conditions it proposed to reform.

It is the opinion of some Italian critics that Italian demoralization began with the reaction against Luther, when the Jesuits rose to supreme power in the Church and gathered the whole education of the young into the hands of the priests. Cesare Cantù, whose book on *Parini ed il suo Secolo* may be read with pleasure and instruction by such as like to know more fully the time of which I speak, was of this mind; he became before his death a leader of the clerical party in Italy, and may be supposed to be without unfriendly prejudice. He alleges that the priestly education made the Italians *literati* rather than citizens; Latinists, poets, instead of good magistrates, workers, fathers of families; it cultivated the memory at the expense of the judgment, the fancy at the cost of the reason, and made them selfish, polished, false; it left a boy " apathetic, irresolute, thoughtless, pusillanimous; he flattered his superiors and hated his fellows, in each of whom he dreaded a spy." He knew the beautiful and loved the grandiose; his pride of family and ancestry was inordinately pampered. What other training he had was in the graces and accomplishments; he was thoroughly instructed in so much of warlike exercise as enabled him to handle a rapier perfectly and to conduct or fight a duel with punctilio.

But he was no warrior; his career was peace. The old medieval Italians who had combated like lions against the French and Germans and against each other, when resting from the labors and the high conceptions which have left us the chief sculptures and architecture of the Peninsula, were dead; and their posterity had almost ceased to know war. Italy had indeed still remained a battle-ground, but not for Italian quarrels nor for Italian swords; the powers which, like Venice, could afford to have quarrels of their own, mostly hired other people to fight them out. All the independent states of the Peninsula had armies, but armies that did nothing; in Lombardy, neither

Frenchman, Spaniard, nor Austrian had been able to recruit or draft soldiers; the flight of young men from the conscription depopulated the province, until at last Francis II. declared it exempt from military service; Piedmont, the Macedon, the Bœotia of that Greece, alone remained warlike, and Piedmont was alone able, when the hour came, to show Italy how to do for herself.

Yet, except in the maritime republics, the army, idle and unwarlike as it was in most cases, continued to be one of the three careers open to the younger sons of good family; the civil service and the Church were the other two. In Genoa, nobles had engaged in commerce with equal honor and profit; nearly every argosy that sailed to or from the port of Venice belonged to some lordly speculator; but in Milan a noble who descended to trade lost his nobility, by a law not abrogated till the time of Charles IV. The nobles had therefore nothing to do. They could not go into business; if they entered the army it was not to fight; the civil service was of course actually performed by subordinates; there were not cures for half the priests, and there grew up that odd, polite rabble of *abbati*, like our good Frugoni, priests without cures, sometimes attached to noble families as chaplains, sometimes devoting themselves to literature or science, sometimes leading lives of mere leisure and fashion; they were mostly of plebeian origin when they did anything at all besides pay court to the ladies.

In Milan the nobles were exempt from many taxes paid by the plebeians; they had separate courts of law, with judges of their own order, before whom a plebeian plaintiff appeared with what hope of justice can be imagined. Yet they were not oppressive; they were at worst only insolent to their inferiors, and they commonly used them with the gentleness which an Italian can hardly fail in. There were many ties of kindness between the classes, the memory of favors and services between master and servant, landlord and tenant, in relations which then lasted a life-time, and even for generations. In Venice, where it was one of the high privileges of the patrician to spit from his box at the theater upon the heads of the people in the pit, the familiar bond of patron and client so endeared the old republican nobles to the populace that the Venetian poor of this day, who know them only by tradition, still lament them. But, on the whole, men have found it at Venice, as elsewhere, better not to be spit upon, even by an affectionate nobility.

The patricians were luxurious everywhere. In Rome they built splendid palaces, in Milan they gave gorgeous dinners. Goldoni, in his charming memoirs, tells us that the Milanese of his time never met anywhere without talking of eating, and they did eat upon all possible occasions, public, domestic, and religious; throughout Italy they have yet the nickname of *lupi lombardi* (Lombard wolves) which their good appetites won them. The nobles of that gay old Milan were very hospitable, easy of access to persons of the proper number of descents, and full of invitations for the stranger. A French writer found their cooking delicate and estimable as that of his own nation; but he adds that many of these friendly, well-dining aristocrats had not good *ton*. One can think of them at our distance of time and place with a kindness which Italian critics, especially those of the bitter period of struggle about the middle of this century, do not affect. Emiliani-Giudici, for example, does not, when he calls them and their order throughout Italy an aristocratic leprosy. He assures us that at the time of that long peace "the moral degradation of what the French call the great world was the inveterate habit of centuries; the nobles wallowed in their filth untouched by remorse"; and he speaks of them as "gilded swine, vain of the glories of their blazons, which they dragged through the mire of their vices."

II

THIS is when he is about to consider a poem in which the Lombard nobility are satirized — if it was satire to paint them to the life. He says that he would be at a loss what passages to quote from it, but fortunately "an unanimous posterity has done Parini due honor"; and he supposes "now there is no man, of whatever sect or opinion, but has read his immortal poem, and has its finest scenes by heart." It is this fact which embarrasses me, however, for how am I to rehabilitate a certain obsolete characteristic figure without quoting from Parini, and constantly wearying people with what they know already so well? The gentle reader, familiar with Parini's immortal poem——

The Gentle Reader.—His immortal poem? What *is* his immortal poem? I never heard even the name of it!

Is it possible? But you, fair reader, who have its finest scenes by heart——

The Fair Reader.—Yes, certainly; of course. But one reads so many things. I don't believe I half remember those striking passages of —— what is the poem? And who did you say the author was?

Oh, madam! And is this undying fame? Is this the immortality for which we waste our time? Is this the remembrance for which the essayist sicklies his visage over with the pale cast of thought? Why, at this rate, even those whose books are favorably noticed by the newspapers will be forgotten in a thousand years. But it is at least consoling to know that you have merely forgotten Parini's poems, the subject of which you will at once recollect when I remind you that it is called The Day, and celebrates The Morning, The Noon, The Evening, and The Night of a gentleman of fashion as Milan knew him for fifty years in the last century.

This gentleman, whatever his nominal business in the world might be, was first and above all a cavaliere servente, and the cavaliere servente was the invention, it is said, of Genoese husbands who had not the leisure to attend their wives to the theater, the promenade, the card-table, the *conversazione*, and so installed their nearest idle friends permanently in the office. The arrangement was found so convenient that the cavaliere servente presently spread throughout Italy; no lady of fashion was thought properly appointed without one; and the office was now no longer reserved to bachelors; it was not at all good form for husband and wife to love each other, and the husband became the cavalier of some other lady, and the whole fine world was thus united, by a usage of which it is very hard to know just how far it was wicked and how far it was only foolish; perhaps it is safest to say that at the best it was apt to be somewhat of the one and always a great deal of the other. In the good society of that day, marriage meant a settlement in life for the girl who had escaped her sister's fate of a sometimes forced religious vocation. But it did not matter so much about the husband if the marriage contract stipulated that she should have her cavaliere servente, and, as sometimes happened, specified him by name. With her husband there was a union of fortunes, with the expectation of heirs; the companionship, the confidence, the faith, was with the cavalier; there could be no domesticity, no family life with either. The cavaliere servente went with his lady to church, where he dipped his finger in the holy-water and offered it her to moisten her own finger at; and he held her prayer-book for her when she rose from her knees and bowed to the high altar. In fact, his place seems to have been as fully acknowledged and honored, if not by the Church, then by all the other competent authorities, as that of the husband. Like other things, his relation to his lady was subject to complication and abuse; no doubt, ladies of fickle minds changed their cavaliers rather often; and in those days following the disorder of the French invasions, the relation suffered deplorable exaggerations and perversions. But when Giuseppe Parini so minutely and graphically depicted the day of a noble Lombard youth, the cavaliere servente was in his most prosperous and illustrious state; and some who have studied Italian social conditions in the past bid us not too virtuously condemn him, since, preposterous as he was, his existence was an amelioration of disorders at which we shall find it better not even to look askance.

Parini's poem is written in the form of instructions to the hero for the politest disposal of his time; and in a strain of polished irony allots the follies of his day to their proper hours. The poet's apparent seriousness never fails him, but he does not suffer his irony to become a burden to the reader, relieving it constantly with pictures, episodes, and excursions, and now and then breaking into a strain of solemn poetry which is fine enough. The work will suggest to the English reader the light mockery of "The Rape of the Lock," and in less degree some qualities of Gay's "Trivia"; but in form and manner it is more like Phillips's "Splendid Shilling" than either of these; and yet it is not at all like the last in being a mere burlesque of the epic style. These resemblances have been noted by Italian critics, who find them as unsatisfactory as myself; but they will serve to make the extracts I am to give a little more intelligible to the reader who does not recur to the whole poem. Parini was not one to break a butterfly upon a wheel; he felt the fatuity of heavily moralizing upon his material; the only way was to treat it with affected gravity, and to use his hero with the respect which best mocks absurdity. One of his arts is to contrast the deeds of his hero with those of his forefathers, of which he is so proud,—of course the contrast is to the disadvantage of the forefathers,—and in these allusions to the past glories of Italy it seems to me that the modern patriotic poetry which has done so much to make Italy begins for the first time to feel its wings.

Parini was in all things a very stanch, brave, and original spirit, and if he was of any school, it was that of the Venetian, Gasparo Gozzi, who wrote pungent and amusing social satires in blank verse, and published at Venice an essay-paper, like the "Spectator," the name of which he turned into *l'Osservatore*. It dealt, like the "Spectator" and all that race of journals, with questions of letters and manners, and was long honored, like the "Spectator," as a model of prose. With an apparent prevalence of French taste, there was in fact much study by Italian authors of English literature at this time, which was encouraged by Dr. Johnson's friend, Baretti, the author of the famous

Frusta Letteraria (Literary Scourge), which drew blood from so many authorlings, now bloodless; it was wielded with more severity than wisdom, and fell pretty indiscriminately upon the bad and the good. It scourged among others Goldoni, the greatest master of the comic art then living, but it spared our Parini, the first part of whose poem Baretti salutes with many kindly phrases, though he cannot help advising him to turn the poem into rhyme. But when did a critic ever know less than a poet about a poet's business?

III

The first part of Parini's Day is Morning, that mature hour at which the hero awakes from the glories and fatigues of the past night. His valet appears, and throwing open the shutters asks whether he will have coffee or chocolate in bed, and when he has broken his fast and risen, the business of the day begins. The earliest comer is perhaps the dancing-master, whose elegant presence we must not deny ourselves:

>   He, entering, stops
> Erect upon the threshold, elevating
> Both shoulders; then contracting like a tortoise
> His neck a little, at the same time drops
> Slightly his chin, and, with the extremest tip
> Of his plumed hat, lightly touches his lips.

In their order come the singing-master and the master of the violin, and, with more impressiveness than the rest, the teacher of French, whose advent hushes all Italian sounds, and who is to instruct the hero to forget his plebeian native tongue. He is to send meanwhile to ask how the lady he serves has passed the night, and attending her response he may read Voltaire in a sumptuous Dutch or French binding, or he may amuse himself with a French romance; or it may happen that the artist whom he has engaged to paint the miniature of his lady (to be placed in the same jeweled case with his own) shall bring his work at this hour for criticism. Then the valets robe him from head to foot in readiness for the hair-dresser and the barber, whose work is completed with the powdering of his hair.

> At last the labor of the learned comb
> Is finished, and the elegant artist strews
> With lightly shaken hand a powdery mist
> To whiten ere their time thy youthful locks.
>
> . . . .
>
>   Now take heart,
> And in the bosom of that whirling cloud
> Plunge fearlessly. O brave! O mighty! Thus
> Appeared thine ancestor through smoke and fire
> Of battle, when his country's trembling gods
> His sword avenged, and shattered the fierce foe
> And put to flight. But he, his visage stained
> With dust and smoke, and smirched with gore and
>   sweat,
> His hair torn and tossed wild, came from the strife
> A terrible vision, even to compatriots

His hand had rescued; milder thou by far,
And fairer to behold, in white array
Shalt issue presently to bless the eyes
Of thy fond country, which the mighty arm
Of thy forefather and thy heavenly smile
Equally keep content and prosperous.

When the hero is finally dressed for the visit to his lady, it is in this splendid figure:

Let purple gaiters clasp thine ankles fine
In noble leather, that no dust or mire
Blemish thy foot; down from thy shoulders flow
Loosely a tunic fair, thy shapely arms
Cased in its closely-fitting sleeves, whose borders
Of crimson or of azure velvet let
The heliotrope's color tinge. Thy slender throat
Encircle with a soft and gauzy band.
. . . . . Thy watch already
Bids thee make haste to go. O me, how fair
The arsenal of tiny charms that hang
With a harmonious tinkling from its chain!
What hangs not there of fairy carriages
And fairy steeds so marvelously feigned
In gold that every charger seems alive?

This magnificent swell, of the times when swells had the world quite their own way, finds his lady already surrounded with visitors when he calls to revere her, as he would have said, and he can therefore make the more effective arrival. Entering her presence he puts on his very finest manner, which I am sure we might all study to our advantage.

Let thy right hand be pressed against thy side
Beneath thy waistcoat, and the other hand

Upon thy snowy linen rest, and hide
Next to thy heart; let the breast rise sublime,
The shoulders broaden both, and bend toward her
Thy pliant neck; then at the corners close
Thy lips a little, pointed in the middle
Somewhat; and from thy mouth thus set exhale
A murmur inaudible. Meanwhile her right
Let her have given, and now softly drop
On the warm ivory a double kiss.
Seat thyself then, and with one hand draw closer
Thy chair to hers, while every tongue is stilled.
Thou only, bending slightly over, with her
Exchange in whisper secret nothings, which
Ye both accompany with mutual smiles
And covert glances that betray, or seem
At least, your tender passion to betray.

It must have been mighty pretty, as Master Pepys says, to look at the life from which this scene was painted, for many a dandy of either sex doubtless sat for it. The scene was sometimes heightened by the different humor in which the lady and the cavalier received each other, as for instance when they met with reproaches and offered the spectacle of a lover's quarrel to the company. In either case, it is for the hero to lead the lady out to dinner.

       With a bound
Rise to thy feet, signor, and give thy hand
Unto thy lady, whom, tenderly drooping,
Support thou with thy strength, and to the table
Accompany, while the guests come after you.
And last of all the husband follows. . .

Or rather—
                If to the husband still
The vestige of a generous soul remain,
Let him frequent another board; beside
Another lady sit, whose husband dines
Yet somewhere else beside another lady,
Whose spouse is likewise absent; and so add
New links unto the chain immense, wherewith
Love, alternating, binds the whole wide world.
. . . .

Behold thy lady seated at the board:
Relinquish now her hand, and while the servant
Places the chair that not too far she sit,
And not so near that her soft bosom press
Too close against the table, with a spring
Stoop thou and gather round thy lady's feet
The wandering volume of her robe. Beside her
Then sit thee down; for the true cavalier
Is not permitted to forsake the side
Of her he serves, except there should arise
Some strange occasion warranting the use
Of so great freedom.

When one reads of these springs and little hops, which were once so elegant, it is almost with a sigh for a world which no longer springs or hops in the service of beauty, or even dreams of doing it. But a passage which will touch the sympathetic with a still keener sense of loss is one which hints how lovely a lady looked when carving, as she then sometimes did:

                Swiftly now the blade,
That sharp and polished at thy right hand lies,
Draw naked forth, and like the blade of Mars

Flash it upon the eyes of all. The point
Press 'twixt thy finger-tips, and bowing low
Offer the handle to her. Now are seen
The soft and delicate playing of the muscles
In the white hand upon its work intent.
The graces that around the lady stoop
Clothe themselves in new forms, and from her fingers
Sportively flying, flutter to the tips
Of her unconscious rosy knuckles, thence
To dip into the hollows of the dimples
That Love beside her knuckles has impressed.

Throughout the dinner it is the part of the wellbred husband — if so ill-bred as to remain at all — to sit impassive and quiescent while the cavalier watches over the wife with tender care, prepares her food, offers what agrees with her, and forbids what harms. He is virtually master of the house; he can order the servants about; if the dinner is not to his mind, it is even his high prerogative to scold the cook.

The poet reports something of the talk at table; and here occurs one of the most admired passages of the poem, the light irony of which it is hard to reproduce in a version. One of the guests, in a strain of affected sensibility, has been denouncing man's cruelty to animals:

Thus he discourses; and a gentle tear
Springs, while he speaks, into thy lady's eyes.
. . . . . . She recalls the day —
Alas, the cruel day! — what time her lap-dog,
Her beauteous lap-dog, darling of the Graces,
Sporting in youthful gayety, impressed
The light mark of her ivory tooth upon

The rude foot of a menial; he, with bold
And sacrilegious toe, flung her away.
Over and over thrice she rolled, and thrice
Rumpled her silken coat, and thrice inhaled
With tender nostril the thick, choking dust,
Then raised imploring cries, and "Help, help, help!"
She seemed to call, while from the gilded vaults
Compassionate Echo answered her again,
And from their cloistral basements in dismay
The servants rushed, and from the upper rooms
The pallid maidens trembling flew; all came.
Thy lady's face was with reviving essence
Sprinkled, and she awakened from her swoon.
Anger and grief convulsed her still; she cast
A lightning glance upon the guilty menial,
And thrice with languid voice she called her pet,
Who rushed to her embrace and seemed to invoke
Vengeance with her shrill tenor. And revenge
Thou hadst, fair poodle, darling of the Graces.
The guilty menial trembled, and with eyes
Downcast received his doom. Naught him availed
His twenty years' desert; naught him availed
His zeal in secret services; for him
In vain were prayer and promise; forth he went,
Spoiled of the livery that till now had made him
Enviable with the vulgar. And in vain
He hoped another lord; the tender dames
Were horror-struck at his atrocious crime,
And loathed the author. The false wretch succumbed
With all his squalid brood, and in the streets
With his lean wife in tatters at his side
Vainly lamented to the passer-by.

It would be quite out of taste for the lover to sit as apathetic as the husband in the presence of his lady's guests, and he is to mingle gracefully in the talk from time to time, turning it to such topics as may best serve to exploit his own accomplishments. As a man of the first fashion, he must be in the habit of seeming to have read Horace a little, and it will be a pretty effect to quote him now; one may also show one's acquaintance with the new French philosophy, and approve its skepticism, while keeping clear of its pernicious doctrines, which insidiously teach —

> That every mortal is his fellow's peer;
> That not less dear to Nature and to God
> Is he who drives thy carriage, or who guides
> The plow across thy field, than thine own self.

But at last the lady makes a signal to the cavalier that it is time to rise from the table :

>   Spring to thy feet
> The first of all, and drawing near thy lady
> Remove her chair and offer her thy hand,
> And lead her to the other rooms, nor suffer longer
> That the stale reek of viands shall offend
> Her delicate sense. Thee with the rest invites
> The grateful odor of the coffee, where
> It smokes upon a smaller table hid
> And graced with Indian webs. The redolent gums
> That meanwhile burn sweeten and purify
> The heavy atmosphere, and banish thence
> All lingering traces of the feast. — Ye sick
> And poor, whom misery or whom hope perchance
> Has guided in the noonday to these doors,
> Tumultuous, naked, and unsightly throng,
> With mutilated limbs and squalid faces,
> In litters and on crutches, from afar

Comfort yourselves, and with expanded nostrils
Drink in the nectar of the feast divine
That favorable zephyrs waft to you;
But do not dare besiege these noble precincts,
Importunately offering her that reigns
Within your loathsome spectacle of woe!
— And now, sir, 'tis your office to prepare
The tiny cup that then shall minister,
Slow sipped, its liquor to thy lady's lips;
And now bethink thee whether she prefer
The boiling beverage much or little tempered
With sweet; or if perchance she like it best
As doth the barbarous spouse, then, when she sits
Upon brocades of Persia, with light fingers
The bearded visage of her lord caressing.

With the dinner the second part of the poem, entitled The Noon, concludes, and The Afternoon begins with the visit which the hero and his lady pay to one of her friends. He has already thought with which of the husband's horses they shall drive out; he has suggested which dress his lady shall wear and which fan she shall carry; he has witnessed the agonizing scene of her parting with her lap-dog,— her children are at nurse and never intrude,— and they have arrived in the palace of the lady on whom they are to call:

And now the ardent friends to greet each other
Impatient fly, and pressing breast to breast
They tenderly embrace, and with alternate kisses
Their cheeks resound; then, clasping hands, they
  drop
Plummet-like down upon the sofa, both

Together. Seated thus, one flings a phrase,
Subtle and pointed, at the other's heart,
Hinting of certain things that rumor tells,
And in her turn the other with a sting
Assails. The lovely face of one is flushed
With beauteous anger, and the other bites
Her pretty lips a little; evermore
At every instant waxes violent
The anxious agitation of the fans.
So, in the age of Turpin, if two knights
Illustrious and well cased in mail encountered
Upon the way, each cavalier aspired
To prove the valor of the other in arms,
And, after greetings courteous and fair,
They lowered their lances and their chargers dashed
Ferociously together; then they flung
The splintered fragments of their spears aside,
And, fired with generous fury, drew their huge,
Two-handed swords and rushed upon each other!
But in the distance through a savage wood
The clamor of a messenger is heard,
Who comes full gallop to recall the one
Unto King Charles, and th' other to the camp
Of the young Agramante. Dare thou, too,
Dare thou, invincible youth, to expose the curls
And the toupet, so exquisitely dressed
This very morning, to the deadly shock
Of the infuriate fans; to new emprises
Thy fair invite, and thus the extreme effects
Of their periculous enmity suspend.

Is not this most charmingly done? It seems to me that the warlike interpretation of the scene is delightful; and those embattled fans — their perfumed breath comes down a hundred years in the verse!

The cavalier and his lady now betake them to the promenade, where all the fair world of Milan is walking or driving, with a punctual regularity which still distinguishes Italians in their walks and drives. The place is full of their common acquaintance, and the carriages are at rest for the exchange of greetings and gossip, in which the hero must take his part. All this is described in the same note of ironical seriousness as the rest of the poem, and The Afternoon closes with a strain of stately and grave poetry which admirably heightens the desired effect:

> Behold the servants
> Ready for thy descent; and now skip down
> And smooth the creases from thy coat, and order
> The laces on thy breast; a little stoop,
> And on thy snowy stockings bend a glance,
> And then erect thyself and strut away
> Either to pace the promenade alone,—
> 'T is thine, if 't please thee walk; or thou mayst draw
> Anigh the carriages of other dames.
> Thou clamberest up, and thrustest in thy head
> And arms and shoulders, half thyself within
> The carriage door. There let thy laughter rise
> So loud that from afar thy lady hear,
> And rage to hear, and interrupt the wit
> Of other heroes who had swiftly run
> Amid the dusk to keep her company
> While thou wast absent. O ye powers supreme,
> Suspend the night, and let the noble deeds
> Of my young hero shine upon the world
> In the clear day! Nay, night must follow still
> Her own inviolable laws, and droop

With silent shades over one half the globe;
And slowly moving on her dewy feet,
She blends the varied colors infinite,
And with the border of her mighty garments
Blots everything; the sister she of Death
Leaves but one aspect indistinct, one guise
To fields and trees, to flowers, to birds and beasts,
And to the great and to the lowly born,
Confounding with the painted cheek of beauty
The haggard face of want, and gold with tatters.
Nor me will the blind air permit to see
Which carriages depart, and which remain,
Secret amidst the shades; but from my hand
The pencil caught, my hero is involved
Within the tenebrous and humid veil.

The concluding section of the poem, by chance or by wise design of the author, remains a fragment. In this he follows his hero from the promenade to the evening party, with an account of which The Night is mainly occupied, so far as it goes. There are many lively pictures in it, with light sketches of expression and attitude; but on the whole it has not so many distinctly quotable passages as the other parts of the poem. The perfunctory devotion of the cavalier and the lady continues throughout, and the same ironical reverence depicts them alighting from their carriage, arriving in the presence of the hostess, sharing in the gossip of the guests, supping, and sitting down at those games of chance with which every fashionable house was provided and at which the lady loses or doubles her pin-money. In Milan long trains were then the mode, and any woman might wear them, but only patricians were allowed to have them carried by servants; the rich plebeian must drag her costly skirts in the dust; and the nobility of our hero's lady is honored by the flunkeys who lift her train as she enters the house. The hostess, seated on a sofa, receives her guests with a few murmured greetings, and then abandons herself to the arduous task of arranging the various partners at cards. When the cavalier serves his lady at supper, he takes his handkerchief from his pocket and spreads it on her lap; such usages and the differences of costume distinguished an evening party at Milan then from the like joy in our time and country.

IV

THE poet who sings this gay world with such mocking seriousness was not himself born to the manner of it. He was born plebeian in 1729 at Bosisio, near Lake Pusiano, and his parents were poor. He himself adds that they were honest, but the phrase has now lost its freshness. His father was a dealer in raw silk, and was able to send him to school in Milan, where his scholarship was not equal to his early literary promise. At least he took no prizes; but this often happens with people whose laurels come abundantly later. He was to enter the Church, and in due time he took orders, but he did not desire a cure, and he became, like so many other accomplished abbati, a teacher in noble families (the great and saintly family Borromeo among others), in whose houses and in those he frequented with them he saw the life he paints in his poem. His father was now dead, and he had already supported himself and his mother by copying law-papers; he had, also, at the age of twenty-three, published a small volume of poems, and had been elected a shepherd of Arcadia; but in a country where one's copyright was good for nothing across the border—scarcely a fair stone's-throw away—of one's own little duchy or province, and the printers everywhere stole a book as soon as it was worth stealing, it is not likely that he made great gains by a volume of verses which, later in life, he repudiated. Baretti had then returned from living in London, where he had seen the prosperity of "the trade of an author" in days which we do not now think so very prosperous, and he viewed with open disgust the abject state of authorship in his own country. So there was nothing for Parini to do but to become a *maestro in casa*. With the Borromei he always remained friends, and in their company he went into society a good deal. Emiliani-Giudici supposes that he came to despise the great world with the same scorn that shows in his poem; but probably he regarded it quite as much with the amused sense of the artist as with the moralist's indignation; some of his contemporaries accused him of a snobbish fondness for the great, but certainly he did not flatter them, and in one passage of his poem he is at the pains to remind his noble acquaintance that not the smallest drop of patrician blood is microscopically discoverable in his veins. His days were rendered more comfortable when he was appointed editor of the government newspaper,—the only newspaper in Milan,—and yet easier when he was made professor of eloquence in the Academy of Fine Arts. In this employment it was his hard duty to write poems from time to time in praise of archdukes and emperors; but by and by the French Revolution arrived in Milan, and Parini was relieved of that labor. The revolution made an end of archdukes and emperors, but the liberty it bestowed was peculiar, and consisted chiefly in not allowing one to do anything that one liked. The altars were abased, and trees of liberty were planted; for making a tumult about an outraged saint a mob was severely handled by the military, and for "insulting" a tree of liberty a poor fellow at Como was shot. Parini was chosen one of the municipal government, which, apparently popular, could really do nothing but register the decrees of the military commandant. He proved so little useful in this government that he was expelled from it, and, giving his salary to his native parish, he fell into something like his old poverty. He who had laughed to scorn the insolence and folly of the nobles could not enjoy the insolence and folly of the plebeians, and he was unhappy in that wild ferment of ideas, hopes, principles, sentiments, which

Milan became in the time of the Cisalpine Republic. He led a retired life, and at last, in 1799, having risen one day to studies which he had never remitted, he died suddenly in his arm-chair.

Many stories are told of his sayings and doings in those troubled days when he tried to serve the public. At the theater once some one cried out, "Long live the republic, death to the aristocrats!" "No," shouted Parini, who abhorred the abominable bloodthirstiness of the liberators, "long live the republic, death to nobody!" They were going to take away a crucifix from a room where he appeared on public business. "Very well," he observed; "where Citizen Christ cannot stay, I have nothing to do," and went out. "Equality does n't consist in dragging me down to your level," he said to one who had impudently given him the *thou*, "but in raising you to mine, if possible. You will always be a pitiful creature, even though you call yourself Citizen; and though you call me Citizen, you can't help my being the Abbate Parini." To another, who reproached him for kindness to an Austrian prisoner, he answered, "I would do as much for a Turk, a Jew, an Arab; I would do it even for you if you were in need." In his closing years many sought him for literary counsel; those for whom there was hope he encouraged; those for whom there was none, he made it a matter of conscience not to praise. A poor fellow came to repeat him two sonnets, in order to be advised which to print; Parini heard the first, and, without waiting further, besought him "Print the other!"

VITTORIO ALFIERI

VITTORIO ALFIERI, the Italian poet whom his countrymen would undoubtedly name next after Dante, Petrarch, Ariosto, and Tasso, and who, in spite of his limitations, was a man of signal and distinct dramatic power, not surpassed if equaled since, is scarcely more than a name to most English readers. He was born in the year 1749, at Asti, a little city of that Piedmont where there has always been a greater regard for feudal traditions than in any other part of Italy; and he belonged by birth to a nobility which is still the proudest in Europe. "What a singular country is ours!" said the Chevalier Nigra, one of the first diplomats of our time, who for many years managed the delicate and difficult relations of Italy with France during the second empire, but who was the son of an apothecary. "In Paris they admit me everywhere; I am asked to court and petted as few Frenchmen are; but here, in my own city of Turin, it would not be possible for me to be received by the Marchioness Doria;" and if this was true in the afternoon of the nineteenth century, one easily fancies what society must have been at Turin in the forenoon of the eighteenth.

I

It was in the order of the things of that day and country that Alfieri should leave home while a child and go to school at the Academy of Turin. Here, as he tells in that most amusing autobiography of his, he spent several years in acquiring a profound ignorance of whatever he was meant to learn; and he came away a stranger not only to the humanities, but to any one language, speaking a barbarous mixture of French and Piedmontese, and reading little or nothing. Doubtless he does not spare color in this statement, but almost anything you like could be true of the education of a gentleman as a gentleman got it from the Italian priests of the last century. "We translated," he says, "the 'Lives of Cornelius Nepos'; but none of us, perhaps not even the masters, knew who these men were whose lives we translated, nor where was their country, nor in what times they lived, nor under what governments, nor what any government was." He learned Latin enough to turn Virgil's "Georgics" into his sort of Italian; but when he read Ariosto by stealth, he atoned for his transgression by failing to understand him. Yet Alfieri tells us that he was one of the first scholars of that admirable academy, and he really had some impulses even then toward literature; for he liked reading Goldoni and Metastasio, though he had never heard of the name of Tasso. This was whilst he was still in the primary classes, under strict priestly control; when he passed to a more advanced grade and found himself free to do what he liked in the manner that pleased him best, in common with the young Russians, Germans, and Englishmen then enjoying the advantages of the Academy of Turin, he says that being grounded in no study, directed by no one, and not understanding any language well, he did not know what study to take up, or how to study. "The reading of many French romances," he goes on, "the constant association with foreigners, and the want of all occasion to speak Italian, or to hear it spoken, drove from my head that small amount of wretched Tuscan which I had contrived to put there in those two or three years of burlesque study of the humanities and asinine rhetoric. In place of it," he says, "the French entered into my empty brain"; but he is careful to disclaim any literary merit for the French he knew, and he afterward came to hate it, with everything else that was French, very bitterly.

It was before this, a little, that Alfieri contrived his first sonnet, which, when he read it to the uncle with whom he lived, made that old soldier laugh unmercifully, so that until his twenty-fifth year the poet made no further attempts in verse. When he left school he spent three years in travel, after the fashion of those grand-touring days when you had to be a gentleman of birth and fortune in order to travel, and when you journeyed by your own conveyance from capital to capital, with letters to your sovereign's ambassadors everywhere, and spent your money handsomely upon the dissipations of the countries through which you passed. Alfieri is constantly at the trouble to have us know that he was a very morose and ill-conditioned young animal, and the figure he makes as a traveler is no more amiable than edifying. He had a ruling passion for horses, and then several smaller passions quite as wasteful and idle. He was driven from place to place by a demon of unrest, and was mainly concerned, after reaching a city, in getting away from it as soon as he could. He gives anecdotes enough in proof of this, and he forgets nothing that can enhance the surprise of his future literary greatness. At the Ambrosian Library in Milan they showed him a manuscript of Petrarch's, which, "like a true barbarian," as he says, he flung aside, declaring that he knew nothing about it, having a rancor against this Petrarch, whom he had once tried to read and had understood as little as Ariosto. At Rome the Sardinian minister innocently affronted him by repeating some verses of Marcellus, which the sulky young noble could not comprehend. In Ferrara he did not remember that it was the city of that divine Ariosto whose poem was the first that came into his hands, and which he had now read in part with infinite pleasure. "But my poor intellect," he says, "was then sleeping a most sordid sleep, and every day, as far as regards letters, rusted more and more. It is true, however, that with respect to knowledge of the world and of men I constantly learned not a little, without taking note of it, so many and diverse were the phases of life and manners that I daily beheld." At

Florence he visited the galleries and churches with much disgust and no feeling for the beautiful, especially in painting, his eyes being very dull to color. "If I liked anything better, it was sculpture a little, and architecture yet a little more"; and it is interesting to note how all his tragedies reflect these preferences, in their lack of color and in their sculpturesque sharpness of outline.

From Italy he passed as restlessly into France, yet with something of a more definite intention, for he meant to frequent the French theater. He had seen a company of French players at Turin, and had acquainted himself with the most famous French tragedies and comedies, but with no thought of writing tragedies of his own. He felt no creative impulse, and he liked the comedies best, though, as he says, he was by nature more inclined to tears than to laughter. But he does not seem to have enjoyed the theater much in Paris, a city for which he conceived at once the greatest dislike, he says, "on account of the squalor and barbarity of the buildings, the absurd and pitiful pomp of the few houses that affected to be palaces, the filthiness and gothicism of the churches, the vandalic structure of the theaters of that time, and the many and many and many disagreeable objects that all day fell under my notice, and worst of all the unspeakably misshapen and beplastered faces of those ugliest of women."

He had at this time already conceived that hatred of kings which breathes, or, I may better say, bellows, from his tragedies; and he was enraged even beyond his habitual fury by his reception at court, where it was etiquette for Louis XV. to stare at him from head to foot and give no sign of having received any impression whatever.

In Holland he fell in love, for the first time, and as was requisite in the polite society of that day, the object of his passion was another man's wife. In England he fell in love the second time, and as fashionably as before. The intrigue lasted for months; in the end it came to a duel with the lady's husband and a great scandal in the newspapers; but in spite of these displeasures, Alfieri liked everything in England. "The streets, the taverns, the horses, the women, the universal prosperity, the life and activity of that island, the cleanliness and convenience of the houses, though extremely little," — as they still strike every one coming from Italy, — these and other charms of "that fortunate and free country" made an impression upon him that never was effaced. He did not at that time, he says, "study profoundly the constitution, mother of so much prosperity," but he "knew enough to observe and value its sublime effects."

Before his memorable sojourn in England, he spent half a year at Turin reading Rousseau, among other philosophers, and Voltaire, whose prose delighted and whose verse wearied him. "But the book of books for me," he says, "and the one which that winter caused me to pass hours of bliss and rapture, was Plutarch, his Lives of the truly great; and some of these, as Timoleon, Cæsar, Brutus, Pelopidas, Cato, and others, I read and

VITTORIO ALFIERI.

read again, with such a transport of cries, tears, and fury, that if any one had heard me in the next room he would surely have thought me mad. In meditating certain grand traits of these supreme men, I often leaped to my feet, agitated and out of my senses, and tears of grief and rage escaped me to think that I was born in Piedmont, and in a time, and under a government, where no high thing could be done or said; and it was almost useless to think or feel it."

These characters had a life-long fascination for Alfieri, and his admiration of such types deeply influenced his tragedies. So great was his scorn of kings at the time he writes of, that he despised even those who liked them, and poor little Metastasio, who lived by the bounty of Maria Theresa, fell under Alfieri's bitterest contempt when in Vienna he saw his brother-poet before the empress in the imperial gardens at Schönbrunn, "performing the customary genuflexions with a servilely contented and adulatory face." This loathing of royalty was naturally intensified beyond utterance in Prussia. "On entering the states of Frederick, I felt redoubled and triplicated my hate for that infamous military trade, most infamous and sole base of arbitrary power." He told his minister that he would be presented only in civil dress, because there were uniforms enough at that court, and he declares that on beholding Frederick he felt "no emotion of wonder, or of respect, but rather of indignation and rage. . . . The king addressed me the three or four customary words; I fixed my eyes respectfully upon his, and inwardly blessed Heaven that I had not been born his slave; and I issued from that universal Prussian barracks . . . abhorring it as it deserved."

In Paris Alfieri bought the principal Italian authors, which he afterwards carried everywhere with him on his travels; but he says that he made very little use of them, having neither the will nor the power to apply his mind to anything. In fact, he knew very little Italian, most of the authors in his collection were strange to him, and at the age of twenty-two he had read nothing whatever of Dante, Petrarch, Tasso, Boccaccio, or Machiavelli.

He made a journey into Spain, among other countries, where he admired the Andalusian horses, and bored himself as usual with what interests educated people; and he signalized his stay at Madrid by a murderous outburst of one of the worst tempers in the world. One night his servant Elia, in dressing his hair, had the misfortune to twitch one of his locks in such a way as to give him a slight pain; on which Alfieri leaped to his feet, seized a heavy candlestick, and without a word struck the valet such a blow upon his temple that the blood gushed out over his face, and over the person of a young Spanish gentleman who had been supping with Alfieri. Elia sprang upon his master, who drew his sword, but the Spaniard after great ado quieted them both; "and so ended this horrible encounter," says Alfieri, "for which I remained deeply afflicted and ashamed. I told Elia that he would have done well to kill me; and he was the man to have done it, being a palm taller than myself, who am very tall, and of a strength and courage not inferior to his height. Two hours later, his wound being dressed and everything put in order, I went to bed, leaving the door from my room into Elia's open as usual, without listening to the Spaniard, who warned me not thus to invite a provoked and outraged man to vengeance: I called to Elia, who had already gone to bed, that he could, if he liked and thought proper, kill me that night, for I deserved it. But he was no less heroic than I, and would take no other revenge than to keep two handkerchiefs, which had been drenched in his blood, and which from time to time he showed me in the course of many years. This reciprocal mixture of fierceness and generosity on both our parts will not be easily understood by those who have had no experience of the customs and of the temper of us Piedmontese;" though here, perhaps, Alfieri does his country too much honor in making his ferocity a national trait. For the rest, he says, he never struck a servant except as he would have done an equal — not with a cane, but with his fist, or a chair, or anything else that came to hand; and he seems to have thought this a democratic if not an amiable habit.

When at last he went back to Turin, he fell once more into his old life of mere vacancy, varied before long by a most unworthy amour, of which he tells us that he finally cured himself by causing his servant to tie him in his chair, and so keep him a prisoner in his own house. A violent distemper followed this treatment, which the light-moraled gossip of the town said Alfieri had invented exclusively for his own use; many days he lay in bed tormented by this anguish; but when he rose he was no longer a slave to his passion. Shortly after, he wrote a tragedy, or a tragic dialogue rather, in Italian blank verse, called Cleopatra, which was played in a Turinese theater with a success of which he tells us he was at once and always ashamed.

Yet apparently it encouraged him to persevere in literature, his qualifications for tragical authorship being "a resolute spirit, very obstinate and untamed, a heart running over with passions of every kind, among which predominated a bizarre mixture of love and all its furies, and a profound and most ferocious rage and abhorrence against all tyranny whatsoever; . . . a very dim and uncertain remembrance of various French tragedies seen in the theaters many years before; . . . an almost total ignorance of all the rules of tragic art, and an unskillfulness almost total in the divine and most necessary art of writing and managing my own language." With this stock in trade, he set about turning his Filippo and his Polinice, which he wrote first in French prose, into Italian verse, making at the same time a careful study of the Italian poets. It was at this period that the poet Ossian was introduced to mankind by the ingenious and self-sacrificing Mr. Macpherson, and Cesarotti's translation of him came into Alfieri's hands. These blank verses were the first that really pleased him;

with a little modification he thought they would be an excellent model for the verse of dialogue.

He had now refused himself the pleasure of reading French, and he had nowhere to turn for tragic literature but to the classics, which he read in literal versions while he renewed his faded Latin with the help of a teacher. But he believed that his originality as a tragic author suffered from his reading, and he determined to read no more tragedies till he had made his own. For this reason he had already given up Shakespeare. " The more that author accorded with my humor (though I very well perceived all his defects), the more I was resolved to abstain," he tells us.

This was during a literary sojourn in Tuscany, whither he had gone to accustom himself " to speak, hear, think, and dream in Tuscan, and not otherwise evermore." Here he versified his first two tragedies, and sketched others ; and here, he says, " I deluged my brain with the verses of Petrarch, of Dante, of Tasso, and of Ariosto, convinced that the day would infallibly come in which all these forms, phrases, and words of others would return from its cells, blended and identified with my own ideas and emotions."

He had now indeed entered with all the fury of his nature into the business of making tragedies, which he did very much as if he had been making love. He abandoned everything else for it—country, home, money, friends; for having decided to live henceforth only in Tuscany, and hating to ask that royal permission to remain abroad, without which, annually renewed, the Piedmontese noble of that day could not reside out of his own country, he gave up his estates at Asti to his sister, keeping for himself a pension that came only to about half his former income. The king of Piedmont was very well, as kings went in that day; and he did nothing to hinder the poet's expatriation. The long period of study and production which followed Alfieri spent chiefly at Florence, but partly also at Rome and Naples. During this time he wrote and printed most of his tragedies; and he formed that relation, common enough in the best society of the eighteenth century, with the Countess of Albany, which continued as long as he lived. The countess's husband was the Pretender Charles Edward, the last of the English Stuarts, who, like all his house, abetted his own evil destiny, and was then drinking himself to death. There were difficulties in the way of her living with Alfieri which would not perhaps have beset a less exalted lady, and which required an especial grace on the part of the Pope. But this the Pope refused ever to bestow, even after being much prayed; and when her husband was dead, she and Alfieri were privately married, or were not married; the fact is still in dispute. Their house became a center of fashionable and intellectual society in Florence, and to be received in it was the best that could happen to any one. The relation seems to have been a sufficiently happy one; neither was painfully scrupulous in observing its ties, and after Alfieri's death the countess gave to the painter

Fabre "a heart which," says Massimo d'Azeglio in his Memoirs, "according to the usage of the time, and especially of high society, felt the invincible necessity of keeping itself in continual exercise." A cynical little story of Alfieri reading one of his tragedies in company, while Fabre stood behind him making eyes at the countess, and from time to time kissing her ring on his finger, was told to D'Azeglio by an aunt of his who witnessed the scene.

In 1787 the poet went to France to oversee the printing of a complete edition of his works, and five years later he found himself in Paris when the Revolution was at its height. The countess was with him, and, after great trouble, he got passports for both, and hurried to the city barrier. The National Guards stationed there would have let them pass, but a party of drunken patriots coming up had their worst fears aroused by the sight of two carriages with sober and decent people in them, and heavily laden with baggage. While they parleyed whether they had better stone the equipages, or set fire to them, Alfieri leaped out, and a scene ensued which placed him in a very characteristic light, and which enables us to see him as it were in person. When the patriots had read the passports, he seized them, and, as he says, "full of disgust and rage, and not knowing at the moment, or in my passion despising the immense peril that attended us, I thrice shook my passport in my hand, and shouted at the top of my voice, 'Look! Listen! Alfieri is my name; Italian and not French; tall, lean, pale, red hair; I am he; look at me: I have my passport, and I have had it legitimately from those who could give it; we wish to pass, and, by Heaven, we *will* pass!'"

They passed, and two days later the authorities that had approved their passports confiscated the horses, furniture, and books that Alfieri had left behind him in Paris, and declared him and the countess—both foreigners—to be refugee aristocrats!

He established himself again in Florence, where, in his forty-sixth year, he took up the study of Greek, and made himself master of that literature, though, till then, he had scarcely known the Greek alphabet. The chief fruit of this study was a tragedy in the manner of Euripides, which he wrote in secret, and which he read to a company so polite that they thought it really was Euripides during the whole of the first two acts.

Alfieri's remaining years were spent in study and the revision of his works, to the number of which he added six comedies in 1800. The presence and domination of the detested French in Florence embittered his life somewhat; but if they had not been there he could never have had the pleasure of refusing to see the French commandant, who had a taste for literary people if not for literature, and would fain have paid his respects to the poet. He must also have found consolation in the thought that if the French had become masters of Europe, many kings had been dethroned, and every tyrant who wore a crown was in a very pitiable state of terror or disaster.

Nothing in Alfieri's life was more like him than his death, of which the Abbate di Caluso gives a full account in his conclusion of the poet's biography. His malady was gout, and amidst its tortures he still labored at the comedies he was then writing. He was impatient at being kept in-doors, and when they added plasters on the feet to the irksomeness of his confinement, he tore away the bandages that prevented him from walking about his room. He would not go to bed, and they gave him opiates to ease his anguish; under their influence his mind was molested by many memories of things long past. "The studies and labors of thirty years," says the Abbate, "recurred to him, and what was yet more wonderful, he repeated in order, from memory, a good number of Greek verses from the beginning of Hesiod, which he had read but once. These he said over to the Signora Contessa, who sat by his side, but it does not appear, for all this, that there ever came to him the thought that death, which he had been for a long time used to imagine near, was then imminent. It is certain at least that he made no sign to the contessa though she did not leave him till morning. About six o'clock he took oil and magnesia without the physician's advice, and near eight he was observed to be in great danger, and the Signora Contessa, being called, found him in agonies that took away his breath. Nevertheless, he rose from his chair, and going to the bed, leaned upon it, and presently the day was darkened to him, his eyes closed and he expired. The duties and consolations of religion were not forgotten, but the evil was not thought so near, nor haste necessary, and so the confessor who was called did not come in time." D'Azeglio relates that the confessor arrived at the supreme moment, and saw the poet bow his head: "He thought it was a salutation, but it was the death of Vittorio Alfieri."

II

I ONCE fancied that a parallel between Alfieri and Byron might be drawn, but their disparities are greater than their resemblances, on the whole. Both, however, were born noble, both lived in voluntary exile, both imagined themselves friends and admirers of liberty, both had violent natures, and both indulged the curious hypocrisy of desiring to seem worse than they were, and of trying to make out a shocking case for themselves when they could. They were men who hardly outgrew their boyishness. Alfieri, indeed, had to struggle against so many defects of training that he could not have reached maturity in the longest life; and he was ruled by passions and ideals; he hated with equal noisiness the tyrants of Europe and the Frenchmen who dethroned them.

When he left the life of a dissolute young noble for that of tragic authorship, he seized upon such histories and fables as would give the freest course to a harsh, narrow, gloomy, vindictive, and declamatory nature; and his dramas reproduce the terrible fatalistic traditions of the Greeks, the stories of Œdipus, Myrrha, Alcestis, Clytemnestra, Orestes, and such passages of Roman history as those relating to the Brutuses and to Virginia. In modern history he has taken such characters and events as those of Philip II., Mary Stuart, Don Garzia, and the Conspiracy of the Pazzi. Two of his tragedies are from the Bible, the Abel and the Saul; one, the Rosmunda, from Longobardic history. And these themes, varying so vastly as to the times, races, and religions with which they originated, are all treated in the same spirit—the spirit Alfieri believed Greek. Their interest comes from the situation and the action; of character, as we have it in the romantic drama, and supremely in Shakespeare, there is scarcely anything; and the language is shorn of all metaphor and picturesque expression. Of course their form is wholly unlike that of the romantic drama; Alfieri holds fast by the famous unities as the chief and saving grace of tragedy. All his actions take place within twenty-four hours; there is no change of scene, and so far as he can master that most obstinate unity, the unity of action, each piece is furnished with a tangible beginning, middle, and ending. The wide stretches of time which the old Spanish and English and all modern dramas cover, and their frequent transitions from place to place, were impossible and abhorrent to him.

Emiliani-Giudici, the Italian critic, writing about the middle of our century, declares that when the fiery love of freedom shall have purged Italy, the Alfierian drama will be the only representation worthy of a great and free people. This critic holds that Alfieri's tragical ideal was of such a simplicity that it would seem derived regularly from the Greek, but for the fact that when he felt irresistibly moved to write tragedy, he probably did not know even the names of the Greek dramatists, and could not have known the structure of their dramas by indirect means, having read then only some Metastasian plays of the French school; so that he created that ideal of his by pure, instinctive force of genius. With him, as with the Greeks, art arose spontaneously; he felt the form of Greek art by inspiration. He believed from the very first that the dramatic poet should assume to render the spectators unconscious of theatrical artifice, and make them take part with the actors; and he banished from the scene everything that could diminish their illusion; he would not mar the intensity of the effect by changing the action from place to place, or by compressing within the brief time of the representation the events of months and years. To achieve the unity of action, he dispensed with all those parts which did not seem to him the most principal, and he studied how to show the subject of the drama in the clearest light. In all this he went to the extreme, but he so wrought " that the print of his cothurnus stamped upon the field of art should remain forever singular and inimitable. Reading his tragedies in order, from the Cleopatra to the Saul, you see how he never changed his tragic ideal, but discerned it more and more distinctly until he fully realized it. Æschylus and Alfieri are two links that unite the chain in a circle. In Alfieri art once more achieved the faultless purity of its proper character; Greek tragedy reached the same height in the Italian's Saul that it touched in the Greek's Prometheus, two dramas which are perhaps the most gigantic creations of any literature." Emiliani-Giudici thinks that the literary ineducation of Alfieri was the principal exterior cause of this prodigious development, that a more regular course of study would have restrained his creative genius, and, while smoothing the way before it, would have subjected it to methods and robbed it of originality of feeling and conception. "Tragedy, born sublime, terrible, vigorous, heroic, the life of liberty, . . . was, as it were, redeemed by Vittorio Alfieri, reassumed the masculine, athletic forms of its original existence, and recommenced the exercise of its lost ministry."

I do not begin to think this is all true. Alfieri himself owns his acquaintance with the French theater before the time when he began to write, and we must believe that he got at least some of his ideas of Athens from Paris, though he liked the Frenchmen none the better for his obligation to them. A less mechanical conception of the Greek idea than his would have prevented its application to historical subjects. In Alfieri's Brutus the First, a far greater stretch of imagination is required from the spectator in order to preserve the unities of time and place than the most capricious changes of scene would have asked. The scene is always in the forum in Rome; the action occurs within twenty-four hours. During this limited time, we see the body of Lucretia borne along in the distance; Brutus harangues the people with the bloody dagger in his hand. The emissaries of Tarquin arrive and organize a conspiracy against the new republic; the sons of Brutus are found in the plot, and are convicted and put to death.

III

But such incongruities as these do not affect us in the tragedies based on the heroic fables; here the poet takes, without offense, any liberty he likes with time and place; the whole affair is in his hands, to do what he will, so long as he respects the internal harmony of his own work. For this reason, I think, we find Alfieri at his best in these tragedies, among which I have liked the Orestes best, as giving the widest range of feeling with the greatest vigor of action. The Agamemnon, which precedes it, and which ought to be read first, closes with its most powerful scene. Agamemnon has returned from Troy to Argos with his captive Cassandra, and Ægisthus has persuaded Clytemnestra that her husband intends to raise Cassandra to the throne. She kills him and reigns with Ægisthus, Electra concealing Orestes on the night of the murder, and sending him secretly away with Strophius, king of Phocis.

In the last scene, as Clytemnestra steals through the darkness to her husband's chamber, she soliloquizes, with the dagger in her hand:

It is the hour; and sunk in slumber now
Lies Agamemnon. Shall he nevermore
Open his eyes to the fair light? My hand,
Once pledge to him of stainless love and faith,
Is it to be the minister of his death?
Did I swear that? Ay, that; and I must keep
My oath. Quick, let me go! My foot, heart, hand—
All over I tremble. Oh, what did I promise?
Wretch! what do I attempt? How all my courage
Hath vanished from me since Ægisthus vanished!
I only see the immense atrocity
Of this, my horrible deed; I only see
The bloody specter of Atrides! Ah,
In vain do I accuse thee! No, thou lovest
Cassandra not. Me, only me, thou lovest,
Unworthy of thy love. Thou hast no blame,
Save that thou art my husband, in the world!
O Heaven! Atrides, thou sent from the arms
Of trustful sleep, to death's arms by my hand?
And where then shall I hide me? O perfidy!
Can I e'er hope for peace? O woful life—
Life of remorse, of madness, and of tears!
How shall Ægisthus, even Ægisthus, dare
To rest beside the parricidal wife
Upon her murder-stainèd marriage-bed,
Nor tremble for himself? Away, away,—
Hence, horrible instrument of all my guilt
And harm, thou execrable dagger, hence!
I 'll lose at once my lover and my life,

But never by this hand betrayed shall fall
So great a hero! Live, honor of Greece
And Asia's terror! Live to glory, live
To thy dear children, and a better wife!
—But what are these hushed steps? Into these rooms
Who is it comes by night? Ægisthus?—Lost,
I am lost!
    Ægisthus. Hast thou not done the deed?
    Cly.   Ægisthus——
    Æg. What, stand'st thou here, wasting thyself in
        tears?
Woman, untimely are thy tears; 't is late,
'T is vain, and it may cost us dear!
    Cly.   Thou here?
But how—woe 's me, what did I promise thee!
What wicked counsel—
    Æg.   Was it not thy counsel?
Love gave it thee and fear annuls it—well!
Since thou repentest, I am glad; and glad
To know thee guiltless shall I be in death.
I told thee that the enterprise was hard,
But thou, unduly trusting in the heart,
That hath not a man's courage in it, chose
Thyself thy feeble hands to strike the blow.
Now may Heaven grant that the intent of evil
Turn not to harm thee! Hither I by stealth
And favor of the darkness have returned
Unseen, I hope. For I perforce must come
Myself to tell thee that irrevocably
My life is dedicated to the vengeance
Of Agamemnon.

    He appeals to her pity for him, and her fear for herself; he reminds her of Agamemnon's consent to the sacrifice of Iphigenia, and goads her on to the crime from which she had recoiled. She goes into Agamemnon's chamber, whence his dying outcries are heard:—

O treachery!
Thou, wife? O heavens, I die! O treachery!

Clytemnestra comes out with the dagger in her hand:
The dagger drips with blood; my hands, my robe,
My face—they all are wet with blood. What vengeance
Shall yet be taken for this blood? Already
I see this very steel turned on my breast,
And by whose hand!

The son whom she forebodes as the avenger of Agamemnon's death passes his childhood and early youth at the court of Strophius in Phocis. The tragedy named for him opens with Electra's soliloquy as she goes to weep at the tomb of their father:—

Night, gloomy, horrible, atrocious night,
Forever present to my thought! each year
For now two lusters I have seen thee come,
Clothed on with darkness and with dreams of blood,
And blood that should have expiated thine
Is not yet spilt! O memory, O sight!
O Agamemnon, hapless father, here
Upon these stones I saw thee murdered lie,
Murdered, and by whose hand! . .
       I swear to thee,
If I in Argos, in thy palace live,
Slave of Ægisthus, with my wicked mother,
Nothing makes me endure a life like this
Saving the hope of vengeance. Far away

Orestes is; but living! I saved thee, brother;
I keep myself for thee, till the day rise
When thou shalt make to stream upon yon tomb
Not helpless tears like these, but our foe's blood.

While Electra fiercely muses, Clytemnestra enters, with the appeal:

Cly. Daughter!
El. What voice! O Heaven, thou here?
Cly. My daughter,
Ah, do not fly me! Thy pious task I fain
Would share with thee. Ægisthus in vain forbids,
He shall not know. Ah, come! go we together
Unto the tomb.
El. Whose tomb?
Thy — hapless — father's.
El. Wherefore not say thy husband's tomb? 'T is well:
Thou darest not speak it. But how dost thou dare
Turn thitherward thy steps — thou that dost reek
Yet with his blood?
Cly. Two lusters now are passed
Since that dread day, and two whole lusters now
I weep my crime.
El. And what time were enough
For that? Ah, if thy tears should be eternal,
They yet were nothing. Look! Seest thou not still
The blood upon these horrid walls the blood
That thou didst splash them with? And at thy presence
Lo, how it reddens and grows quick again!
Fly, thou, whom I must never more call mother!

. . . .

Cly. Oh, woe is me! What can I answer? Pity—
But I merit none! — And yet if in my heart,

Daughter, thou couldst but read—ah, who could look
Into the secret of a heart like mine,
Contaminated with such infamy,
And not abhor me? I blame not thy wrath,
No, nor thy hate. On earth I feel already
The guilty pangs of hell. Scarce had the blow
Escaped my hand before a swift remorse,
Swift but too late, fell terrible upon me.
From that hour still the sanguinary ghost
By day and night, and ever horrible,
Hath moved before mine eyes. Whene'er I turn
I see its bleeding footsteps trace the path
That I must follow; at table, on the throne,
It sits beside me; on my bitter pillow
If e'er it chance I close mine eyes in sleep,
The specter — fatal vision! — instantly
Shows itself in my dreams, and tears the breast,
Already mangled, with a furious hand,
And thence draws both its palms full of dark blood,
To dash it in my face! On dreadful nights
Follow more dreadful days. In a long death
I live my life. Daughter, — whate'er I am,
Thou art my daughter still, — dost thou not weep
At tears like mine?

Clytemnestra confesses that Ægisthus no longer loves her, but she loves him, and she shrinks from Electra's fierce counsel that she shall kill him. He enters to find her in tears, and a violent scene between him and Electra follows, in which Clytemnestra interposes.

Cly. O daughter, he is my husband. Think, Ægis-
    thus,
She is my daughter.

Æg. She is Atrides' daughter!
El. He is Atrides' murderer!
Cly. Electra!
Have pity, Ægisthus! Look—the tomb! Oh, look,
The horrible tomb!—and art thou not content?
    Æg. Woman, be less unlike thyself. Atrides,—
Tell me by whose hand in yon tomb he lies?
    Cly. O mortal blame! What else is lacking now
To my unhappy, miserable life?
Who drove me to it now upbraids my crime!
    El. O marvelous joy! O only joy that's blessed
My heart in these ten years! I see you both
At last the prey of anger and remorse;
I hear at last what must the endearments be
Of love so blood-stained.

    The first act closes with a scene between Ægisthus and Clytemnestra, in which he urges her to consent that he shall send to have Orestes murdered, and reminds her of her former crimes when she revolts from this. The scene is very well managed, with that sparing phrase which in Alfieri is quite as apt to be touchingly simple as bare and poor. In the opening scene of the second act, Orestes has returned in disguise to Argos with Pylades the son of Strophius, to whom he speaks:

We are come at last. Here Agamemnon fell,
Murdered, and here Ægisthus reigns. Here rose
In memory still, though I a child departed,
These natal walls, and the just Heaven in time
Leads me back hither.
                  Twice five years have passed
This very day since that dread night of blood,
When, slain by treachery, my father made

The whole wide palace with his dolorous cries
Echo again. Oh, well do I remember!
Electra swiftly bore me through this hall
Thither where Strophius in his pitying arms
Received me—Strophius, less by far thy father
Than mine, thereafter—and fled onward with me
By yonder postern-gate, all tremulous;
And after me there ran upon the air
Long a wild clamor and a lamentation
That made me weep and shudder and lament,
I knew not why, and weeping Strophius ran,
Preventing with his hand my outcries shrill,
Clasping me close, and sprinkling all my face
With bitter tears; and to the lonely coast,
Where only now we landed, with his charge
He came apace; and eagerly unfurled
His sails before the wind.

Pylades strives to restrain the passion for revenge in Orestes, which imperils them both. The friend proposes that they shall feign themselves messengers sent by Strophius with tidings of Orestes' death, and Orestes has reluctantly consented, when Electra re-appears, and they recognize each other. Pylades discloses their plan, and when her brother urges, "The means is vile," she answers, all woman,—

Less vile than is Ægisthus. There is none
Better or surer, none, believe me. When
You are led to him, let it be mine to think
Of all—the place, the manner, time, and arms,
To kill him. Still I keep, Orestes, still
I keep the steel that in her husband's breast
She plunged whom nevermore we might call mother.

Orestes. How fares it with that impious woman?
Electra. Ah,
Thou canst not know how she drags out her life!
Save only Agamemnon's children, all
Must pity her — and even we must pity.
Full ever of suspicion and of terror,
And held in scorn even by Ægisthus' self,
Loving Ægisthus though she know his guilt;
Repentant, and yet ready to renew
Her crime, perchance, if the unworthy love
Which is her shame and her abhorrence, would;
Now wife, now mother, never wife nor mother,
Bitter remorse gnaws at her heart by day
Unceasingly, and horrible shapes by night
Scare slumber from her eyes. — So fares it with her.

In the third scene of the following act Clytemnestra meets Orestes and Pylades, who announce themselves as messengers from Phocis to the king; she bids them deliver their tidings to her, and they finally do so, Pylades struggling to prevent Orestes from revealing himself. There are touchingly simple and natural passages in the lament that Clytemnestra breaks into over her son's death, and there is fire, with its true natural extinction in tears, when she upbraids Ægisthus, who now enters:

My fair fame and my husband and my peace,
My only son beloved, I gave thee all.
. . . .
All that I gave thou did'st account as nothing
While aught remained to take. Who ever saw
At once so cruel and so false a heart?
The guilty love that thou did'st feign so ill

And I believed so well, what hindrance to it,
What hindrance, tell me, was the child Orestes?
Yet scarce had Agamemnon died before
Thou did'st cry out for his son's blood; and searched
Through all the palace in thy fury. Then
The blade thou durst not wield against the father,
Then thou didst brandish! Ay, bold wast thou then
Against a helpless child! . . .
Unhappy son, what booted it to save thee
From thy sire's murderer, since thou hàst found
Death ere thy time in strange lands far away?
Ægisthus, villainous usurper! Thou,
Thou hast slain my son! Ægisthus—Oh forgive!
I was a mother, and am so no more.

Throughout this scene, and in the soliloquy preceding it, Alfieri paints very forcibly the struggle in Clytemnestra between her love for her son and her love for Ægisthus, to whom she clings even while he exults in the tidings that wring her heart. It is all too baldly presented, doubtless, but it is very effective and affecting.

Orestes and Pylades are now brought before Ægisthus, and he demands how and where Orestes died, for after his first rejoicing he has come to doubt the fact. Pylades responds in one of those speeches with which Alfieri seems to carve the scene in bas-relief:

Every fifth year an ancient use renews
In Crete the games and offerings unto Jove.
The love of glory and innate ambition
Lure to that coast the youth; and by his side
Goes Pylades, inseparable from him.

In the light car upon the arena wide,
The hopes of triumph urge him to contest
The proud palm of the flying-footed steeds,
And, too intent on winning, there his life
He gives for victory.
 Æg.   But how? Say on.
 Pyl. Too fierce, impatient, and incautious, he
Now frights his horses on with threatening cries,
Now whirls his blood-stained whip, and lashes them,
Till past the goal the ill-tamed coursers fly
Faster and faster. Reckless of the rein,
Deaf to the voice that fain would soothe them now,
Their nostrils breathing fire, their loose manes tossed
Upon the wind, and in thick clouds involved
Of choking dust, round the vast circle's bound,
As lightning swift they whirl and whirl again.
Fright, horror, mad confusion, death, the car
Spreads in its crooked circles everywhere,
Until at last, the smoking axle dashed
With horrible shock against a marble pillar,
Orestes headlong falls —
 Cly.   No more! Ah, peace!
His mother hears thee.
 Pyl.   It is true. Forgive me.
I will not tell how, horribly dragged on,
His streaming life-blood soaked the arena's dust —
Pylades ran — in vain — within his arms
His friend expired.
 Cly.   O wicked death!
 Pyl.   In Crete
All men lamented him, so potent in him
Were beauty, grace, and daring.
 Cly.   Nay, who would not
Lament him save this wretch alone? Dear son,
Must I then never, never see thee more?

O me! too well I see thee crossing now
The Stygian stream to clasp thy father's shade:
Both turn your frowning eyes askance on me,
Burning with dreadful wrath! Yea, it was I,
'T was I that slew you both. Infamous mother
And guilty wife!—Now art content, Ægisthus?

Ægisthus still doubts, and pursues the pretended messengers with such insulting question that Orestes, goaded beyond endurance, betrays that their character is assumed. They are seized and about to be led to prison in chains, when Electra enters and in her anguish at the sight exclaims, "Orestes led to die!" Then ensues a heroic scene, in which each of the friends claims to be Orestes. At last Orestes shows the dagger Electra has given him, and offers it to Clytemnestra, that she may stab Ægisthus with the same weapon with which she killed Agamemnon:

-To thee I give my dagger
Whom then I would call mother. Take it; thou know'st how
To wield it; plunge it in Ægisthus' heart!
Leave me to die; I care not, if I see
My father avenged. I ask no other proof
Of thy maternal love from thee. Quick, now,
Strike! Oh, what is it that I see? Thou tremblest?
Thou growest pale? Thou weepest? From thy hand
The dagger falls? Thou lov'st Ægisthus, lov'st him
And art Orestes' mother? Madness! Go
And never let me look on thee again!

Ægisthus dooms Electra to the same death with Orestes and Pylades, but on the way to prison the guards liberate them all, and the Argives rise against the usurper with the beginning of the fifth act, which I shall give entire, because I think it very characteristic of Alfieri, and necessary to a conception of his vehement, if somewhat arid, genius. I translate as heretofore almost line for line, and word for word, keeping the Italian order as nearly as I can.

Scene I.

ÆGISTHUS *and* Soldiers.

Æg. O treachery unforeseen! O madness! Freed, Orestes freed? Now we shall see . . .

Enter CLYTEMNESTRA.

Cly. Ah! turn Backward thy steps.
Æg. Ah, wretch, dost thou arm too Against me?
Cly. I would save thee. Hearken to me, I am no longer —
Æg. Traitress —
Cly. Stay!
Æg. Thou 'st promised Haply to give me to that wretch alive?
Cly. To keep thee, save thee from him, I have sworn,
Though I should perish for thee! Ah, remain
And hide thee here in safety. I will be
Thy stay against his fury —
Æg. Against his fury My sword shall be my stay. Go, leave me! I go —
Cly. Whither?

Æg.   To kill him!
Cly.   To thy death thou goest!
O me! What dost thou? Hark! Dost thou not hear
The yells and threats of the whole people? Hold!
I will not leave thee.
  Æg.   Nay, thou hop'st in vain
To save thy impious son from death. Hence! Peace!
Or I will else —
  Cly.   Oh, yes, Ægisthus, kill me,
If thou believest me not. "Orestes!" Hark!
"Orestes!" How that terrible name on high
Rings everywhere! I am no longer mother
When thou 'rt in danger. Against my blood I grow
Cruel once more.
  Æg.   Thou knowest well the Argives
Do hate thy face, and at the sight of thee
The fury were redoubled in their hearts.
The tumult rises. Ah, thou wicked wretch,
Thou wast the cause! For thee did I delay
Vengeance that turns on me now.
  Cly.   Kill me, then!
Æg. I'll find escape some other way.
Cly.   I follow —
Æg. Ill shield wert thou for me. Leave me — away,
  away!
At no price would I have thee by my side!   [*Exit.*
 Cly. All hunt me from them! O most hapless state!
My son no longer owns me for his mother,
My husband for his wife: and wife and mother
I still must be! O misery! Afar
I'll follow him, nor lose the way he went.

      Enter ELECTRA.

 El. Mother, where goest thou! Turn thy steps again
Into the palace. Danger —

Cly.   Orestes — speak!
Where is he? What does he do?
   El.   Orestes,
Pylades, and myself, we are all safe.
Even Ægisthus' minions pitied us.
They cried, "This is Orestes!" and the people,
"Long live Orestes! Let Ægisthus die!"
   Cly. What do I hear?
   El.   Calm thyself, mother; soon
Thou shalt behold thy son again, and soon
Th' infamous tyrant's corse —
   Cly.   Ah, cruel, leave me!
I go —
   El. No, stay! The people rage, and cry
Out on thee for a parricidal wife.
Show thyself not as yet, or thou incurrest
Great peril. 'T was for this I came. In thee
A mother's agony appeared, to see
Thy children dragged to death, and thou hast now
Atoned for thy misdeed. My brother sends me
To comfort thee, to succor and to hide thee
From dreadful sights. To find Ægisthus out,
All armed meanwhile, he and his Pylades
Search everywhere. Where is the wicked wretch?
   Cly. Orestes is the wicked wretch!
   El.   O Heaven!
   Cly. I go to save him or to perish with him.
   El. Nay, mother, thou shalt never go. Thou ravest —
   Cly. The penalty is mine. I go —
   El.   O mother!
The monster that but now thy children doomed
To death, wouldst thou —
   Cly.   Yes, I would save him — I!
Out of my path! My terrible destiny

I must obey. He is my husband. All
Too dear he cost me. I will not, can not lose him.
You I abhor, traitors, not children to me!
I go to him. Loose me, thou wicked girl!
At any risk I go, and may I only
Reach him in time! [*Exit.*
  El. Go to thy fate, then, go,
If thou wilt so, but be thy steps too late!
Why can not I, too, arm me with a dagger,
To pierce with stabs a thousand-fold the breast
Of infamous Ægisthus! O blind mother, oh,
How art thou fettered to his baseness! Yet,
And yet, I tremble— If the angry mob
Avenge their murdered king on her— O Heaven!
Let me go after her— But who comes here?
Pylades, and my brother not beside him?

Enter PYLADES.

Oh, tell me! Orestes—?
  Pyl. Compasses the palace
About with swords. And now our prey is safe.
Where lurks Ægisthus! Hast thou seen him?
  El. Nay,
I saw and strove in vain a moment since
To stay his maddened wife. She flung herself
Out of this door, crying that she would make
Herself a shield unto Ægisthus. He
Already had fled the palace.
  Pyl. Durst he then
Show himself in the sight of Argos? Why,
Then he is slain ere this! Happy the man
That struck him first. Nearer and louder yet
I hear their yells.
  El. "Orestes!" Ah, were 't so!
  Pyl. Look at him in his fury where he comes!

Enter ORESTES *and his followers.*

Or. No man of you attempt to slay Ægisthus:
There is no wounding sword here save my own.
Ægisthus, ho! Where art thou, coward! Speak!
Ægisthus, where art thou? Come forth: it is
The voice of Death that calls thee! Thou comest not?
Ah, villain, dost thou hide thyself? In vain:
The midmost deep of Erebus should not hide thee!
Thou shalt soon see if I be Atrides' son.
  El. He is not here; he —
  Or.   Traitors! You perchance
Have slain him without me?
  Pyl.   Before I came
He had fled the palace.
  Or.   In the palace still
Somewhere he lurks; but I will drag him forth;
By his soft locks I 'll drag him with my hand:
There is no prayer, nor god, nor force of hell
Shall snatch thee from me. I will make thee plow
The dust with thy vile body to the tomb
Of Agamemnon, — I will drag thee thither
And pour out there all thine adulterous blood.
  El. Orestes, dost thou not believe me? — me!
  Or. Who 'rt thou? I want Ægisthus.
  El.   He is fled.
  Or. He 's fled, and you, ye wretches, linger here?
But I will find him.

Enter CLYTEMNESTRA.

  Cly.   Oh, have pity, son!
  Or. Pity? Whose son am I? Atrides' son
Am I.
  Cly. Ægisthus, loaded with chains —
  Or.   He lives yet?
O joy! Let me go slay him!

Cly. Nay, kill me!
I slew thy father — I alone. Ægisthus
Had no guilt in it.
 Or. Who, who grips my arm!
Who holds me back? O madness! Ah, Ægisthus!
I see him; they drag him hither — Off with thee!
 Cly. Orestes, dost thou not know thy mother?
 Or. Die,
Ægisthus! By Orestes' hand, die, villain! [*Exit.*
 Cly. Ah, thou 'st escaped me! Thou shalt slay me
first! [*Exit.*
 El. Pylades, go! Run, run! Oh, stay her! fly;
Bring her back hither! [*Exit* PYLADES.
      I shudder! She is still
His mother, and he must have pity on her.
Yet only now she saw her children stand
Upon the brink of an ignoble death;
And was her sorrow and her daring then
As great as they are now for him? At last
The day so long desired has come; at last,
Tyrant, thou diest; and once more I hear
The palace all resound with wails and cries,
As on that horrible and bloody night,
Which was my father's last, I heard it ring.
Already hath Orestes struck the blow,
The mighty blow; already is Ægisthus
Fallen — the tumult of the crowd proclaims it.
Behold Orestes conqueror, his sword
Dripping with blood!

    Enter ORESTES.

     O brother mine, oh come,
Avenger of the king of kings, our father,
Argos, and me, come to my heart!

Or. Sister,
At last thou seest me Atrides' worthy son.
Look, 't is Ægisthus' blood! I hardly saw him
And ran to slay him where he stood, forgetting
To drag him to our father's sepulcher.
Full twice seven times I plunged and plunged my sword
Into his cowardly and quaking heart;
Yet have I slaked not my long thirst of vengeance!
  El. Then Clytemnestra did not come in time
To stay thine arm?
  Or. And who had been enough
For that? To stay my arm? I hurled myself
Upon him; not more swift the thunderbolt.
The coward wept, and those vile tears the more
Filled me with hate. A man that durst not die
Slew thee, my father!
  El. Now is our sire avenged!
Calm thyself now, and tell me, did thine eyes
Behold not Pylades?
  Or. I saw Ægisthus;
None other. Where is dear Pylades? And why
Did he not second me in this glorious deed?
  El. I had confided to his care our mad
And desperate mother.
  Or. I knew nothing of them.

Enter PYLADES.

  El. See, Pylades returns—O heavens, what do I see?
Returns alone?
  Or. And sad? Oh wherefore sad,
Part of myself, art thou? Know'st not I 've slain
Yon villain? Look, how with his life-blood yet

My sword is dripping! Ah, thou did'st not share
His death-blow with me! Feed then on this sight
Thine eyes, my Pylades!
 Pyl.   O sight! Orestes,
Give me that sword.
 Or.   And wherefore?
 Pyl.   Give it me.
 Or. Take it.
 Pyl.   Oh listen! We may not tarry longer
Within these borders; come —
 Or.   But what —
 El.   Oh speak!
Where's Clytemnestra?
 Or.   Leave her; she is perchance
Kindling the pyre unto her traitor husband.
 Pyl. Oh, thou hast far more than fulfilled thy ven-
  geance.
Come, now, and ask no more.
 Or.   What dost thou say?
 El. Our mother! I beseech thee yet again!
Pylades — Oh what chill is this that creeps
Through all my veins?
 Pyl.   The heavens —
 El.   Ah, she is dead!
 Or. Hath turned her dagger, maddened, on herself?
 El. Alas, Pylades! Why dost thou not answer?
 Or. Speak! What hath been?
 Pyl.   Slain —
 Or.   And by whose hand?
 Pyl.   Come!
 El. (*To* ORESTES.) Thou slewest her!
 Or.   I parricide?
 Pyl.   Unknowing
Thou plungèdst in her heart thy sword, as blind
With rage thou rannest on Ægisthus —

Or.   Oh,
What horror seizes me! I parricide?
My sword! Pylades, give it me; I 'll have it —
  Pyl. It shall not be.
  El.   Brother—
  Or.   Who calls me brother?
Thou, haply, impious wretch, thou that didst save me
To life and matricide? Give me my sword!
My sword! O fury! Where am I? What is it
That I have done? Who stays me? Who follows
    me?
Ah, whither shall I fly, where hide myself? —
O father, dost thou look on me askance?
Thou wouldst have blood of me, and this is blood;
For thee alone — for thee alone I shed it!
  El. Orestes, Orestes — miserable brother!
He hears us not! ah, he is mad! Forever,
Pylades, we must go beside him.
  Pyl.   Hard,
Inevitable law of ruthless Fate!

IV

ALFIERI himself wrote a critical comment on each of his tragedies, discussing their qualities and the question of their failure or success dispassionately enough. For example, he frankly says of his Maria Stuarda that it is the worst tragedy he ever wrote, and the only one that he could wish not to have written; of his Agamennone, that all the good in it came from the author and all the bad from the subject; of his Fillippo II., that it may make a very terrible impression indeed of mingled pity and horror, or that it may disgust, through the cold atrocity of Philip, even to the point of nausea. On the Orestes, we may very well consult him more at length. He declares: "This tragic action has no other motive or development, nor admits any other passion, than an implacable revenge; but the passion of revenge (though very strong by nature), having become greatly enfeebled among civilized peoples, is regarded as a vile passion, and its effects are wont to be blamed and looked upon with loathing. Nevertheless, when it is just, when the offense received is very atrocious, when the persons and the circumstances are such that no human law can indemnify the aggrieved and punish the aggressor, then revenge, under the names of war, invasion, conspiracy, the duel, and the like, ennobles itself, and so works upon our minds as not only to be endured but to be admirable and sublime."

In his Orestes he confesses that he sees much to praise and very little to blame: "Orestes, to my thinking, is ardent in sublime degree, and this daring character of his, together with the perils he confronts, may greatly diminish in him the atrocity and coldness of a meditated revenge. . . . Let those who do not believe in the force of a passion for high and just revenge add to it, in the heart of Orestes, private interest, the love of power, rage at beholding his natural heritage occupied by a murderous usurper, and then they will have a sufficient reason for all his fury. Let them consider, also, the ferocious ideas in which he must have been nurtured by Strophius, king of Phocis, the persecutions which he knows to have been everywhere moved against him by the usurper,—his being, in fine, the son of Agamemnon, and greatly priding himself thereon,—and all these things will certainly account for the vindictive passion of Orestes. . . . Clytemnestra is very difficult to treat in this tragedy, since she must be here,

Now wife, now mother, never wife nor mother,

which is much easier to say in a verse than to manage in the space of five acts. Yet I believe that Clytemnestra, through the terrible remorse she feels, the vile treatment which she receives from Ægisthus, and the awful perplexity in which she lives . . . will be considered sufficiently punished by the spectator. Ægisthus is never able to elevate his soul; . . . he will always be an unpleasing, vile, and difficult personage to manage well; a character that brings small praise to the author when made sufferable, and much blame if not made so. . . . I believe the fourth and fifth acts would produce the highest effect on the stage if well represented. In the fifth, there is a movement, a brevity, a rapidly operating heat, that ought to touch, agitate, and singularly surprise the spirit. So it seems to me, but perhaps it is not so."

This analysis is not only very amusing for the candor with which Alfieri praises himself, but it is also remarkable for the justice with which the praise is given, and the strong, conscious hold which it shows him to have had upon his creations. It leaves one very little to add, but I cannot help saying that I think the management of Clytemnestra especially admirable throughout. She loves Ægisthus with the fatal passion which no scorn or cruelty on his part can quench; but while he is in power and triumphant, her heart turns tenderly to her hapless children, whom she abhors as soon as his calamity comes; then she has no thought but to save him. She can join her children in hating the murder which she has herself done on Agamemnon, but she cannot avenge it on Ægisthus, and thus expiate her crime in their eyes. Ægisthus is never able to conceive of the unselfishness of her love; he believes her ready to betray him when danger threatens and to shield herself behind him from the anger of the Argives; it is a deep knowledge of human nature that makes him interpose the memory of her unatoned-for crime between her and any purpose of good.

Orestes always sees his revenge as something sacred, and that is a great scene in which he offers his dagger to Clytemnestra and bids her kill Ægisthus with it, believing for the instant that even she must exult to share his vengeance. His feeling towards Ægisthus never changes; it is not revolting to the spectator, since Orestes is so absolutely unconscious of wrong in putting him to death. He shows his blood-stained sword to Pylades with a real sorrow that his friend should not also have enjoyed the rapture of killing the usurper. His story of his escape on the night of Agamemnon's murder is as simple and grand in movement as that of figures in an antique bas-relief. Here and elsewhere one feels how Alfieri does not paint, but sculptures his scenes and persons, cuts their outlines deep, and strongly carves their attitudes and expression.

Electra is the worthy sister of Orestes, and the family likeness between them is sharply traced. She has all his faith in the sacredness of his purpose, while she has, woman-like, a far keener and more specific hatred of Ægisthus. The ferocity of her exultation when Clytemnestra and Ægisthus upbraid each other is terrible, but the picture she draws for Orestes of their mother's life is touched with an exquisite filial pity. She seems to me studied with marvelous success.

The close of the tragedy is full of fire and life, yet never wanting in a sort of lofty, austere grace, that lapses at last into a truly statuesque despair. Orestes mad, with Electra and Pylades on either side: it is the attitude and gesture of Greek sculpture, a group forever fixed in the imperishable sorrow of stone.

In reading Alfieri, I am always struck with what I may call the narrowness of his tragedies. They have height and depth, but not breadth. The range of sentiment is as limited in any one of them as the range of phrase in this Orestes, where the recurrence of the same epithets, horrible, bloody, terrible, fatal, awful, is not apparently felt by the poet as monotonous. Four or five persons, each representing a purpose or a passion, occupy the scene, and obviously contribute by every word and deed to the advancement of the tragic action; and this narrowness and rigidity of intent would be intolerable, if the tragedies were not so brief: I do not think any of them is much longer than a single act of one of Shakespeare's plays. They are in all other ways equally unlike Shakespeare's plays. When you read Macbeth or Hamlet, you find yourself in a world where the interests and passions are complex and divided against themselves, as they are here and now. The action progresses fitfully, as events do in life; it is promoted by the things that seem to retard it; and it includes long stretches of time and many places. When you read Orestes, you find yourself attendant upon an imminent calamity, which nothing can avert or delay. In a solitude like that of dreams, those hapless phantasms, dark types of remorse, of cruel ambition, of inexorable revenge, move swiftly on the fatal end. They do not grow or develop on the imagination; their character is stamped at once, and they have but to act it out. There is no lingering upon episodes, no digressions, no reliefs. They cannot stir from that spot where they are doomed to expiate or consummate their crimes; one little day is given them, and then all is over.

Mr. Lowell, in his essay on Dryden, speaks of "a style of poetry whose great excellence was that it was in perfect sympathy with the genius of the people among whom it came into being;" and this I conceive to be the virtue of the Alfierian poetry. The Italians love beauty of form, and we Goths love picturesque effect; and Alfieri has little or none of the kind of excellence which we enjoy. But while

<blockquote>I look and own myself a happy Goth,</blockquote>

I have moods, in the presence of his simplicity and severity, when I feel that he and all the classicists may be right. When I see how much he achieves with his sparing phrase, his sparsely populated scene, his narrow plot and angular design, when I find him perfectly sufficient in expression and entirely adequate in suggestion, the Classic alone appears elegant and true — till I read Shakespeare again; or till I turn to Nature, whom I do not find sparing or severe, but full of variety and change and relief, and yet having a sort of elegance and truth of her own.

In the treatment of historical subjects Alfieri allowed himself every freedom. He makes Lorenzo de' Medici, a brutal and very insolent tyrant, a tyrant after the high Roman fashion, a tyrant almost after the fashion of the late Edwin Forrest. Yet there are some good passages in the Congiura dei Pazzi, of the peculiarly hard Alfierian sort:

<blockquote>
An enemy insulted and not slain!
What breast in triple iron armed, but needs
Must tremble at him?
</blockquote>

is a saying of Giuliano de' Medici, who, when asked if he does not fear one of the conspirators, puts the whole political wisdom of the sixteenth century into his answer,—

Being feared, I fear.

The Filippo of Alfieri must always have an interest for English readers because of its chance relation to Keats, who, sick to death of consumption, bought a copy of Alfieri when on his way to Rome. As Mr. Lowell relates in his sketch of the poet's life, the dying man opened the book at the second page, and read the lines—perhaps the tenderest that Alfieri ever wrote—

Misero me! sollievo a me non resta
Altro che il pianto, e il pianto è delitto!

Keats read these words, and then laid down the book and opened it no more. The closing scene of the fourth act of this tragedy can well be studied as a striking example of Alfieri's power of condensation.

Some of the non-political tragedies of Alfieri are still played; Ristori has played his Mirra, and Salvini his Saul; but I believe there is now no Italian critic who praises him so entirely as Giudici did. Yet the poet finds a warm defender against the French and German critics in De Sanctis,[*] a very clever and brilliant Italian, who accounts for Alfieri in a way that helps to make all Italian things more intelligible to us. He is speaking of Alfieri's epoch and social circumstances: "Education had been

[*] Saggi Critici. Di Francesco de Sanctis. Napoli: Antonio Morano. 1859.

classic for ages. Our ideal was Rome and Greece, our heroes Brutus and Cato, our books Livy, Tacitus, and Plutarch; and if this was true of all Europe, how much more so of Italy, where this history might be called domestic, a thing of our own, a part of our traditions, still alive to the eye in our cities and monuments. From Dante to Machiavelli, from Machiavelli to Metastasio, our classical tradition was never broken. . . . In the social dissolution of the last century, all disappeared except this ideal. In fact, in that first enthusiasm, when the minds of men confidently sought final perfection, it passed from the schools into life, ruled the imagination, inflamed the will. People lived and died Romanly. . . . The situations that Alfieri has chosen in his tragedies have a visible relation to the social state, to the fears and to the hopes of his own time. It is always resistance to oppression, of man against man, of people against tyrant. . . . In the classicism of Alfieri there is no positive side. It is an ideal Rome and Greece, outside of time and space, floating in the vague, . . . which his contemporaries filled up with their own life."

Giuseppe Arnaud, in his admirable criticisms on the Patriotic Poets of Italy, has treated of the literary side of Alfieri in terms that seem to me, on the whole, very just: "He sacrificed the foreshortening, which has so great a charm for the spectator, to the sculptured full figure that always presents itself face to face with you, and in entire relief. The grand passions, which are commonly sparing of words, are in his system condemned to speak much, and to explain themselves too much. . . . To what shall we attribute that respectful somnolence which nowadays reigns over the audience during the recitation of Alfieri's tragedies, if they are not sustained by some theatrical celebrity? You will certainly say, to the mediocrity of the actors. But I hold that the tragic effect can be produced even by mediocre actors, if this effect truly abounds in the plot of the tragedy. . . . I know that these opinions of mine will not be shared by the great majority of the Italian public, and so be it. The contrary will always be favorable to one who greatly loved his country, always desired to serve her, and succeeded in his own time and own manner. Whoever should say that Alfieri's tragedies, in spite of many eminent merits, were constructed on a theory opposed to grand scenic effects and to one of the two bases of tragedy, namely, compassion, would certainly not say what was far from the truth. And yet, with all this, Alfieri will still remain that dry, harsh blast which swept away the noxious miasms with which the Italian air was infected. He will still remain that poet who aroused his country from its dishonorable slumber, and inspired its heart with intolerance of servile conditions and with regard for its dignity. Up to his time we had bleated, and he roared." "In fact," says D'Azeglio, " one of the merits of that proud heart was to have found Italy Metastasian and left it Alfierian; and his first and greatest merit was, to my thinking, that he discovered Italy, so to speak, as Columbus discovered America, and initiated the idea of Italy as a nation. I place this merit far beyond that of his verses and his tragedies."

Besides his tragedies, Alfieri wrote, as I have already stated, some comedies in his last years; but I must own my ignorance of all six of them; and he wrote various satires, odes, sonnets, epigrams, and other poems. Most of these are of political interest; the Miso-Gallo is an expression of his scorn and hatred of the French nation; the America Liberata celebrates our separation from England; the Etruria Vendicata praises the murder of the abominable Alessandro de' Medici by his kinsman, Lorenzaccio. None of the satires, whether on kings, aristocrats, or people, have lent themselves easily to my perusal; the epigrams are signally unreadable, but some of the sonnets are very good. He seems to find in their limitations the same sort of strength that he finds in his restricted tragedies; and they are all in the truest sense sonnets.

Here is one, which loses, of course, by translation. In this and other of my versions, I have rarely found the English too concise for the Italian, and often not concise enough:

HE IMAGINES THE DEATH OF HIS LADY.

The sad bell that within my bosom aye
   Clamors and bids me still renew my tears,
Doth stun my senses and my soul bewray
   With wandering fantasies and cheating fears;

The gentle form of her that is but ta'en
  A little from my sight I seem to see
At life's bourne lying faint and pale with pain,—
  My love that to these tears abandons me.
"O my own true one," tenderly she cries,
  "I grieve for thee, love, that thou winnest naught
Save hapless life with all thy many sighs."
  Life? Never! Though thy blessed steps have taught
My feet the path in all well-doing, stay!—
At this last pass 't is mine to lead the way.

There is a still more characteristic sonnet of Alfieri's, with which I shall close, as I began, in the very open air of his autobiography:

HIS PORTRAIT.

Thou mirror of veracious speech sublime,
  What I am like in soul and body, show:
Red hair,— in front grown somewhat thin with time;
  Tall stature, with an earthward head bowed low;
A meager form, with two straight legs beneath;
  An aspect good; white skin with eyes of blue;
A proper nose; fine lips and choicest teeth;
  Face paler than a thronèd king's in hue;
Now hard and bitter, yielding now and mild;
  Malignant never, passionate alway,
With mind and heart in endless strife embroiled;
  Sad mostly, and then gayest of the gay.
Achilles now, Thersites in his turn:
Man, art thou great or vile? Die and thou 'lt learn!

VINCENZO MONTI AND UGO FOSCOLO

I

The period of Vincenzo Monti and Ugo Foscolo is that covered in political history by the events of the French revolution, the French invasion of Italy and the Napoleonic wars there against the Austrians, the establishment of the Cisalpine Republic and of the kingdom of Italy, the final overthrow of the French dominion, and the restoration of the Austrians. During all these events, the city of Milan remained the literary as well as the political center of Italy, and whatever were the moral reforms wrought by the disasters of which it was also the center, there is no doubt that intellectually a vast change had taken place since the days when Parini's satire was true concerning the life of the Milanese nobles. The transformation of national character by war is never, perhaps, so immediate or entire as we are apt to expect. When our own war broke out, those who believed that we were to be purged and ennobled in all our purposes by calamity looked for a sort of total and instant conversion. This, indeed, seemed to take place, but there was afterward the inevitable reaction, and it appears that there are still some small blemishes upon our political and social state. Yet, for all this, each of us is conscious of some vast and inestimable difference in the nation.

It is instructive, if it is not ennobling, to be moved by great and noble impulses, to feel one's self part of a people, and to recognize country for once as the supreme interest; and these were the privileges the French revolution gave the Italians. It shed their blood, and wasted their treasure, and stole their statues and pictures, but it bade them believe themselves men; it forced them to think of Italy as a nation, and the very tyranny in which it ended was a realization of unity, and more to be desired a thousand times than the shameless tranquillity in which it had found them. It is imaginable that when the revolution advanced upon Milan it did not seem the greatest and finest thing in life to serve a lady; when the battles of Marengo and Lodi were fought, and Mantua was lost and won, to court one's neighbor's wife must have appeared to some gentlemen rather a waste of time; when the youth of the Italian legion in Napoleon's campaign perished amidst the snows of Russia, their brothers and sisters, and fathers and mothers, must have found intrigues and operas and fashions but a poor sort of distraction. By these terrible means the old forces of society were destroyed, not quickly, but irreparably. The cavaliere servente was extinct early in this century; and men and women opened their eyes upon an era of work, the most industrious age that the world has ever seen.

The change took place slowly; much of the material was old and hopelessly rotten; but in the new generation the growth towards better and greater things was more rapid.

Yet it would not be well to conjure up too heroic an image of Italian revolutionary society: we know what vices fester and passions rage in war-time, and Italy was then almost constantly involved in war. Intellectually, men are active, but the great poems are not written in war-time, nor the highest effects of civilization produced. There is a taint of insanity and of instability in everything, a mark of feverishness and haste and transition. The revolution gave Italy a chance for new life, but this was the most the revolution could do. It was a great gift, not a perfect one; and as it remained for the Italians to improve the opportunity, they did it partially, fitfully, as men do everything.

II

The poets who belong to this time are numerous enough, but those best known are Vincenzo Monti and Ugo Foscolo. These men were long the most conspicuous literati in the capital of Lombardy, but neither was Lombard. Monti was educated in the folds of Arcadia at Rome; Foscolo was a native of one of the Greek islands dependent on Venice, and passed his youth and earlier manhood in the lagoons. The accident of residence at Milan brought the two men together, and made friends of those who had naturally very little in common. They can only be considered together as part of the literary history of the time in which they both happened to be born, and as one of its most striking contrasts.

In 1802, Napoleon bestowed a republican constitution on Lombardy and the other provinces of Italy which had been united under the name of the Cisalpine Republic, and Milan became the capital of the new state. Thither at once turned all that was patriotic, hopeful, and ambitious in Italian life; and though one must not judge this phase of Italian civilization from Vincenzo Monti, it is an interesting comment on its effervescent, unstable, fictitious, and partial nature that he was its most conspicuous poet. Few men appear so base as Monti; but it is not certain that he was of more fickle and truthless soul than many other contemplative and cultivated men of the poetic temperament who are never confronted with exigent events, and who therefore never betray the vast difference that lies between the ideal heroism of the poet's vision and the actual heroism of occasion. We all have excellent principles until we are tempted, and it was Monti's misfortune to be born in an age which put his principles to the test, with a prospect of more than the usual prosperity in reward for servility and compliance, and more than the usual want, suffering, and danger in punishment of candor and constancy.

He was born near Ferrara in 1754; and having early distinguished himself in poetry, he was conducted to Rome by the Cardinal-Legate Borghesi. At Rome he entered the Arcadian fold of course, and piped by rule there with extraordinary acceptance, and might have died a Shepherd but for the French Revolution, which broke out and gave him a chance to be a Man. The secretary of the French Legation at Naples, appearing in Rome with the tri-color of the Republic, was attacked by the foolish populace, and killed; and Monti, the petted and caressed of priests, the elegant and tuneful young poet in the train of Cardinal Borghesi, seized the event of Ugo Bassville's death, and turned it to epic account. In the moment of dissolution, Bassville, repenting his republicanism, receives pardon; but, as a condition of his acceptance into final bliss, he is shown, through several cantos of *terza rima*, the woes which the Revolution has brought upon France and the world. The bad people of the poem are naturally the French Revolutionists; the good people, those who hate them. The most admired episode is that descriptive of poor Louis XVI.'s ascent into heaven from the scaffold.

There is some reason to suppose that Monti was sincerer in this poem than in any other of political bearing which he wrote; and the Dantesque plan of the work gave it, with the occasional help of Dante's own phraseology and many fine turns of

VINCENZO MONTI.

expression picked up in the course of a multifarious reading, a dignity from which the absurdity of the apotheosis of priests and princes detracted nothing among its readers. At any rate, it was received by Arcadia with rapturous acclaim, though its theme was *not* the Golden Age; and on the *Bassvilliana* the little that is solid in Monti's fame rests at this day. His lyric poetry is seldom quoted; his tragedies are no longer played, not even his *Galeoto Manfredi*, in which he has stolen almost enough from Shakespeare to vitalize one of the characters. After a while the Romans wearied of their idol, and began to attack him in politics and literature; and in 1797 Monti, after a sojourn of twenty years in the Papal capital, fled from Rome to Milan. Here he was assailed in one of the journals by a fanatical Neapolitan, who had also written a *Bassvilliana*, but with celestial powers, heroes and martyrs of French politics, and who now accused Monti of enmity to the rights of man. Monti responded by a letter to this poet, in which he declared that his *Bassvilliana* was no expression of his own feelings, but that he had merely written it to escape the fury of Bassville's murderers, who were incensed against him as Bassville's friend! But for all this the *Bassvilliana* was publicly burnt before the cathedral in Milan, and Monti was turned out of a government place he had got, because "he had published books calculated to inspire hatred of democracy, or predilection for the government of kings, of theocrats and aristocrats." The poet was equal to this exigency; and he now reprinted his works, and made them praise the French and the revolutionists wherever they had blamed them before; all the bad systems and characters were depicted as monarchies and kings and popes, instead of anarchies and demagogues. Bonaparte was exalted, and poor Louis XVI., sent to heaven with so much ceremony in the *Bassvilliana*, was abased in a later ode on Superstition.

Monti was amazed that all this did not suffice "to overcome that fatal combination of circumstances which had caused him to be judged as the courtier of despotism." "How gladly," he writes, "would I have accepted the destiny which envy could not reach! But this scourge of honest men clings to my flesh, and I cannot hope to escape it, except I turn scoundrel to become fortunate!" When the Austrians returned to Milan, the only honest man unhanged in Italy fled with other democrats to Paris, whither the fatal combination of circumstances followed him, and caused him to be looked on with coldness and suspicion by the republicans. After Bonaparte was made First Consul, Monti invoked his might against the Germans in Italy, and carried his own injured virtue back to Milan in the train of the conqueror. When Bonaparte was crowned emperor, this democrat and patriot was the first to hail and glorify him; and the emperor rewarded the poet's devotion with a chair in the University of Pavia, and a pension attached to the place of Historiographer. Monti accepted the honors and emoluments due to long-suffering integrity and inalterable virtue, and continued in the enjoyment of them till the Austrians came back to Milan a second time, in 1815, when his chaste muse was stirred to a new passion by the charms of German despotism, and celebrated as "the wise, the just, the best of kings, Francis Augustus," who, if one were to believe Monti, "in war was a whirlwind and in peace a zephyr." But the heavy Austrian, who knew he was nothing of the kind, thrust out his surly under lip at these blandishments, said that this muse's favors were mercenary, and cut off Monti's pension. Stung by such ingratitude, the victim of his own honesty retired forever from courts, and thenceforward sang only the merits of rich persons in private station, who could afford to pay for spontaneous and incorruptible adulation. He died in 1826, having probably endured more pain and run greater peril in his desire to avoid danger and suffering than the bravest and truest man in a time when courage and truth seldom went in company. It is not probable that he thought himself despicable or other than unjustly wretched.

Perhaps, after all, he was not so greatly to blame. As De Sanctis subtly observes: "He was always a liberal. How not be liberal in those days when even the reactionaries shouted for liberty — of course, *true* liberty, as they called it? And in that name he glorified all governments. . . . And it was not with hypocrisy. . . . He was a man who would have liked to reconcile the old and the new ideas, all opinions, yet, being forced to choose, he clung to the majority, with no desire to play the martyr. So he became the secretary of the dominant feeling, the poet of success. Kindly, tolerant, sincere, a good friend, a courtier more from necessity and weakness than perversity or wickedness; if he could have retired into his own heart, he might have come out a poet."

Monti, in fact, was always an *improvvisatore*, and the subjects which events cast in his way were like the themes which the improvvisatore receives from his audience. He applied his poetic faculty to their celebration with marvelous facility, and, doubtless, regarded the results as rhetorical feats. His poetry was an art, not a principle; and perhaps he was really surprised when people thought him in earnest, and held him personally to account for what he wrote. "A man of sensation, rather than sentiment," says Arnaud, " Monti cared only for the objective side of life. He poured out melodies, colors, and chaff in the service of all causes; he was the poet-advocate, the Siren of the Italian Parnassus." Of course such a man instinctively hated the ideas of the Romantic school, and he contested their progress in literature with great bitterness. He believed that poetry meant feigning, not making; and he declared that "the hard truth was the grave of the beautiful." The latter years of his life were spent in futile battle with the "audacious boreal school" and in noxious revival of the foolish old disputes of the Italian grammarians; and Emiliani-Giudici condemns him for having done more than any enemy of his country to turn Italian thought from questions of patriotic interest to questions of philology, from the unity of Italy to the unity of the language, from the usurpations and tyranny of Austria to the assumptions of Della Crusca. But Monti could scarcely help any cause which he espoused; and it seems to me that he was as well employed in disputing the claims of the Tuscan dialect to be considered the Italian language as he would have been in any other way. The wonderful facility, no less than the unreality, of the man appears in many things, but in none more remarkably than his translation of Homer, which is the translation universally accepted and approved in Italy. He knew little more than the Greek alphabet, and produced his translation from the preceding versions in Latin and Italian, submitting the work to the correction of eminent scholars before he printed it. His poems fill many volumes; and all display the ease, perspicuity, and obvious beauty of the improvvisatore. From a fathomless memory, he drew felicities which had clung to it in his vast reading, and gave them a new excellence by the art with which he presented them as new. The commonplace Italians long continued to speak awfully of Monti as a great poet, because the commonplace mind regards everything established as great. He is a classic of those classics common to all languages — dead corpses which retain their forms perfectly in the coffin, but crumble to dust as soon as exposed to the air.

III

From the *Bassvilliana* I have translated the passage descriptive of Louis XVI.'s ascent to heaven; and I offer this, perhaps not quite justly, in illustration of what I have been saying of Monti as a poet. There is something of his curious verbal beauty in it, and his singular good luck of phrase, with his fortunate reminiscences of other poets; the collocation of the different parts is very comical, and the application of it all to Louis XVI. is one of the most preposterous things in literature. But one must remember that the poor king was merely a subject, a theme, with the poet.

> As when the sun uprears himself among
>   The lesser dazzling substances, and drives
>   His eager steeds along the fervid curve,—
>
> When in one only hue is painted all
>   The heavenly vault, and every other star
>   Is touched with pallor and doth veil its front,
>
> So with sidereal splendor all aflame
>   Amid a thousand glad souls following,
>   High into heaven arose that beauteous soul.
>
> Smiled, as he passed them, the majestical,
>   Tremulous daughters of the light, and shook
>   Their glowing and dewy tresses as they moved.
>
> He among all with longing and with love
>   Beaming, ascended until he was come
>   Before the triune uncreated life;

> There his flight ceases, there the heart, become
>   Aim of the threefold gaze divine, is stilled,
>   And all the urgence of desire is lost;
>
> There on his temples he receives the crown
>   Of living amaranth immortal, on
>   His cheek the kiss of everlasting peace.
>
> And then were heard consonances and notes
>   Of an ineffable sweetness, and the orbs
>   Began again to move their starry wheels.
>
> More swiftly yet the steeds that bore the day
>   Exulting flew, and with their mighty tread,
>   Did beat the circuit of their airy way.

In this there are three really beautiful lines; namely, those which describe the arrival of the spirit in the presence of God:

> There his flight ceases, there the heart, become
>   Aim of the threefold gaze divine, is stilled,
>   And all the urgence of desire is lost;

Or, as it stands in the Italian:

> Ivi queta il suo vol, ivi s'appunta
>   In tre sguardi beata, ivi il cor tace,
>   E tutta perde del desio la punta.

It was the fortune of Monti, as I have said, to sing all round and upon every side of every subject, and he was governed only by knowledge of which side was for the moment uppermost. If a poem attacked the French when their triumph seemed doubtful, the offending verses were erased as soon as the

French conquered, and the same poem unblushingly exalted them in a new edition;—now religion and the Church were celebrated in Monti's song, now the goddess of Reason and the reign of liberty; the Pope was lauded in Rome, and the Inquisition was attacked in Milan; England was praised whilst Monti was in the anti-French interest, and as soon as the poet could turn his coat of many colors, the sun was urged to withdraw from England the small amount of light and heat which it vouchsafed the foggy island; and the Rev. Henry Boyd, who translated the *Bassvilliana* into our tongue, must have been very much dismayed to find this eloquent foe of revolutions assailing the hereditary enemy of France in his next poem, and uttering the hope that she might be surrounded with waves of blood and with darkness, and shaken with earthquakes. But all this was nothing to Monti's treatment of the shade of poor King Louis XVI. We have seen with how much ceremony the poet ushered that unhappy prince into eternal bliss, and in Mr. Boyd's translation of the *Bassvilliana*, we can read the portents with which Monti makes the heavens recognize the crime of his execution in Paris.

> Then from their houses, like a billowy tide,
> Men rush enfrenzied, and, from every breast
> Banished shrinks Pity, weeping, terrified.
> Now the earth quivers, trampled and oppressed
> By wheels, by feet of horses and of men;
> The air in hollow moans speaks its unrest;
> Like distant thunder's roar, scarce within ken.

Like the hoarse murmurs of the midnight surge,
Like the north wind rushing from its far-off den.
. . . .

Through the dark crowds that round the scaffold flock
The monarch see with look and gait appear
That might to soft compassion melt a rock;
Melt rocks, from hardest flint draw pity's tear,—
But not from Gallic tigers; to what fate,
Monsters, have ye brought him who loved you dear?

It seems scarcely possible that a personage so flatteringly attended from the scaffold to the very presence of the Trinity, could afterward have been used with disrespect by the same master of ceremonies; yet in his Ode on Superstition, Monti has later occasion to refer to the French monarch in these terms:

> The tyrant has fallen. Ye peoples
> Oppressèd, rise! Nature breathes freely.
> Proud kings, bow before them and tremble;
> Yonder crumbles the greatest of thrones!
> *(Repeat.)* There was stricken the vile perjurer Capet,

(He will only give Louis his family name!)

> Who had worn out the patience of God!
> In that pitiless blood dip thy fingers,
> France, delivered from fetters unworthy!
> 'T is blood sucked from the veins of thy children
> Whom the despot has cruelly wronged!
> O freemen to arms that are flying,
> Bathe, bathe in that blood your bright weapons,
> Triumph rests 'mid the terror of battle
> Upon swords that have smitten a king!

This, every one must allow, was a very unhandsome way of treating an ex-martyr, but at the time Monti wrote he was in Milan, in the midst of most revolutionary spirits, and he felt obliged to be rude to the memory of the unhappy king. After all, probably it did not hurt the king so much as the poet.

IV

The troubled life of Ugo Foscolo is a career altogether wholesomer than Monti's to contemplate. There is much of violence, vanity, and adventure in it, to remind of Byron; but Foscolo had neither the badness of Byron's heart nor the greatness of his talent. He was, moreover, a better scholar and a man of truer feeling. Coming to Venice from Zante, in 1793, he witnessed the downfall of a system which Venetians do not yet know whether to lament or execrate; and he was young and generous enough to believe that Bonaparte really meant to build up a democratic republic on the ruins of the fallen oligarchy. Foscolo had been one of the popular innovators before the Republic perished, and he became the secretary of the provisional government, and was greatly beloved by the people. It is related that they were so used to his voice, and so fond of hearing it, that one day, when they heard another reading in his place, they became quite turbulent, till the president called out with that deliciously caressing Venetian familiarity, *Popolo, ste cheto; Foscolo xe rochio!* "People, be quiet; Foscolo is hoarse." While in this office, he brought out his first tragedy, which met with great success; and at the same time Napoleon played the cruel farce with which he had beguiled the Venetians, by selling them to Austria, at Campo-Formio. Foscolo then left Venice, and went to Milan, where he established a patriotic journal, in which a genuine love of country found expression, and in which he defended unworthy Monti against the attacks of the red republicans. He also defended the Latin language, when the legislature, which found time in a season of great public peril and anxiety to regulate philology, fulminated a decree against that classic tongue; and he soon afterward quitted Milan, in despair of the Republic's future. He had many such fits of disgust, and in one of them he wrote that the wickedness and shame of Italy were so great, that they could never be effaced till the two seas covered her. There was fighting in those days, for such as had stomach for it, in every part of Italy; and Foscolo, being enrolled in the Italian Legion, was present at the battle of Cento, and took part in the defense of Genoa, but found time, amid all his warlike occupations, for literature. He had written, in the flush of youthful faith and generosity, an ode to Bonaparte Liberator; and he employed the leisure of the besieged in republishing it at Genoa, affixing to the verses a reproach to Napoleon for the treaty of Campo-Formio, and menacing him with a Tacitus. He returned to Milan after the battle of Marengo, but his enemies procured his removal to Boulogne, whither the Italian Legion had been ordered, and where Foscolo cultivated his knowledge of English and his hatred of Napoleon. After travel in Holland and marriage with an Englishwoman there, he again came back to Milan, which he found full as ever of folly, intrigue, baseness, and envy. Leaving the capital, says Arnaud, "he took up his abode on the hills of Brescia, and for two weeks was seen wandering over the heights, declaiming and gesticulating. The mountaineers thought him mad. One morning he descended to the city with the manuscript of the *Sepolcri*. It was in 1807. Not Jena, not Friedland, could dull the sensation it imparted to the Italian republic of letters."

V

It is doubtful whether this poem, which Giudici calls the sublimest lyrical composition modern literature has produced, will stir the English reader to enthusiastic admiration. The poem is of its age — declamatory, ambitious, eloquent; but the ideas do not seem great or new, though that, perhaps, is because they have been so often repeated since. De Sanctis declares it the "earliest lyrical note of the new literature, the affirmation of the rehabilitated conscience of the new manhood. A law of the Republic"— the French Republic— "prescribed the equality of men before death. The splendor of monuments seemed a privilege of the nobles and the rich, and the Republicans contested the privilege, the distinction of classes, even in this form. . . . This revolutionary logic driven to its ultimate corollaries clouded the poetry of life for him. . . . He lacked the religious idea, but the sense of humanity in its progress and its aims, bound together by the family, the state, liberty, glory— from this Foscolo drew his harmonies, a new religion of the tomb." . . .

He touches in it on the funeral usages of different times and peoples, with here and there an episodic allusion to the fate of heroes and poets, and disquisitions on the æsthetic and spiritual significance of posthumous honors. The most-admired passage of the poem is that in which the poet turns to the monuments of Italy's noblest dead, in the church of Santa Croce, at Florence:

> The urnèd ashes of the mighty kindle
> The great soul to great actions, Pindemonte,
> And fair and holy to the pilgrim make
> The earth that holds them. When I saw the tomb
> Where rests the body of that great one,* who,

---

* Question of Machiavelli. Whether "The Prince" was written in earnest, with a wish to serve the Devil, or in irony, with a wish to serve the people, is still in dispute.

Tempering the scepter of the potentate,
Strips off its laurels, and to the people shows
With what tears it doth reek, and with what blood;
When I beheld the place of him who raised
A new Olympus to the gods in Rome,* —
Of him † who saw the worlds wheel through the heights
Of heaven, illumined by the moveless sun,
And to the Anglian ‡ oped the skyey ways
He swept with such a vast and tireless wing,—
O happy!§ I cried, in thy life-giving air,
And in the fountains that the Apennine
Down from his summit pours for thee! The moon,
Glad in thy breath, laps in her clearest light
Thy hills with vintage laughing; and thy vales,
Filled with their clustering cots and olive-groves,
Send heavenward th' incense of a thousand flowers.
And thou wert first, Florence, to hear the song
With which the Ghibelline exile charmed his wrath,‖
And thou his language and his ancestry
Gavest that sweet lip of Calliope,¶
Who clothing on in whitest purity
Love in Greece nude and nude in Rome, again
Restored him unto the celestial Venus; —
But happiest I count thee that thou keep'st
Treasured beneath one temple-roof the glories
Of Italy,— now thy sole heritage,
Since the ill-guarded Alps and the inconstant
Omnipotence of human destinies
Have rent from thee thy substance and thy arms,
Thy altars, country,— save thy memories, all.

* Michelàngelo.   † Galileo.
‡ Newton.   § Florence.
‖ It is the opinion of many historians that the *Divina Commedia* was commenced before the exile of Dante.—*Foscolo.*
¶ Petrarch was born in exile of Florentine parents.—*Ibid.*

Ah! here, where yet a ray of glory lingers,
Let a light shine unto all generous souls,
And be Italia's hope! Unto these stones
Oft came Vittorio * for inspiration,
Wroth to his country's gods. Dumbly he roved
Where Arno is most lonely, anxiously
Brooding upon the heavens and the fields;
Then when no living aspect could console,
Here rested the Austere, upon his face
Death's pallor and the deathless light of hope.
Here with these great he dwells for evermore,
His dust yet quick with love of country. Yes,
A god speaks to us from this sacred peace,
That nursed for Persians upon Marathon,
Where Athens gave her heroes sepulture,
Greek ire and virtue. There the mariner
That sailed the sea under Euboea saw
Flashing amidst the wide obscurity
The steel of helmets and of clashing brands,
The smoke and lurid flame of funeral pyres,
And phantom warriors, clad in glittering mail,
Seeking the combat. Through the silences
And horror of the night, along the field,
The tumult of the phalanxes arose,
Mixing itself with sound of warlike tubes,
And clatter of the hoofs of steeds, that rushed
Trampling the helms of dying warriors,—
And sobs, and hymns, and the wild Parcæ's songs! †

The poem ends with the prophecy that poetry, after time destroys the sepulchers, shall preserve

* Alfieri. So Foscolo saw him in his last years.

† The poet, quoting Pausanias, says: "The sepulture of the Athenians who fell in the battle took place on the plain of Marathon, and there every night is heard the neighing of the steeds, and the phantoms of the combatants appear."

the memories of the great and the unhappy, and invokes the shades of Greece and Troy to give an illusion of sublimity to the close. The poet doubts if there be any comfort to the dead in monumental stones, but declares that they keep memories alive, and concludes that only those who leave no love behind should have little joy of their funeral urns. He blames the promiscuous burial of the good and bad, the great and base; he dwells on the beauty of the ancient cemeteries and the pathetic charm of English churchyards. The poem of *I Sepolcri* has peculiar beauties, yet it does not seem to me the grand work which the Italians have esteemed it; though it has the pensive charm which attaches to all elegiac verse. De Sanctis attaches a great political and moral value to it. "The revolution, in the horror of its excesses, was passing. More temperate ideas prevailed; the need of a moral and religious restoration was felt. Foscolo's poem touched these chords . . . which vibrated in all hearts."

The tragedies of Foscolo are little read, and his unfinished but faithful translation of Homer did not have the success which met the facile paraphrase of Monti. His other works were chiefly critical, and are valued for their learning. The Italians claim that in his studies of Dante he was the first to reveal him to Europe in his political character, "as the inspired poet, who availed himself of art for the civil regeneration of the people speaking the language which he dedicated to supreme song"; and they count as among their best critical works, Foscolo's "exquisite essays on Petrarch and Boccaccio." His romance, "The Last Letters of Jacopo Ortis," is a novel full of patriotism, suffering, and suicide, which found devoted readers among youth affected by "The Sorrows of Werther," and which was the first cry of Italian disillusion with the French. Yet it had no political effect, De Sanctis says, because it was not in accord with the popular hopefulness of the time. It was, of course, wildly romantic, of the romantic sort that came before the school had got its name, and it was supposed to celebrate one of Foscolo's first loves. He had a great many loves, first and last, and is reproached with a dissolute life by the German critic, Gervinius.

He was made Professor of Italian Eloquence at the University of Pavia in 1809; but, refusing to flatter Napoleon in his inaugural address, his professorship was abolished. When the Austrians returned to Milan, in 1815, they offered him the charge of their official newspaper; but he declined it, and left Milan for the last time. He wandered homeless through Switzerland for a while, and at last went to London, where he gained a livelihood by teaching the Italian language and lecturing on its literature; and where, tormented by homesickness and the fear of blindness, he died, in 1827. "Poverty would make even Homer abject in London," he said.

One of his biographers, however, tells us that he was hospitably welcomed at Holland House in London, and "entertained by the most illustrious islanders; but the indispensable etiquette of the country, grievous to all strangers, was intolerable to Foscolo, and he soon withdrew from these elegant circles, and gave himself up to his beloved books." Like Alfieri, on whom he largely modeled his literary ideal, and whom he fervently admired, Foscolo has left us his portrait drawn by himself, which the reader may be interested to see.

A furrowed brow, with cavernous eyes aglow;
  Hair tawny; hollow cheeks; looks resolute;
Lips pouting, but to smiles and pleasance slow;
  Head bowed, neck beautiful, and breast hirsute;
Limbs shapely; simple, yet elect, in dress;
  Rapid my steps, my thoughts, my acts, my tones;
Grave, humane, stubborn, prodigal to excess;
  To the world adverse, fortune me disowns.
Shame makes me vile, and anger makes me brave,
  Reason in me is cautious, but my heart
Doth, rich in vices and in virtues, rave;
  Sad for the most, and oft alone, apart;
Incredulous alike of hope and fear,
Death shall bring rest and honor to my bier.

Cantù thinks that Foscolo succeeded, by imitating unusual models, in seeming original, and probably more with reference to the time in which he wrote than to the qualities of his mind, classes him with the school of Monti. Although his poetry is full of mythology and classic allusion, the use of the well-worn machinery is less mechanical than in Monti; and Foscolo, writing always with one high purpose, was essentially different in inspiration from the poet who merchandised his genius and sold his

UGO FOSCOLO.

song to any party threatening hard or paying well. Foscolo was a brave man, and faithfully loved freedom, and he must be ranked with those poets who, in later times, have devoted themselves to the liberation of Italy. He is classic in his forms, but he is revolutionary, and he hoped for some ideal Athenian liberty for his country, rather than the English freedom she enjoys. But we cannot venture to pronounce dead or idle the Greek tradition, and we must confess that the romanticism which brought into literary worship the trumpery picturesqueness of the Middle Ages was a lapse from generous feeling.

ALESSANDRO MANZONI

I

It was not till the turbulent days of the Napoleonic age were past, that the theories and thoughts of Romance were introduced into Italy. When these days came to an end, the whole political character of the peninsula reverted, as nearly as possible, to that of the times preceding the revolutions. The Bourbons were restored to Naples, the Pope to Rome, the Dukes and Grand Dukes to their several states, the House of Savoy to Piedmont, and the Austrians to Venice and Lombardy; and it was agreed among all these despotic governments that there was to be no Italy save, as Metternich suggested, in a geographical sense. They encouraged a relapse, among their subjects, into the follies and vices of the past, and they largely succeeded. But, after all, the age was against them; and people who have once desired and done great things are slow to forget them, though the censor may forbid them to be named, and the prison and the scaffold may enforce his behest.

With the restoration of the Austrians, there came a tranquillity to Milan which was not the apathy it seemed. It was now impossible for literary patriotism to be openly militant, as it had been in Alfieri and Foscolo, but it took on the retrospective phase of Romance, and devoted itself to the celebration of the past glories of Italy. In this way it still fulfilled its educative and regenerative mission. It dwelt on the victories which Italians had won in other days over their oppressors, and it tacitly reminded them that they were still oppressed by foreign governments; it portrayed their own former corruption and crimes, and so taught them the virtues which alone could cure the ills their vices had brought upon them. Only secondarily political, and primarily moral, it forbade the Italians to hope to be good citizens without being good men. This was Romance in its highest office, as Manzoni, Grossi, and D'Azeglio conceived it. Æsthetically, the new school struggled to overthrow the classic traditions; to liberate tragedy from the bondage of the unities, and let it concern itself with any tragical incident of life; to give comedy the generous scope of English and Spanish comedy; to seek poetry in the common experiences of men and to find beauty in any theme; to be utterly free, untrammeled, and abundant; to be in literature what the Gothic is in architecture. It perished because it came to look for Beauty only, and all that was good in it became merged in Realism which looks for Truth.

These were the purposes of Romance, and the masters in whom the Italian Romanticists had studied them were the great German and English poets.

The tragedies of Shakespeare were translated and admired, and the dramas of Schiller were reproduced in Italian verse; the poems of Byron and of Scott were made known, and the ballads of such lyrical Germans as Bürger. But, of course, so quick and curious a people as the Italians had been sensitive to all preceding influences in the literary world, and before what we call Romance came in from Germany, a breath of nature had already swept over the languid elegance of Arcady from the northern lands of storms and mists; and the effects of this are visible in the poetry of Foscolo's period.

The enthusiasm with which Ossian was received in France remained, or perhaps only began, after the hoax was exploded in England. In Italy, the misty essence of the Caledonian bard was hailed as a substantial presence. The king took his spear, and struck his deeply sounding shield, as it hung on the willows over the neatly kept garden-walks, and the Shepherds and Shepherdesses promenading there in perpetual *villeggiatura* were alarmed and perplexed out of a composure which many noble voices had not been able to move. Emiliani-Giudici declares that Melchiorre Cesarotti, a professor in the University of Padua, dealt the first blow against the power of Arcadia. This professor of Greek made the acquaintance of George Sackville, who inflamed him with a desire to read Ossian's poems, then just published in England; and Cesarotti studied the English language in order to acquaint himself with a poet whom he believed greater than Homer. He translated Macpherson into Italian verse, retaining, however, in extraordinary degree, the genius of the language in which he found the poetry. He is said (for I have not read his version) to have twisted the Italian into our curt idioms, and indulged himself in excesses of compound words, to express the manner of his original. He believed that the Italian language had become "sterile, timid, and superstitious," through the fault of the grammarians; and in adopting the blank verse for his translation, he ventured upon new forms, and achieved complete popularity, if not complete success. "In fact," says Giudici, "the poems of Ossian were no sooner published than Italy was filled with uproar by the new methods of poetry, clothed in all the magic of magnificent forms till then unknown. The Arcadian flocks were thrown into tumult, and proclaimed a crusade against Cesarotti as a subverter of ancient order and a mover of anarchy in the peaceful republic—it was a tyranny, and they called it a republic—of letters. Cesarotti was called corrupter, sacrilegious, profane, and assailed with titles of obscene contumely; but the poems of Ossian were read by all, and the name of the translator, till then little known, became famous in and out of Italy." In fine, Cesarotti founded a school; but, blinded by his marvelous success, he attempted to translate Homer into the same fearless Italian which had received his Ossian. He failed, and was laughed at.

Ossian, however, remained a power in Italian letters, though Cesarotti fell; and his influence was felt for romance before the time of the Romantic

School. Monti imitated him as he found him in Italian; yet, though Monti's verse abounds, like Ossian, in phantoms and apparitions, they are not northern specters, but respectable shades, classic, well-mannered, orderly, and have no kinship with anything but the personifications, Vice, Virtue, Fear, Pleasure, and the rest of their genteel allegorical company. Unconsciously, however, Monti had helped to prepare the way for romantic realism by his choice of living themes. Louis XVI., though decked in epic dignity, was something that touched and interested the age; and Bonaparte, even in pagan apotheosis, was so positive a subject that the improvvisatore acquired a sort of truth and sincerity in celebrating him. Bonaparte might not be the Sun he was hailed to be, but even in Monti's verse he was a soldier, ambitious, unscrupulous, irresistible, recognizable in every guise.

In Germany, where the great revival of romantic letters took place,—where the poets and scholars, studying their own Minnesingers and the ballads of England and Scotland, reproduced the simplicity and directness of thought characteristic of young literatures,—the life as well as the song of the people had once been romantic. But in Italy there had never been such a period. The people were municipal, mercantile; the poets burlesqued the tales of chivalry, and the traders made money out of the Crusades. In Italy, moreover, the patriotic instincts of the people, as well as their habits and associations, were opposed to those which fostered romance in Germany; and the poets and novelists, who sought to naturalize the new element of literature, were naturally accused of political friendship with the hated Germans. The obstacles in the way of the Romantic School at Milan were very great, and it may be questioned if, after all, its disciples succeeded in endearing to the Italians any form of romantic literature except the historical novel, which came from England, and the untrammeled drama, which was studied from English models. They produced great results for good in Italian letters; but, as usual, these results were indirect, and not just those at which the Romanticists aimed.

In Italy the Romantic School was not so sharply divided into a first and second period as in Germany, where it was superseded for a time by the classicism following the study of Winckelmann. Yet it kept, in its own way, the general tendency of German literature. For the "Sorrows of Werther," the Italians had the "Last Letters of Jacopo Ortis"; for the brood of poets who arose in the fatherland to defy the Revolution, incarnate in Napoleon, with hymn and ballad, a retrospective national feeling in Italy found the same channels of expression through the Lombard group of lyrists and dramatists, while the historical romance flourished as richly as in England, and for a much longer season.

De Sanctis studies the literary situation in the concluding pages of his history; they are almost the most brilliant pages, and they embody a conception of it so luminous that it would be idle to pretend to offer the reader anything better than a résumé of his work. The revolution had passed away under the horror of its excesses; more temperate ideas prevailed; the need of a religious and moral restoration was felt. "Foscolo died in 1827, and Pellico, Manzoni, Grossi, Berchet, had risen above the horizon. The Romantic School, 'the audacious boreal school,' had appeared. 1815 is a memorable date. . . . It marks the official manifestation of a reaction, not only political, but philosophical and literary. . . . The reaction was as rapid and violent as the revolution. . . . The white terror succeeded to the red."

Our critic says that there were at this time two enemies, materialism and skepticism, and that there rose against them a spirituality carried to idealism, to mysticism. "To the right of nature was opposed the divine right, to popular sovereignty legitimacy, to individual rights the State, to liberty authority or order. The middle ages returned in triumph. . . . Christianity, hitherto the target of all offense, became the center of every philosophical investigation, the banner of all social and religious progress. . . . The criterions of art were changed. There was a pagan art and a Christian art, whose highest expression was sought in the Gothic, in the glooms, the mysteries, the vague, the indefinite, in a beyond which was called the ideal, in an aspiration towards the infinite, incapable of fruition and therefore melancholy. . . . To Voltaire and Rousseau succeeded Chateaubriand, De Staël, Lamartine, Victor Hugo, Lamennais. And in 1815 appeared the Sacred Hymns of the young Manzoni."

The Romantic movement was as universal then as the Realistic movement is now, and as irresistible. It was the literary expression of monarchy and aristocracy, as Realism is the literary expression of republicanism and democracy. What De Sanctis shows is that out of the political tempest absolutism issued stronger than ever, that the clergy and the nobles, once its rivals, became its creatures; the prevailing bureaucracy interested the citizen class in the perpetuity of the state, but turned them into office-seekers; the police became the main-spring of power; the office-holder, the priest and the soldier became spies. "There resulted an organized corruption called government, absolute in form, or under a mask of constitutionalism. . . . Such a reaction, in violent contradiction of modern ideas, could not last." There were outbreaks in Spain, Naples, Piedmont, the Romagna; Greece and Belgium rose; legitimacy fell; citizen-kings came in; and a long quiet followed, in which the sciences and letters flourished. Even in Austria-ridden Italy, where constitutionalism was impossible, the middle class was allowed a part in the administration. "Little by little the new and the old learned to live together: the divine right and the popular will were associated in laws and writs. . . . The movement was the same revolution as before, mastered by experience and self-disciplined. . . . Chateaubriand, Lamartine, Victor Hugo, Lamennais, Manzoni, Grossi, Pellico, were liberal no less than Voltaire and Rousseau, Alfieri and Foscolo. . . . The religious sentiment, too deeply offended, vindicated itself; yet it could not escape from the lines of the revolution . . . it was a reaction transmuted into a reconciliation."

The literary movement was called Romantic as against the old Classicism; medieval and Christian, it made the papacy the hero of its poetry; it abandoned Greek and Roman antiquity for national antiquity, but the modern spirit finally informed Romanticism as it had informed Classicism; Parini and Manzoni were equally modern men. Religion is restored, but, "it is no longer a creed, it is an artistic motive. . . . It is not enough that there are saints, they must be beautiful; the Christian idea returns as art. . . . Providence comes back to the world, the miracle re-appears in story, hope and prayer revive, the heart softens, it opens itself to gentle influences. . . . Manzoni reconstructs the ideal of the Christian Paradise and reconciles it with the modern spirit. Mythology goes, the classic remains; the eighteenth century is denied, its ideas prevail."

The pantheistic idealism which resulted pleased the citizen-fancy; the notion of "evolution succeeded to that of revolution"; one said civilization, progress, culture, instead of liberty. "Louis Philippe realized the citizen ideal. . . . The problem was solved, the skein untangled. God might rest. . . . The supernatural was not believed, but it was explained and respected. One did not accept Christ as divine, but a human Christ was exalted to the stars; religion was spoken of with earnestness, and the ministers of God with reverence."

A new criticism arose, and bade literature draw

from life, while a vivid idealism accompanied anxiety for historical truth. In Italy, where the liberals could not attack the governments, they attacked Aristotle, and a tremendous war arose between the Romanticists and the Classicists. The former grouped themselves at Milan chiefly, and battled through the Conciliatore, a literary journal famous in Italian annals. They vaunted the English and Germans; they could not endure mythology; they laughed the three unities to scorn. At Paris Manzoni had imbibed the new principles, and made friends with the new masters; for Goethe and Schiller he abandoned Alfieri and Monti. "Yet if the Romantic School, by its name, its ties, its studies, its impressions, was allied to German traditions and French fashions, it was at bottom Italian in accent, aspiration, form, and motive. . . . Every one felt our hopes palpitating under the medieval robe; the least allusion, the remotest meanings, were caught by the public, which was in the closest accord with the writers. The middle ages were no longer treated with historical and positive intention; they became the garments of our ideals, the transparent expression of our hopes."

It is this fact which is especially palpable in Manzoni's work, and Manzoni was the chief poet of the Romantic School in that land where it found the most realistic development, and set itself seriously to interpret the emotions and desires of the nation. When these were fulfilled, even the form of Romanticism ceased to be.

III

ALESSANDRO MANZONI was born at Milan in 1784, and inherited from his father the title of Count, which he always refused to wear; from his mother, who was the daughter of Beccaria, the famous and humane writer on Crimes and Punishments, he may have received the nobility which his whole life has shown.

In his youth he was a liberal thinker in matters of religion; the stricter sort of Catholics used to class him with the Voltaireans, and there seems to have been some ground for their distrust of his orthodoxy. But in 1808 he married Mlle. Louisa Henriette Blondel, the daughter of a banker of Geneva, who, having herself been converted from Protestantism to the Catholic faith on coming to Milan, converted her husband in turn, and thereafter there was no question concerning his religion. She was long remembered in her second country "for her fresh blond head, and her blue eyes, her lovely eyes," and she made her husband very happy while she lived. The young poet signalized his devotion to his young bride, and the faith to which she restored him, in his Sacred Hymns, published in this devout and joyous time. But Manzoni was never a Catholic of those Catholics who believed in the temporal power of the Pope. He said to Madam Colet, the author of "L' Italie des Italiens," a silly and gossiping but entertaining book, "I bow humbly to the Pope, and the Church has no more respectful son; but why confound the interests of earth and

ALESSANDRO MANZONI.

those of heaven? The Roman people are right in asking their freedom—there are hours for nations, as for governments, in which they must occupy themselves, not with what is convenient, but with what is just. Let us lay hands boldly upon the temporal power, but let us not touch the doctrine of the Church. The one is as distinct from the other as the immortal soul from the frail and mortal body. To believe that the Church is attacked in taking away its earthly possessions is a real heresy to every true Christian."

The Sacred Hymns were published in 1815, and in 1820 Manzoni gave the world his first tragedy, *Il Conte di Carmagnola*, a romantic drama written in the boldest defiance of the unities of time and place. He dispensed with these hitherto indispensable conditions of dramatic composition among the Italians eight years before Victor Hugo braved their tyranny in his Cromwell; and in an introduction to his tragedy he gave his reasons for this audacious innovation. Following the Carmagnola, in 1822, came his second and last tragedy, *Adelchi*. In the mean time he had written his magnificent ode on the Death of Napoleon, "Il Cinque Maggio," which was at once translated by Goethe, and recognized by the French themselves as the last word on the subject. It placed him at the head of the whole continental Romantic School.

In 1825 he published his romance, "I Promessi Sposi," known to every one knowing anything of Italian, and translated into all modern languages. Besides these works, and some earlier poems, Manzoni wrote only a few essays upon historical and literary subjects, and he always led a very quiet and uneventful life. He was very fond of the country; early every spring he left the city for his farm, whose labors he directed and shared. His life was so quiet, indeed, and his fate so happy, in contrast with that of Pellico and other literary contemporaries at Milan, that he was accused of indifference in political matters by those who could not see the subtler tendency of his whole life and works. Marc Monnier says, "There are countries where it is a shame not to be persecuted," and this is the only disgrace which has ever fallen upon Manzoni.

When the Austrians took possession of Milan, after the retirement of the French, they invited the patricians to inscribe themselves in a book of nobility, under pain of losing their titles, and Manzoni preferred to lose his. He constantly refused honors offered him by the Government, and he sent back the ribbon of a knightly order with the answer that he had made a vow never to wear any decoration. When Victor Emanuel in turn wished to do him a like honor, he held himself bound by his excuse to the Austrians, but accepted the honorary presidency of the Lombard Institute of Sciences, Letters and Arts. In 1860 he was elected a Senator of the realm; he appeared in order to take the oath and then he retired to a privacy never afterwards broken.

IV

"Goethe's praise," says a sneer turned proverb, "is a brevet of mediocrity." Manzoni must rest under this damaging applause, which was not too freely bestowed upon other Italian poets of his time, or upon Italy at all, for that matter.

Goethe could not laud Manzoni's tragedies too highly; he did not find one word too much or too little in them; the style was free, noble, full and rich. As to the religious lyrics, the manner of their treatment was fresh and individual although the matter and the significance were not new; and the poet was "a Christian without fanaticism, a Roman Catholic without bigotry, a zealot without hardness."

The tragedies had no success upon the stage. The Carmagnola was given in Florence in 1828, but in spite of the favor of the court, and the open rancor of the friends of the Classic School, it failed; at Turin, where the Adelchi was tried, Pellico regretted that the attempt to play it had been made, and deplored the "vile irreverence of the public."

Both tragedies deal with patriotic themes, but they are both concerned with occurrences of remote epochs. The time of the Carmagnola is the fifteenth century; that of the Adelchi the eighth century; and however strongly marked are the characters,— and they are very strongly marked, and differ widely from most persons of Italian classic tragedy in this respect,— one still feels that they are subordinate to the great contests of elements and principles for which the tragedy furnishes a scene. In the Carmagnola the pathos is chiefly in the feeling embodied by the magnificent chorus lamenting the slaughter of Italians by Italians at the battle of Maclodio; in the Adelchi we are conscious of no emotion so strong as that we experience when we hear the wail of the Italian people, to whom the overthrow of their Longobard oppressors by the Franks is but the signal of a new enslavement. This chorus is almost as fine as the more famous one in the Carmagnola; both are incomparably finer than anything else in the tragedies and are much more dramatic than the dialogue. It is in the emotion of a spectator belonging to our own time rather than in that of an actor of those past times that the poet shows his dramatic strength; and whenever he speaks abstractly for country and humanity he moves us in a way that permits no doubt of his greatness.

After all, there is but one Shakespeare, and in the drama below him Manzoni holds a high place. The faults of his tragedies are those of most plays which are not acting plays, and their merits are much greater than the great number of such plays can boast. I have not meant to imply that you want sympathy with the persons of the drama, but only less sympathy than with the ideas embodied in them. There are many affecting scenes, and the whole of each tragedy is conceived in the highest and best ideal.

V

IN the Carmagnola, the action extends from the moment when the Venetian Senate, at war with the Duke of Milan, places its armies under the command of the count, who is a soldier of fortune and has formerly been in the service of the Duke. The Senate sends two commissioners into his camp to represent the state there, and to be spies upon his conduct. This was a somewhat clumsy contrivance of the Republic to give a patriotic character to its armies, which were often recruited from mercenaries and generaled by them; and, of course, the hireling leaders must always have chafed under the surveillance. After the battle of Maclodio, in which the Venetian mercenaries defeated the Milanese, the victors, according to the custom of their trade, began to free their comrades of the other side whom they had taken prisoners. The commissioners protested against this waste of results, but Carmagnola answered that it was the usage of his soldiers, and he could not forbid it; he went further, and himself liberated some remaining prisoners. His action was duly reported to the Senate, and as he had formerly been in the service of the Duke of Milan, whose kinswoman he had married, he was suspected of treason. He was invited to Venice, and received with great honor, and conducted with every flattering ceremony to the hall of the Grand Council. After a brief delay, sufficient to exclude Carmagnola's followers, the Doge ordered him to be seized, and upon a summary trial he was put to death. From this tragedy I give first a translation of that famous chorus of which I have already spoken; I have kept the measure and the movement of the original at some loss of literality. The poem is introduced into the scene immediately succeeding the battle of Maclodio, where the two bands of those Italian *condottieri* had met to butcher each other in the interests severally of the Duke of Milan and the Signory of Venice.

CHORUS.

On the right hand a trumpet is sounding,
  On the left hand a trumpet replying,
The field upon all sides resounding
    With the trampling of foot and of horse.
Yonder flashes a flag; yonder flying
Through the still air a bannerol glances;
Here a squadron embattled advances,
    There another that threatens its course.

The space 'twixt the foes now beneath them
  Is hid, and on swords the sword ringeth;
In the hearts of each other they sheathe them;
    Blood runs, they redouble their blows.
Who are these? To our fair fields what bringeth
To make war upon us, this stranger?
Which is he that hath sworn to avenge her,
    The land of his birth, on her foes?

They are all of one land and one nation,
  One speech; and the foreigner names them
All brothers, of one generation;
    In each visage their kindred is seen;
This land is the mother that claims them,

This land that their life blood is steeping,
That God, from all other lands keeping,
   Set the seas and the mountains between.

Ah, which drew the first blade among them
  To strike at the heart of his brother?
What wrong, or what insult hath stung them
  To wipe out what stain, or to die?
  They know not; to slay one another
They come in a cause none hath told them;
A chief that was purchased hath sold them;
  They combat for him, nor ask why.

Ah, woe for the mothers that bare them,
  For the wives of these warriors maddened!
Why come not their loved ones to tear them
  Away from the infamous field?
  Their sires, whom long years have saddened,
And thoughts of the sepulcher chastened,
In warning why have they not hastened
  To bid them to hold and to yield?

As under the vine that embowers
  His own happy threshold, the smiling
Clown watches the tempest that lowers
  On the furrows his plow has not turned,
  So each waits in safety, beguiling
The time with his count of those falling
Afar in the fight, and the appalling
  Flames of towns and of villages burned.

There, intent on the lips of their mothers,
  Thou shalt hear little children with scorning
Learn to follow and flout at the brothers
  Whose blood they shall go forth to shed;
Thou shalt see wives and maidens adorning

Their bosoms and hair with the splendor
Of gems but now torn from the tender,
   Hapless daughters and wives of the dead.

Oh, disaster, disaster, disaster!
   With the slain the earth's hidden already;
With blood reeks the whole plain, and vaster
   And fiercer the strife than before!
But along the ranks, rent and unsteady,
Many waver — they yield, they are flying!
With the last hope of victory dying
   The love of life rises again.

As out of the fan, when it tosses
   The grain in its breath, the grain flashes,
So over the field of their losses
   Fly the vanquished. But now in their course
Starts a squadron that suddenly dashes
Athwart their wild flight and that stays them,
While hard on the hindmost dismays them
   The pursuit of the enemy's horse.

At the feet of the foe they fall trembling,
   And yield life and sword to his keeping;
In the shouts of the victors assembling,
   The moans of the dying are drowned.
To the saddle a courier leaping,
Takes a missive, and through all resistance,
Spurs, lashes, devours the distance;
   Every hamlet awakes at the sound.

Ah, why from their rest and their labor
   To the hoof-beaten road do they gather?
Why turns every one to his neighbor
   The jubilant tidings to hear?
Thou know'st whence he comes, wretched father?

And thou long'st for his news, hapless mother?
In fight brother fell upon brother!
These terrible tidings *I* bring.

All around I hear cries of rejoicing;
　The temples are decked; the song swelleth
From the hearts of the fratricides, voicing
　　Praise and thanks that are hateful to God.
Meantime from the Alps where he dwelleth
The Stranger turns hither his vision,
And numbers with cruel derision
　　The brave that have bitten the sod.

Leave your games, leave your songs and exulting;
　Fill again your battalions and rally
Again to your banners! Insulting
　　The stranger descends, he is come!
Are ye feeble and few in your sally,
Ye victors? For this he descendeth!
'T is for this that his challenge he sendeth
　　From the fields where your brothers lie dumb!

Thou that strait to thy children appearedst,
　Thou that knew'st not in peace how to tend them,
Fatal land! now the stranger thou fearedst
　　Receive, with the judgment he brings!
A foe unprovoked to offend them
At thy board sitteth down, and derideth,
The spoil of thy foolish divideth,
　　Strips the sword from the hand of thy kings.

Foolish he, too! What people was ever
　For bloodshedding blest, or oppression?
To the vanquished alone comes harm never;
　　To tears turns the wrong-doer's joy!
　Though he 'scape through the years' long progression,
7

Yet the vengeance eternal o'ertaketh
Him surely; it waiteth and waketh;
　　It seizes him at the last sigh!

We are all made in one Likeness holy,
　　Ransomed all by one only redemption;
Near or far, rich or poor, high or lowly,
　　Wherever we breathe in life's air,
We are brothers, by one great preëmption
Bound all; and accursed be its wronger,
Who would ruin by right of the stronger,
　　Wring the hearts of the weak with despair.

Here is the whole political history of Italy. In this poem the picture of the confronted hosts, the vivid scenes of the combat, the lamentations over the ferocity of the embattled brothers, and the indifference of those that behold their kinsmen's carnage, the strokes by which the victory, the rout, and the captivity are given, and then the apostrophe to Italy, and finally the appeal to conscience—are all masterly effects. I do not know just how to express my sense of near approach through that last stanza to the heart of a very great and good man, but I am certain that I have such a feeling.

The noble, sonorous music, the solemn movement of the poem are in great part lost by its version into English; yet, I hope that enough are left to suggest the original. I think it quite unsurpassed in its combination of great artistic and moral qualities, which I am sure my version has not wholly obscured, bad as it is.

VI

THE scene following first upon this chorus also strikes me with the grand spirit in which it is wrought; and in its revelations of the motives and ideas of the old professional soldier-life, it reminds me of Schiller's Wallenstein's Camp. Manzoni's canvas has not the breadth of that of the other master, but he paints with as free and bold a hand, and his figures have an equal heroism of attitude and motive. The generous soldierly pride of Carmagnola, and the strange *esprit du corps* of the mercenaries, who now stood side by side, and now front to front in battle; who sold themselves to any buyer that wanted killing done, and whose noblest usage was in violation of the letter of their bargains, are the qualities on which the poet touches, in order to waken our pity for what has already raised our horror. It is humanity in either case that inspires him—a humanity characteristic of many Italians of this century, who have studied so long in the school of suffering that they know how to abhor a system of wrong, and yet excuse its agents.

The scene I am to give is in the tent of the great *condottiere*. Carmagnola is speaking with one of the Commissioners of the Venetian Republic, when the other suddenly enters:

Commissioner. My lord, if instantly
You haste not to prevent it, treachery
Shameless and bold will be accomplished, making
Our victory vain, as 't partly hath already.

Count. How now?

Com. The prisoners leave the camp in troops!
The leaders and the soldiers vie together
To set them free; and nothing can restrain them
Saving command of yours.

Count. Command of mine?

Com. You hesitate to give it?

Count. 'T is a use,
This, of the war, you know. It is so sweet
To pardon when we conquer; and their hate
Is quickly turned to friendship in the hearts
That throb beneath the steel. Ah, do not seek
To take this noble privilege from those
Who risked their lives for your sake, and to-day
Are generous because valiant yesterday.

Com. Let him be generous who fights for himself,
My lord! But these — and it rests upon their honor —
Have fought at our expense, and unto us
Belong the prisoners.

Count. You may well think so,
Doubtless, but those who met them front to front,
Who felt their blows, and fought so hard to lay
Their bleeding hands upon them, they will not
So easily believe it.

Com. And is this
A joust for pleasure then? Doth not Venice
Conquer to keep? And shall her victory
Be all in vain?

Count. Already I have heard it.
And I must hear that word again? 'T is bitter;
Importunate it comes upon me, like an insect
That, driven once away, returns to buzz
About my face. . . . The victory is in vain!
The field is heaped with corpses; scattered wide,
And broken are the rest — a most flourishing

Army, with which, if it were still united,
And it were mine, mine truly, I 'd engage
To overrun all Italy! Every design
Of the enemy baffled; even the hope of harm
Taken away from him; and from my hand
Hardly escaped, and glad of their escape,
Four captains against whom but yesterday
It were a boast to show resistance; vanished
Half of the dread of those great names; in us
Doubled the daring that the foe has lost;
The whole choice of the war now in our hands;
And ours the lands they 've left — is 't nothing?
Think you that they will go back to the Duke,
Those prisoners; and that they love him, or
Care more for *him* than *you?* that they have fought
In *his* behalf? Nay, they have combatted
Because a sovereign voice within the heart
Of men that follow any banner cries,
"Combat and conquer!" they have lost and so
Are set at liberty; they 'll sell themselves —
O, such is now the soldier! — to the first
That seeks to buy them — Buy them; they are yours!
  1st Com. When we paid those that were to fight with
    them,
We then believed ourselves to have purchased them.
  2d Com. My lord, Venice confides in you; in you
She sees a son; and all that to her good
And to her glory can redound, expects
Shall be done by you.
  Count.   Everything I can.
  2d Com. And what can you not do upon this field?
  Count. The thing you ask. An ancient use, a use
Dear to the soldier, I can not violate.
  2d Com. You, whom no one resists, on whom so
    promptly

Every will follows, so that none can say,
Whether for love or fear it yield itself;
You, in this camp, you are not able, you,
To make a law, and to enforce it?
  Count.   I said
I could not; now I rather say, I *will* not!
No further words; with friends this hath been ever
My ancient custom; satisfy at once
And gladly all just prayers, and for all other
Refuse them openly and promptly. Soldier!
  Com. Nay — what is your purpose?
  Count.   You will see anon.
                    [*To a soldier who enters.*
How many prisoners still remain?
  Soldier.   I think,
My lord, four hundred.
  Count.   Call them hither — call
The bravest of them — those you meet the first;
Send them here quickly.   [*Exit soldier.*
              Surely, I might do it —
If I gave such a sign, there were not heard
A murmur in the camp. But these, my children,
My comrades amid peril, and in joy,
Those who confide in me, believe they follow
A leader ever ready to defend
The honor and advantage of the soldier;
I play them false, and make more slavish yet,
More vile and base their calling, than 't is now?
Lords, I am trustful, as the soldier is,
But if you now insist on that from me
Which shall deprive me of my comrades' love,
If you desire to separate me from them,
And so reduce me that I have no stay
Saving yourselves — in spite of me I say it,
You force me, you, to doubt —

Com. What do you say?
  [*The prisoners, among them young Pergola, enter.*
Count (To the prisoners). O brave in vain! Unfortunate! To you,
Fortune is cruelest, then? And you alone
Are to a sad captivity reserved?
  A prisoner. Such, mighty lord, was never our belief.
When we were called into your presence, we
Did seem to hear a messenger that gave
Our freedom to us. Already, all of those
That yielded them to captains less than you
Have been released, and only we —
  Count. Who was it,
That made you prisoners?
  Prisoner. We were the last
To give our arms up. All the rest were taken
Or put to flight, and for a few brief moments
The evil fortune of the battle weighed
On us alone. At last you made a sign
That we should draw nigh to your banner, — we
Alone not conquered, relics of the lost.
  Count. You are those? I am very glad, my friends,
To see you again, and I can testify
That you fought bravely; and if so much valor
Were not betrayed, and if a captain equal
Unto yourselves had led you, it had been
No pleasant thing to stand before you.
  Prisoner. And now
Shall it be our misfortune to have yielded
Only to you, my lord? And they that found
A conqueror less glorious, shall they find
More courtesy in him? In vain we asked
Our freedom of your soldiers — no one durst
Dispose of us without your own assent,
But all did promise it. "O, if you can,

Show yourselves to the Count," they said. "Be sure,
He 'll not embitter fortune to the vanquished;
An ancient courtesy of war will never
Be ta'en away by him; he would have been
Rather the first to have invented it."
  Count (To the Coms). You hear them, lords? Well,
   then, what do you say?
What would you do, you? *(To the prisoners)*
        Heaven forbid that any
Should think more highly than myself of me!
You are all free, my friends; farewell! Go, follow
Your fortune, and if e'er again it lead you
Under a banner that 's adverse to mine,
Why, we shall see each other. *(The Count observes
   young Pergola and stops him.)*
         Ho, young man,
Thou art not of the vulgar! Dress, and face
More clearly still, proclaims it; yet with the others
Thou minglest and art silent?
  Pergola.   Vanquished men
Have nought to say, O captain.
  Count.   This ill-fortune
Thou bearest so, that thou dost show thyself
Worthy a better. What 's thy name?
  Pergola.   A name
Whose fame 't were hard to greaten, and that lays
On him who bears it a great obligation.
Pergola is my name.
  Count.   What! thou 'rt the son
Of that brave man?
  Pergola.   I am he.
  Count.   Come, embrace
Thy father's ancient friend! Such as thou art
That I was when I knew him first. Thou bringest

Happy days back to me! the happy days
Of hope. And take thou heart! Fortune did give
A happier beginning unto me;
But fortune's promises are for the brave,
And soon or late she keeps them. Greet for me
Thy father, boy, and say to him that I
Asked it not of thee, but that I was sure
This battle was not of his choosing.
 Pergola.   Surely,
He chose it not; but his words were as wind.
 Count. Let it not grieve thee; 't is the leader's shame
Who is defeated; he begins well ever
Who like a brave man fights where he is placed.
Come with me, *(takes his hand)*
     I would show thee to my comrades.
I 'd give thee back thy sword. Adieu, my lords;
         (To the Coms.)
I never will be merciful to your foes
Till I have conquered them.

 A notable thing in this tragedy of Carmagnola is that the interest of love is entirely wanting to it, and herein it differs very widely from the play of Schiller. The soldiers are simply soldiers; and this singleness of motive is in harmony with the Italian conception of art. Yet the Carmagnola of Manzoni is by no means like the heroes of the Alfierian tragedy. He is a man, not merely an embodied passion or mood; his character is rounded, and has all the checks and counterpoises, the inconsistencies, in a word, without which nothing actually lives in literature, or usefully lives in the world. In his generous and magnificent illogicality, he comes the nearest being a woman of all the characters in the tragedy. There is no other personage in it equaling him in interest; but he also is subordinated to the author's purpose of teaching his countrymen an enlightened patriotism. I am loath to blame this didactic aim, which, I suppose, mars the æsthetic excellence of the piece.

Carmagnola's liberation of the prisoners was not forgiven him by Venice, who, indeed, never forgave anything; he was in due time entrapped in the hall of the Grand Council, and condemned to die. The tragedy ends with a scene in his prison, where he awaits his wife and daughter, who are coming with one of his old comrades, Gonzago, to bid him a last farewell. These passages present the poet in his sweeter and tenderer moods, and they have had a great charm for me.

Scene — The Prison.

Count (speaking of his wife and daughter). By this time
    they must know my fate. Ah! why
Might I not die far from them? Dread, indeed,
Would be the news that reached them, but, at least,
The darkest hour of agony would be past,
And now it stands before us. We must needs
Drink the draft drop by drop. O open fields,
O liberal sunshine, O uproar of arms,
O joy of peril, O trumpets, and the cries
Of combatants, O my true steed! 'midst you
'T were fair to die; but now I go rebellious
To meet my destiny, driven to my doom

Like some vile criminal, uttering on the way
Impotent vows, and pitiful complaints.

. . . .

But I shall see my dear ones once again
And, alas! hear their moans; the last adieu
Hear from their lips—shall find myself once more
Within their arms—then part from them forever.
They come! O God, bend down from heaven on them
One look of pity.
        [*Enter* ANTONIETTA, MATILDE, *and* GONZAGA.
Antonietta.   My husband!
Matilde.   O my father!
Antonietta. Ah, thus thou comest back! Is this the moment
So long desired?
Count.   O poor souls! Heaven knows
That only for your sake is it dreadful to me.
I who so long am used to look on death,
And to expect it, only for your sakes
Do I need courage. And you, you will not surely
Take it away from me? God, when he makes
Disaster fall on the innocent, he gives, too,
The heart to bear it. Ah! let *yours* be equal
To your affliction now! Let us enjoy
This last embrace—it likewise is Heaven's gift.
Daughter, thou weepest; and thou, wife! Oh, when
I chose thee mine, serenely did thy days
Glide on in peace; but made I thee companion
Of a sad destiny. And it is this thought
Embitters death to me. Would that I could not
See how unhappy I have made thee!
    Antonietta.   O husband
Of my glad days, thou mad'st them glad! My heart,—
Yes, thou may'st read it!—I die of sorrow! Yet
I could not wish that I had not been thine.

Count. O love, I know how much I lose in thee:
Make me not feel it now too much.
    Matilde.   The murderers!
Count. No, no, my sweet Matilde; let not those
Fierce cries of hatred and of vengeance rise
From out thine innocent soul. Nay, do not mar
These moments; they are holy; the wrong's great,
But pardon it, and thou shalt see in midst of ills
A lofty joy remaining still. My death,
The cruelest enemy could do no more
Than hasten it. Oh surely men did never
Discover death, for they had made it fierce
And insupportable! It is from Heaven
That it doth come, and Heaven accompanies it,
Still with such comfort as men cannot give
Nor take away. O daughter and dear wife,
Hear my last words! All bitterly, I see,
They fall upon your hearts. But you one day will
    have
Some solace in remembering them together.
Dear wife, live thou; conquer thy sorrow, live;
Let not this poor girl utterly be orphaned.
Fly from this land, and quickly; to thy kindred
Take her with thee. She is their blood; to them
Thou once wast dear, and when thou didst become
Wife of their foe, only less dear; the cruel
Reasons of state have long time made adverse
The names of Carmagnola and Visconti;
But thou go'st back unhappy; the sad cause
Of hate is gone. Death's a great peacemaker!
And thou, my tender flower, that to my arms
Wast wont to come and make my spirit light,
Thou bow'st thy head? Aye, aye, the tempest roars
Above thee! Thou dost tremble, and thy breast
Is shaken with thy sobs. Upon my face

I feel thy burning tears fall down on me,
And cannot wipe them from thy tender eyes.
                . . . Thou seem'st to ask
Pity of me, Matilde. Ah! thy father
Can do naught for thee. But there is in heaven,
There is a Father thou know'st for the forsaken;
Trust him and live on tranquil if not glad.

. . . .

Gonzaga, I offer thee this hand, which often
Thou hast pressed upon the morn of battle, when
We knew not if we e'er should meet again:
Wilt press it now once more, and give to me
Thy faith that thou wilt be defense and guard
Of these poor women, till they are returned
Unto their kinsmen?
   Gonzaga.   I do promise thee.
   Count. When thou go'st back to camp,
Salute my brothers for me; and say to them
That I die innocent; witness thou hast been
Of all my deeds and thoughts — thou knowest it.
Tell them that I did never stain my sword
With treason — I did never stain it — and
I am betrayed. — And when the trumpets blow,
And when the banners beat against the wind,
Give thou a thought to thine old comrade then!
And on some mighty day of battle, when
Upon the field of slaughter the priest lifts
His hands amid the doleful noises, offering up
The sacrifice to heaven for the dead,
Bethink thyself of me, for I too thought
To die in battle.
   Antonietta.   O God, have pity on us!
   Count. O wife! Matilde! now the hour is near
We needs must part. Farewell!

158   MODERN ITALIAN POETS.

  Matilde.   No, father —
  Count.   Yet
Once more, come to my heart! Once more, and now,
In mercy, go!
  Antonietta. Ah, no! they shall unclasp us
By force!
     [*A sound of armed men is heard without.*
  Matilde. What sound is that?
  Antonietta.   Almighty God!
    [*The door opens in the middle; armed men
    are seen. Their leader advances toward
    the Count; the women swoon.*
  Count. Merciful God! Thou hast removed from them
This cruel moment, and I thank Thee! Friend,
Succor them, and from this unhappy place
Bear them! And when they see the light again,
Tell them that nothing more is left to fear.

VII

In the Carmagnola having dealt with the internal wars which desolated medieval Italy, Manzoni in the Adelchi takes a step further back in time, and evolves his tragedy from the downfall of the Longobard kingdom and the invasion of the Franks. These enter Italy at the bidding of the priests, to sustain the Church against the disobedience and contumacy of the Longobards.

Desiderio and his son Adelchi are kings of the Longobards, and the tragedy opens with the return to their city Pavia of Ermenegarda, Adelchi's sister, who was espoused to Carlo, king of the Franks, and has been repudiated by him. The Longobards have seized certain territories belonging to the Church, and as they refuse to restore them, the ecclesiastics send a messenger, who crosses the Alps on foot, to the camp of the Franks, and invites their king into Italy to help the cause of the Church. The Franks descend into the valley of Susa, and soon after defeat the Longobards. It is in this scene that the chorus of the Italian peasants, who suffer, no matter which side conquers, is introduced. The Longobards retire to Verona, and Ermenegarda, whose character is painted with great tenderness and delicacy, and whom we may take for a type of the what little goodness and gentleness, sorely puzzled, there was in the world at that time (which was really one of the worst of all the bad times in the world), dies in a convent near Brescia, while the war rages all round her retreat. A defection takes place among the Longobards; Desiderio is captured; a last stand is made by Adelchi at Verona, where he is mortally wounded, and is brought prisoner to his father in the tent of Carlo. The tragedy ends with his death; and I give the whole of the last scene:

Enter CARLO *and* DESIDERIO.

Desiderio. Oh, how heavily
Hast thou descended upon my gray head,

Thou hand of God! How comes my son to me!
My son, my only glory, here I languish,
And tremble to behold thee! Shall I see
Thy deadly wounded body, I that should
Be wept by thee? I, miserable, alone,
Dragged thee to this; blind dotard I, that fain
Had made earth fair to thee, I digged thy grave.
If only thou amidst thy warriors' songs
Hadst fallen on some day of victory,
Or had I closed upon thy royal bed
Thine eyes amidst the sobs and reverent grief
Of thy true liegemen, ah; it still had been
Anguish ineffable! And now thou diest,
No king, deserted, in thy foeman's land,
With no lament, saving thy father's, uttered
Before the man that doth exult to hear it.

Carlo. Old man, thy grief deceives thee. Sorrowful,
And not exultant do I see the fate
Of a brave man and king. Adelchi's foe
Was I, and he was mine, nor such that I
Might rest upon this new throne, if he lived
And were not in my hands. But now he is
In God's own hands, whither no enmity
Of man can follow him.

Des. 'T is a fatal gift
Thy pity, if it never is bestowed
Save upon those fallen beyond all hope—
If thou dost never stay thine arm until
Thou canst find no place to inflict a wound!

(Adelchi is brought in, mortally wounded.)

Des. My son!

Adelchi. And do I see thee once more, father?
Oh come, and touch my hand!

Des. 'T is terrible
For me to see thee so!

Ad.   Many in battle
Did fall so by my sword.
 Des.   Ah, then, this wound
Thou hast, it is incurable?
 Ad.   Incurable.
 Des.   Alas, atrocious war!
And cruel I that made it. 'T is I kill thee.
 Ad. Not thou nor he *(pointing to Carlo)*, but the
  Lord God of all.
 Des. Oh, dear unto those eyes! how far away
From thee I suffered! and it was one thought
Among so many woes upheld me. 'T was the hope
To tell thee all one day in some safe hour
Of peace —
 Ad. That hour of peace has come to me.
Believe it, father, save that I leave thee
Crushed with thy sorrow here below.
 Des.   O front
Serene and bold! O fearless hand! O eyes
That once struck terror!
 Ad.   Cease thy lamentations,
Cease, father, in God's name! For was not this
The time to die? But thou that shalt live captive,
And hast lived all thy days a king, oh listen:
Life 's a great secret that is not revealed
Save in the latest hour. Thou 'st lost a kingdom;
Nay, do not weep! Trust me, when to this hour
Thou also shalt draw nigh, most jubilant
And fair shall pass before thy thought the years
In which thou wast not king — the years in which
No tears shall be recorded in the skies
Against thee, and thy name shall not ascend
Mixed with the curses of the unhappy. Oh,
Rejoice that thou art king no longer! that
All ways are closed against thee! There is none

For innocent action, and there but remains
To do wrong or to suffer wrong. A power
Fierce, pitiless, grasps the world, and calls itself
The right. The ruthless hands of our forefathers
Did sow injustice, and our fathers then
Did water it with blood; and now the earth
No other harvest bears. It is not meet
To uphold crime, thou 'st proved it, and if 't were,
Must it not end thus? Nay, this happy man
Whose throne my dying renders more secure,
Whom all men smile on and applaud, and serve,
He is a man and he shall die.
 Des.   But I
That lose my son, what shall console me?
 Ad.   God!
Who comforts us for all things. And oh, thou
Proud foe of mine! *(Turning to Carlo.)*
 Carlo.   Nay, by this name, Adelchi,
Call me no more; I was so, but toward death
Hatred is impious and villainous. Nor such,
Believe me, knows the heart of Carlo.
 Ad.   Friendly
My speech shall be, then, very meek and free
Of every bitter memory to both.
For this I pray thee, and my dying hand
I lay in thine! I do not ask that thou
Should'st let go free so great a captive — no,
For I well see that my prayer were in vain
And vain the prayer of any mortal. Firm
Thy heart is — must be — nor so far extends
Thy pity. That which thou can'st not deny
Without being cruel, that I ask thee! Mild
As it can be, and free of insult, be
This old man's bondage, even such as thou
Would'st have implored for thy father, if the heavens

Had destined thee the sorrow of leaving him
In others' power. His venerable head
Keep thou from every outrage; for against
The fallen many are brave; and let him not
Endure the cruel sight of any of those
His vassals that betrayed him.
   Carlo.   Take in death
This glad assurance, Adelchi! and be Heaven
My testimony, that thy prayer is as
The word of Carlo!
   Ad.   And thy enemy,
In dying, prays for thee!

              Enter ARVINO.

   Arvino. (Impatiently) O mighty king, thy warriors
      and chiefs
Ask entrance.
   Ad. (Appealingly.) Carlo!
   Carlo.   Let not any dare
To draw anigh this tent; for here Adelchi
Is sovereign; and no one but Adelchi's father
And the meek minister of divine forgiveness
Have access here.
   Des.   O my beloved son!
   Ad.   O my father,
The light forsakes these eyes.
   Des.   Adelchi,—No!
Thou shalt not leave me!
   Ad.   O King of kings! betrayed
By one of Thine, by all the rest abandoned:
I come to seek Thy peace, and do Thou take
My weary soul!
   Des.   He heareth thee, my son,
And thou art gone, and I in servitude
Remain to weep.

I wish to give another passage from this tragedy: the speech which the emissary of the Church makes to Carlo when he reaches his presence after his arduous passage of the Alps. I suppose that all will note the beauty and reality of the description in the story this messenger tells of his adventures; and I feel, for my part, a profound effect of wildness and loneliness in the verse, which has almost the solemn light and balsamy perfume of those mountain solitudes:

> From the camp,
> Unseen, I issued, and retraced the steps
> But lately taken. Thence upon the right
> I turned toward Aquilone. Abandoning
> The beaten paths, I found myself within
> A dark and narrow valley; but it grew
> Wider before my eyes as further on
> I kept my way. Here, now and then, I saw
> The wandering flocks, and huts of shepherds. 'T was
> The furthermost abode of men. I entered
> One of the huts, craved shelter, and upon
> The woolly fleece I slept the night away.
> Rising at dawn, of my good shepherd host
> I asked my way to France. "Beyond those heights
> Are other heights," he said, "and others yet;
> And France is far and far away; but path
> There 's none, and thousands are those mountains —
> Steep, naked, dreadful, uninhabited
> Unless by ghosts, and never mortal man
> Passed over them." "The ways of God are many,
> Far more than those of mortals," I replied,
> "And God sends me." "And God guide you!" he said.
> Then, from among the loaves he kept in store,

He gathered up as many as a pilgrim
May carry, and in a coarse sack wrapping them,
He laid them on my shoulders. Recompense
I prayed from Heaven for him, and took my way.
Reaching the valley's top, a peak arose,
And, putting faith in God, I climbed it. Here
No trace of man appeared, only the forests
Of untouched pines, rivers unknown, and vales
Without a path. All hushed, and nothing else
But my own steps I heard, and now and then
The rushing of the torrents, and the sudden
Scream of the hawk, or else the eagle, launched
From his high nest, and hurtling through the dawn,
Passed close above my head; or then at noon,
Struck by the sun, the crackling of the cones
Of the wild pines. And so three days I walked,
And under the great trees, and in the clefts,
Three nights I rested. The sun was my guide;
I rose with him, and him upon his journey
I followed till he set. Uncertain still,
Of my own way I went; from vale to vale
Crossing forever; or, if it chanced at times
I saw the accessible slope of some great height
Rising before me, and attained its crest,
Yet loftier summits still, before, around,
Towered over me; and other heights with snow
From foot to summit whitening, that did seem
Like steep, sharp tents fixed in the soil; and others
Appeared like iron, and arose in guise
Of walls insuperable. The third day fell
What time I had a mighty mountain seen
That raised its top above the others; 't was
All one green slope, and all its top was crowned
With trees. And thither eagerly I turned
My weary steps. It was the eastern side,

Sire, of this very mountain on which lies
Thy camp that faces toward the setting sun.
While I yet lingered on its spurs the darkness
Did overtake me; and upon the dry
And slippery needles of the pine that covered
The ground, I made my bed, and pillowed me
Against their ancient trunks. A smiling hope
Awakened me at day-break; and all full
Of a strange vigor, up the steep I climbed.
Scarce had I reached the summit when my ear
Was smitten with a murmur that from far
Appeared to come, deep, ceaseless; and I stood
And listened motionless. 'T was not the waters
Broken upon the rocks below; 't was not the wind
That blew athwart the woods and whistling ran
From one tree to another, but verily
A sound of living men, an indistinct
Rumor of words, of arms, of trampling feet,
Swarming from far away; an agitation
Immense, of men! My heart leaped, and my steps
I hastened. On that peak, O king, that seems
To us like some sharp blade to pierce the heaven,
There lies an ample plain that 's covered thick
With grass ne'er trod before. And this I crossed
The quickest way; and now at every instant
The murmur nearer grew, and I devoured
The space between; I reached the brink, I launched
My glance into the valley and I saw,
I saw the tents of Israel, the desired
Pavilion of Jacob; on the ground
I fell, thanked God, adored him, and descended.

VIII

I COULD easily multiply beautiful and effective passages from the poetry of Manzoni; but I will give only one more version, "The Fifth of May," that ode on the death of Napoleon, which, if not the most perfect lyric of modern times as the Italians vaunt it to be, is certainly very grand. I have followed the movement and kept the meter of the Italian, and have at the same time reproduced it quite literally; yet I feel that any translation of such a poem is only a little better than none. I think I have caught the shadow of this splendid lyric; but there is yet no photography that transfers the splendor itself, the life, the light, the color; I can give you the meaning, but not the feeling, that pervades every syllable as the blood warms every fiber of a man, not the words that flashed upon the poet as he wrote, nor the yet more precious and inspired words that came afterward to his patient waiting and pondering, and touched the whole with fresh delight and grace. If you will take any familiar passage from one of our poets in which every motion of the music is endeared by long association and remembrance, and every tone is sweet upon the tongue, and substitute a few strange words for the original, you will have some notion of the wrong done by translation.

THE FIFTH OF MAY.

He passed; and as immovable
  As, with the last sigh given,
Lay his own clay, oblivious,
  From that great spirit riven,

So the world stricken and wondering
  Stands at the tidings dread:
Mutely pondering the ultimate
  Hour of that fateful being,
And in the vast futurity
  No peer of his foreseeing
Among the countless myriads
    Her blood-stained dust that tread.

Him on his throne and glorious
  Silent saw I, that never —
When with awful vicissitude
  He sank, rose, fell forever —
Mixed my voice with the numberless
  Voices that pealed on high;
Guiltless of servile flattery
  And of the scorn of coward,
Come I when darkness suddenly
  On so great light hath lowered,
And offer a song at his sepulcher
    That haply shall not die.

From the Alps unto the Pyramids,
  From Rhine to Manzanares
Unfailingly the thunderstroke
  His lightning purpose carries;
Bursts from Scylla to Tanais, —
  From one to the other sea.
Was it true glory? — Posterity,
  Thine be the hard decision;
Bow we before the mightiest,
  Who willed in him the vision
Of his creative majesty
    Most grandly traced should be.

The eager and tempestuous
　Joy of the great plan's hour,
The throe of the heart that controllessly
　Burns with a dream of power,
And wins it, and seizes victory
　　It had seemed folly to hope —
All he hath known: the infinite
　Rapture after the danger,
The flight, the throne of sovereignty,
　The salt bread of the stranger;
Twice 'neath the feet of the worshipers,
　　Twice 'neath the altar's cope.

He spoke his name; two centuries,
　Armèd and threatening either,
Turned unto him submissively,
　As waiting fate together;
He made a silence, and arbiter
　　He sat between the two.
He vanished; his days in the idleness
　Of his island-prison spending,
Mark of immense malignity,
　And of a pity unending,
Of hatred inappeasable,
　　Of deathless love and true.

As on the head of the mariner,
　Its weight some billow heaping,
Falls even while the castaway,
　With strainèd sight far sweeping,
Scanneth the empty distances
　　For some dim sail in vain;
So over his soul the memories
　Billowed and gathered ever!

How oft to tell posterity
    Himself he did endeavor,
And on the pages helplessly
    Fell his weary hand again.

How many times, when listlessly
    In the long, dull day's declining —
Downcast those glances fulminant,
    His arms on his breast entwining —
He stood assailed by the memories
    Of days that were passed away;
He thought of the camps, the arduous
    Assaults, the shock of forces,
The lightning-flash of the infantry,
    The billowy rush of horses,
The thrill in his supremacy,
    The eagerness to obey.

Ah, haply in so great agony
    His panting soul had ended
Despairing, but that potently
    A hand, from heaven extended,
Into a clearer atmosphere
    In mercy lifted him.
And led him on by blossoming
    Pathways of hope ascending
To deathless fields, to happiness
    All earthly dreams transcending,
Where in the glory celestial
    Earth's fame is dumb and dim.

Beautiful, deathless, beneficent
    Faith! used to triumphs, even
This also write exultantly:
    No loftier pride 'neath heaven

Unto the shame of Calvary
  Stooped ever yet its crest.
Thou from his weary mortality
  Disperse all bitter passions:
The God that humbleth and hearteneth,
  That comforts and that chastens,
Upon the pillow else desolate
  To his pale lips lay pressed!

IX

GIUSEPPE ARNAUD says that in his sacred poetry Manzoni gave the Catholic dogmas the most moral explanation, in the most attractive poetical language; and he suggests that Manzoni had a patriotic purpose in them, or at least a sympathy with the effort of the Romantic writers to give priests and princes assurance that patriotism was religious, and thus win them to favor the Italian cause. It must be confessed that such a temporal design as this would fatally affect the devotional quality of the hymns, even if the poet's consciousness did not; but I am not able to see any evidence of such sympathy in the poems themselves. I detect there a perfectly sincere religious feeling, and nothing of devotional rapture. The poet had, no doubt, a satisfaction in bringing out the beauty and sublimity of his faith; and, as a literary artist, he had a right to be proud of his work, for its spirit is one of which the tuneful piety of Italy had long been void. In truth, since David, king of Israel, left making psalms, religious songs have been poorer than any other sort of songs; and it is high praise of Manzoni's "Inni Sacri" to say that they are in irreproachable taste, and unite in unaffected poetic appreciation of the grandeur of Christianity as much reason as may coexist with obedience.

The poetry of Manzoni is so small in quantity, that we must refer chiefly to excellence of quality the influence and the fame it has won him, though I do not deny that his success may have been partly owing at first to the errors of the school which preceded him. It could be easily shown, from literary history, that every great poet has appeared at a moment fortunate for his renown, just as we might prove, from natural science, that it is felicitous for the sun to get up about day-break. Manzoni's art was very great, and he never gave his thought defective expression, while the expression was always secondary to the thought. For the self-respect, then, of an honest man, which would not permit him to poetize insincerity and shape the void, and for the great purpose he always cherished of making literature an agent of civilization and Christianity, the Italians are right to honor Manzoni. Arnaud thinks that the school he founded lingered too long on the educative and religious ground he chose; and Marc Monnier declares Manzoni to be the poet of resignation, thus distinguishing him from the poets of revolution. The former critic is the nearer right of the two, though neither is quite just, as it seems to me; for I do not understand how any one can read the romance and the dramas of Manzoni without finding him full of sympathy for all Italy has suffered, and a patriot very far from resigned; and I think political conditions—or the Austrians in Milan, to put it more concretely—scarcely left to the choice of the Lombard school that attitude of aggression which others assumed under a weaker, if not a milder, despotism at Florence. The utmost allowed the Milanese poets was the expression of a retrospective patriotism, which celebrated the glories of Italy's past, which deplored her errors, and which denounced her crimes, and thus contributed to keep the sense of nationality alive. Under such governments as endured in Piedmont until 1848, in Lombardy until 1859, in Venetia until 1866, literature must remain educative, or must cease to be. In the works, therefore, of Manzoni and of nearly all his immediate followers, there is nothing directly revolutionary except in Giovanni Berchet. The line between them and the directly revolutionary poets is by no means to be traced with exactness, however, in their literature, and in their lives they were all alike patriotic.

Manzoni lived to see all his hopes fulfilled, and died two years after the fall of the temporal power, in 1873. "Toward mid-day," says a Milanese journal at the time of his death, "he turned suddenly to the household friends about him, and said: 'This man is failing—sinking—call my confessor!'

The confessor came, and he communed with him half an hour, speaking, as usual, from a mind calm and clear. After the confessor left the room, Manzoni called his friends and said to them: 'When I am dead, do what I did every day: pray for Italy—pray for the king and his family—so good to me!' His country was the last thought of this great man dying as in his whole long life it had been his most vivid and constant affection."

SILVIO PELLICO, TOMMASO GROSSI, LUIGI CARRER, AND GIOVANNI BERCHET

I

As I have noted, nearly all the poets of the Romantic School were Lombards, and they had nearly all lived at Milan under the censorship and espionage of the Austrian government. What sort of life this must have been, we, born and reared in a free country, can hardly imagine. We have no experience by which we can judge it, and we never can do full justice to the intellectual courage and devotion of a people who, amid inconceivable obstacles and oppressions, expressed themselves in a new and vigorous literature. It was not, I have explained, openly revolutionary; but whatever tended to make men think and feel was a sort of indirect rebellion against Austria. When a society of learned Milanese gentlemen once presented an address to the Emperor, he replied, with brutal insolence, that he wanted obedient subjects in Italy, nothing more; and it is certain that the activity of the Romantic School was regarded with jealousy and dislike by the government from the first. The authorities awaited only a pretext for striking a deadly blow at the poets and novelists, who ought to have been satisfied with being good subjects, but who, instead, must needs even found a newspaper, and discuss in it projects for giving the Italians a literary life, since they could not have a political existence. The perils of contributing to the *Conciliatore* were such as would attend house-breaking and horse-stealing in happier countries and later times. The government forbade any of its employees to write for it, under pain of losing their places; the police, through whose hands every article intended for publication had to pass, not only struck out all possibly offensive expressions, but informed one of the authors that if his articles continued to come to them so full of objectionable things, he should be banished, even though those things never reached the public.

At last the time came for suppressing this journal and punishing its managers. The chief editor was a young Piedmontese poet, who politically was one of the most harmless and inoffensive of men; his literary creed obliged him to choose Italian subjects for his poems, and he thus erred by mentioning Italy; yet Arnaud, in his "Poeti Patriottici," tells us he could find but two lines from which this poet could be suspected of patriotism, and he altogether refuses to class him with the poets who have promoted revolution. Nevertheless, it is probable that this poet wished Freedom well. He was indefinitely hopeful for Italy; he was young, generous, and credulous of goodness and justice. His youth, his generosity, his truth, made him odious to Austria. One day he returned from a visit to Turin, and was arrested. He could have escaped when danger first threatened, but his faith in his own innocence ruined him. After a tedious imprisonment, and repeated examinations in Milan, he was taken to Venice, and lodged in the famous *piombi*, or cells in the roof of the Ducal Palace. There, after long delays, he had his trial, and was sentenced to twenty years in the prison of Spielberg. By a sort of poetical license which the imperial clemency sometimes used, the nights were counted as days, and the term was thus reduced to ten years. Many other young and gifted Italians suffered at the same time; most of them came to this country at the end of their long durance; this Piedmontese poet returned to his own city of Turin, an old and broken-spirited man, doubting of the political future, and half a Jesuit in religion. He was devastated, and for once a cruel injustice seemed to have accomplished its purpose.

Such is the grim outline of the story of Silvio Pellico. He was arrested for no offense, save that he was an Italian and an intellectual man; for no other offense he was condemned and suffered. His famous book, " My Prisons," is the touching and forgiving record of one of the greatest crimes ever perpetrated.

Few have borne wrong with such Christlike meekness and charity as Pellico. One cannot read his *Prigioni* without doing homage to his purity and goodness, and cannot turn to his other works without the misgiving that the sole poem he has left the world is the story of his most fatal and unmerited suffering. I have not the hardihood to pretend that I have read all his works. I must confess that I found it impossible to do so, though I came to their perusal inured to drought by travel through Saharas of Italian verse. I can boast only of having read the *Francesca da Rimini,* among the tragedies, and two or three of the canticles,— or romantic stories of the Middle Ages, in blank verse,— which now refuse to be identified. I know, from a despairing reference to his volume, that his remaining poems are chiefly of a religious cast.

II

A MUCH better poet of the Romantic School was Tommaso Grossi, who, like Manzoni and Pellico, is now best known by a prose work — a novel which enjoys a popularity as great as that of "Le Mie Prigioni," and which has been nearly as much read in Italy as "I Promessi Sposi." The "Marco Visconti" of Grossi is a romance of the thirteenth century; and though not, as Cantù says, an historic "episode, but a succession of episodes, which do not leave a general and unique impression," it yet contrives to bring you so pleasantly acquainted with the splendid, squalid, poetic, miserable Italian life in Milan, and

TOMMASO GROSSI.

on its neighboring hills and lakes, during the Middle Ages, that you cannot help reading it to the end. I suppose that this is the highest praise which can be bestowed upon an historical romance, and that it implies great charm of narrative and beauty of style. I can add, that the feeling of Grossi's " Marco Visconti " is genuine and exalted, and that its morality is blameless. It has scarcely the right to be analyzed here, however, and should not have been more than mentioned, but for the fact that it chances to be the setting of the author's best thing in verse. I hope that, even in my crude English version, the artless pathos and sweet natural grace of one of the tenderest little songs in any tongue have not wholly perished.

THE FAIR PRISONER TO THE SWALLOW.

Pilgrim swallow! pilgrim swallow!
  On my grated window's sill,
Singing, as the mornings follow,
  Quaint and pensive ditties still,
What would'st tell me in thy lay?
Prithee, pilgrim swallow, say!

All forgotten, com'st thou hither
  Of thy tender spouse forlorn,
That we two may grieve together,
  Little widow, sorrow worn?
Grieve then, weep then, in thy lay!
Pilgrim swallow, grieve alway!

Yet a lighter woe thou weepest:
  Thou at least art free of wing,

And while land and lake thou sweepest,
  May'st make heaven with sorrow ring,
Calling his dear name alway,
Pilgrim swallow, in thy lay.

Could I too! that am forbidden
  By this low and narrow cell,
Whence the sun's fair light is hidden,
  Whence thou scarce can'st hear me tell
Sorrows that I breathe alway,
While thou pip'st thy plaintive lay.

Ah! September quickly coming,
  Thou shalt take farewell of me,
And, to other summers roaming,
  Other hills and waters see,—
Greeting them with songs more gay,
Pilgrim swallow, far away.

Still, with every hopeless morrow,
  While I ope mine eyes in tears,
Sweetly through my brooding sorrow
  Thy dear song shall reach mine ears,—
Pitying me, though far away,
Pilgrim swallow, in thy lay.

Thou, when thou and spring together
  Here return, a cross shalt see,—
In the pleasant evening weather,
  Wheel and pipe, here, over me!
Peace and peace! the coming May,
Sing me in thy roundelay!

It is a great good fortune for a man to have written a thing so beautiful as this, and not a singular fortune that he should have written nothing else comparable to it. The like happens in all literatures; and no one need be surprised to learn that I found the other poems of Grossi often difficult, and sometimes almost impossible to read.

Grossi was born in 1791, at Bellano, by lovely Como, whose hills and waters he remembers in all his works with constant affection. He studied law at the University of Pavia, but went early to Milan, where he cultivated literature rather than the austerer science to which he had been bred, and soon became the fashion, writing tales in Milanese and Italian verse, and making the women cry by his pathetic art of story-telling. "Ildegonda," published in 1820, was the most popular of all these tales, and won Grossi an immense number of admirers, every one (says his biographer Cantù) of the fair sex, who began to wear Ildegonda dresses and Ildegonda bonnets. The poem was printed and reprinted; it is the heart-breaking story of a poor little maiden in the middle ages, whom her father and brother shut up in a convent because she is in love with the right person and will not marry the wrong one — a common thing in all ages. The cruel abbess and wicked nuns, by the order of Ildegonda's family, try to force her to take the veil; but she, supported by her own repugnance to the cloister, and by the secret counsels of one of the sisters, with whom force had succeeded, resists persuasion, reproach, starvation, cold, imprisonment, and chains. Her lover attempts to rescue her by means of a subterranean vault under the convent; but the plot is discovered, and the unhappy pair are assailed by armed men at the very moment of escape. Ildegonda is dragged back to her dungeon; and Rizzardo, already under accusation of heresy, is quickly convicted and burnt at the stake. They bring the poor girl word of this, and her sick brain turns. In her delirium she sees her lover in torment for his heresy, and, flying from the hideous apparition, she falls and strikes her head against a stone. She wakes in the arms of the beloved sister who had always befriended her. The cruel efforts against her cease now, and she writes to her father imploring his pardon, which he gives, with a prayer for hers. At last she dies peacefully. The story is pathetic; and it is told with art, though its lapses of taste are woful, and its faults those of the whole class of Italian poetry to which it belongs. The agony is tedious, as Italian agony is apt to be, the passion is outrageously violent or excessively tender, the description too often prosaic; the effects are sometimes produced by very "rough magic." The more than occasional infelicity and awkwardness of diction which offend in Byron's poetic tales are not felt, so much in those of Grossi; but in "Ildegonda" there is horror more material even than in "Parisina." Here is a picture of Rizzardo's apparition, for which my faint English has no stomach:

> Chè dalla bocca fuori gli pendea
> La coda smisurata d' un serpente,
> E il flagellava per la faccia, mentre
> Il capo e il tronco gli scendean nel ventre.

Fischia la biscia nell' orribil lutta
Entro il ventre profondo del dannato,
Che dalla bocca lacerata erutta
Un torrente di sangue aggruppato;
E bava gialla, venenosa e brutta,
Dalle narici fuor manda col fiato,
La qual pel mento giù gli cola, e lassa
Insolcata la carne, ovunque passa.

It seems to have been the fate of Grossi as a poet to achieve fashion, and not fame; and his great poem in fifteen cantos, called "I Lombardi alla Prima Crociata," which made so great a noise in its day, was eclipsed in reputation by his subsequent novel of "Marco Visconti." Since the "Gerusalemma" of Tasso, it is said that no poem has made so great a sensation in Italy as "I Lombardi," in which the theme treated by the elder poet is celebrated according to the æsthetics of the Romantic School. Such parts of the poem as I have read have not tempted me to undertake the whole; but many people must have at least bought it, for it gave the author thirty thousand francs in solid proof of popularity.

After the "Marco Visconti," Grossi seems to have produced no work of importance. He married late, but happily; and he now devoted himself almost exclusively to the profession of the law, in Milan, where he died in 1853, leaving the memory of a good man, and the fame of a poet unspotted by reproach. As long as he lived, he was the beloved friend of Manzoni. He dwelt many years under the great master's roof, subject to the influence of the stronger mind, but not servile to it; adopting its literary principles, but giving them his own expression.

III

Luigi Carrer of Venice was the first of that large number of minor poets and dramatists to which the states of the old Republic have given birth during the present century. His life began with our century, and he died in 1850. During this time he witnessed great political events — the retirement of the French after the fall of Napoleon; the failure of all the schemes and hopes of the Carbonari to shake off the yoke of the stranger; and that revolution in 1848 which drove out the Austrians, only that, a year later, they should return in such force as to make the hope of Venetian independence through the valor of Venetian arms a vain dream forever. There is not wanting evidence of a tender love of country in the poems of Carrer, and probably the effectiveness of the Austrian system of repression, rather than his own indifference, is witnessed by the fact that he has scarcely a line to betray a hope for the future, or a consciousness of political anomaly in the present.

Carrer was poor, but the rich were glad to be his friends, without putting him to shame; and as long as the once famous *conversazioni* were held in the great Venetian houses, he was the star of whatever place assembled genius and beauty. He had a professorship in a private school, and while he was young he printed his verses in the journals. As he grew older, he wrote graceful books of prose, and drew his slender support from their sale and from the minute pay of some offices in the gift of his native city.

Carrer's ballads are esteemed the best of his poems; and I may offer an idea of the quality and manner of some of his ballads by the following translation, but I cannot render his peculiar elegance, nor give the whole range of his fancy:

THE DUCHESS.

From the horrible profound
  Of the voiceless sepulcher
Comes, or seems to come, a sound;
  Is't his Grace, the Duke, astir?
In his trance he hath been laid
As one dead among the dead!

The relentless stone he tries
  With his utmost strength to move;
Fails, and in his fury cries,
  Smiting his hands, that those above.
If any shall be passing there,
Hear his blasphemy, or his prayer.

And at last he seems to hear
  Light feet overhead go by;
"O, whoever passes near
  Where I am, the Duke am I!

All my states and all I have
To him that takes me from this grave."

There is no one that replies;
　　Surely, some one seemed to come!
On his brow the cold sweat lies,
　　As he waits an instant dumb;
Then he cries with broken breath,
"Save me, take me back from death!"

"Where thou liest, lie thou must,
　　Prayers and curses alike are vain:
Over thee dead Gismond's dust—
　　Whom thy pitiless hand hath slain—
On this stone so heavily
Rests, we cannot set thee free."

From the sepulcher's thick walls
　　Comes a low wail of dismay,
And, as when a body falls,
　　A dull sound;—and the next day
In a convent the Duke's wife
Hideth her remorseful life.

Of course, Carrer wrote much poetry besides his ballads. There are idyls, and romances in verse, and hymns; sonnets of feeling and of occasion; odes, sometimes of considerable beauty; apologues, of such exceeding fineness of point, that it often escapes one; satires and essays, or *sermoni*, some of which I have read with no great relish. The same spirit dominates nearly all—the spirit of pensive disappointment which life brings to delicate and sensitive natures, and which they love to affect even more than they feel. Among Carrer's many sonnets, I think I like best the following, of which the sentiment seems to me simple and sweet, and the expression very winning:

> I am a pilgrim swallow, and I roam
> Beyond strange seas, of other lands in quest,
> Leaving the well-known lakes and hills of home,
> And that dear roof where late I hung my nest;
> All things beloved and love's eternal woes
> I fly, an exile from my native shore:
> I cross the cliffs and woods, but with me goes
> The care I thought to abandon evermore.
> Along the banks of streams unknown to me,
> I pipe the elms and willows pensive lays,
> And call on her whom I despair to see,
> And pass in banishment and tears my days.
> Breathe, air of spring, for which I pine and yearn,
> That to his nest the swallow may return!

The prose writings of Carrer are essays on æsthetics and morals, and sentimentalized history. His chief work is of the latter nature. "I Sette Gemm di Venezia" are sketches of the lives of the seven Venetian women who have done most to distinguish the name of their countrywomen by their talents, or misfortunes, or sins. You feel, in looking through the book, that its interest is in great part factitious. The stories are all expanded, and filled up with facile but not very relevant discourse, which a pleasant fancy easily supplies, and which is always best left to the reader's own thought. The style is somewhat florid; but the author contrives to retain in his fantastic strain much of the grace of simplicity. It is the work of a cunning artist; but it has a certain insipidity, and it wearies. Carrer did well in the limit which he assigned himself, but his range was circumscribed. At the time of his death, he had written sixteen cantos of an epic poem called "La Fata Vergine," which a Venetian critic has extravagantly praised, and which I have not seen. He exercised upon the poetry of his day an influence favorable to lyric naturalness, and his ballads were long popular.

IV

GIOVANNI BERCHET was a poet who alone ought to be enough to take from the Lombard romanticists the unjust reproach of "resignation." "Where our poetry," says De Sanctis, "throws off every disguise, romantic or classic, is in the verse of Berchet. ... If Giovanni Berchet had remained in Italy, probably his genius would have remained enveloped in the allusions and shadows of romanticism. But in his exile at London he uttered the sorrow and the wrath of his betrayed and vanquished country. It was the accent of the national indignation which, leaving the generalities of the sonnets and the ballads, dramatized itself and portrayed our life in its most touching phases."

Berchet's family was of French origin, but he was the most Italian of Italians, and nearly all his poems are of an ardent political tint and temperature. Naturally, he spent a great part of his life in exile after the Austrians were reëstablished in Milan; he was some time in England, and I believe he died in Switzerland.

I have most of his patriotic poems in a little book which is curiously historical of a situation forever past. I picked it up, I do not remember where or when, in Venice; and as it is a collection of pieces all meant to embitter the spirit against Austria, it had doubtless not been brought into the city with the connivance of the police. There is no telling where it was printed, the mysterious date of publication being "Italy, 1861," and nothing more, with the English motto: "Adieu, my native land, adieu!"

The principal poem here is called "Le Fantasie," and consists of a series of lyrics in which an Italian exile contrasts the Lombards, who drove out Frederick Barbarossa in the twelfth century, with the Lombards of 1829, who crouched under the power defied of old. It is full of burning reproaches, sarcasms, and appeals; and it probably had some influence in renewing the political agitation which in Italy followed the French revolution of 1830. Other poems of Berchet represent social aspects of the Austrian rule, like one entitled "Remorse," which paints the isolation and wretchedness of an Italian woman married to an Austrian; and another, "Giulia," which gives a picture of the frantic misery of an Austrian conscription in Italy. A very impressive poem is that called "The Hermit of Mt. Cenis." A traveler reaches the summit of the pass, and, looking over upon the beauty and magnificence of the Italian plains, and seeing only their loveliness and peace, his face is lighted up with an involuntary smile, when suddenly the hermit who knows all the invisible disaster and despair of the scene suddenly accosts him with, "Accursed be he who approaches without tears this home of sorrow!"

At the time the Romantic School rose in Italian literature, say from 1815 till 1820, society was brilliant, if not contented or happy. In Lombardy and Venetia, immediately after the treaties of the Holy Alliance had consigned these provinces to Austria, there flourished famous *conversazioni* at many noble houses. In those of Milan many distinguished literary men of other nations met. Byron and Hobhouse were frequenters of the same *salons* as Pellico, Manzoni, and Grossi; the Schlegels represented the German Romantic School, and Madame de Staël the sympathizing movement in France. There was very much that was vicious still, and very much that was ignoble in Italian society, but this was by sufferance and not as of old by approval; and it appears that the tone of the highest life was intellectual. It cannot be

claimed that this tone was at all so general as the
badness of the last century. It was not so easily
imitated as that, and it could not penetrate so subtly
into all ranks and conditions. Still it was very observable, and mingled with it in many leading
minds was the strain of religious resignation,
audible in Manzoni's poetry. That was a time
when the Italians might, if ever, have adapted
themselves to foreign rule; but the Austrians, so
far from having learned political wisdom during
the period of their expulsion from Italy, had actually retrograded; from being passive authorities
whom long sojourn was gradually Italianizing,
they had, in their absence, become active and relentless tyrants, and they now seemed to study
how most effectually to alienate themselves. They
found out their error later, but when too late to
repair it, and from 1820 until 1859 in Milan, and
until 1866 in Venice, the hatred, which they had
themselves enkindled, burned fiercer and fiercer
against them. It is not extravagant to say that if
their rule had continued a hundred years longer
the Italians would never have been reconciled to
it. Society took the form of habitual and implacable defiance to them. The life of the whole people
might be said to have resolved itself into a protest against their presence. This hatred was
the heritage of children from their parents, the
bond between friends, the basis of social faith;
it was a thread even in the tie between lovers; it
was so intense and so pervasive that it cannot be
spoken.

Berchet was the vividest, if not the earliest, expression of it in literature, and the following poem, which I have already mentioned, is, therefore, not only intensely true to Italian feeling, but entirely realistic in its truth to a common fact.

REMORSE.

Alone in the midst of the throng,
  'Mid the lights and the splendor alone,
Her eyes, dropped for shame of her wrong,
  She lifts not to eyes she has known:
Around her the whirl and the stir
  Of the light-footing dancers she hears;
None seeks her; no whisper for her
  Of the gracious words filling her ears.

The fair boy that runs to her knees,
  With a shout for his mother, and kiss
For the tear-drop that welling he sees
  To her eyes from her sorrow's abyss, —
Though he blooms like a rose, the fair boy,
  No praise of his beauty is heard;
None with him stays to jest or to toy,
  None to her gives a smile or a word.

If, unknowing, one ask who may be
  This woman, that, as in disgrace,
O'er the curls of the boy at her knee
  Bows her beautiful, joyless face,
A hundred tongues answer in scorn,
  A hundred lips teach him to know —
"Wife of one of our tyrants, forsworn
  To her friends in her truth to their foe."

At the play, in the streets, in the lanes,
  At the fane of the merciful God,
'Midst a people in prison and chains,
  Spy-haunted, at home and abroad —
Steals through all like the hiss of a snake
  Hate, by terror itself unsuppressed:
"Cursèd be the Italian could take
  The Austrian foe to her breast!"

Alone — but the absence she mourned
  As widowhood mourneth, is past:
Her heart leaps for her husband returned
  From his garrison far-off at last?
Ah, no! For this woman forlorn
  Love is dead, she has felt him depart:
With far other thoughts she is torn,
  Far other the grief at her heart.

When the shame that has darkened her days
  Fantasmal at night fills the gloom,
When her soul, lost in wildering ways,
  Flies the past, and the terror to come —
When she leaps from her slumbers to hark,
  As if for her little one's call,
It is then to the pitiless dark
  That her woe-burdened soul utters all:

"Woe is me! It was God's righteous hand
  My brain with its madness that smote:
At the alien's flattering command
  The land of my birth I forgot!
I, the girl who was loved and adored,
  Feasted, honored in every place.
Now what am I? The apostate abhorred,
  Who was false to her home and her race!

"I turned from the common disaster;
  My brothers oppressed I denied;
I smiled on their insolent master;
  I came and sat down by his side.
Wretch! a mantle of shame thou hast wrought;
  Thou hast wrought it—it clingeth to thee,
And for all that thou sufferest, naught
  From its meshes thy spirit can free.

"Oh, the scorn I have tasted! They know not,
  Who pour it on me, how it burns;
How it galls the meek spirit, whose woe not
  Their hating with hating returns!
Fool! I merit it: I have not holden
  My feet from their paths! Mine the blame:
I have sought in their eyes to embolden
  This visage devoted to shame!

"Rejected and followed with scorn,
  My child, like a child born of sin,
In the land where my darling was born,
  He lives exiled! A refuge to win
From their hatred, he runs in dismay
  To my arms. But the day may yet be
When my son shall the insult repay,
  I have nurtured him in, unto me!

"If it chances that ever the slave
  Snaps the shackles that bind him, and leaps
Into life in the heart of the brave
  The sense of the might that now sleeps—
To which people, which side shall I cleave?
  Which fate shall I curse with my own?
To which banner pray Heaven to give
  The triumph? Which desire o'erthrown?

"Italian, and sister, and wife,
  And mother, unfriended, alone,
Outcast, I wander through life,
  Over shard and bramble and stone!
Wretch! a mantle of shame thou hast wrought;
  Thou hast wrought it — it clingeth to thee,
And for all that thou sufferest, naught
  From its meshes thy spirit shall free!"

GIAMBATTISTA NICCOLINI

I

THE school of Romantic poets and novelists was practically dispersed by the Austrian police after the Carbonari disturbances in 1821-22, and the literary spirit of the nation took refuge under the mild and careless despotism of the grand dukes at Florence.

In 1821 Austria was mistress of pretty near all Italy. She held in her own grasp the vast provinces of Lombardy and Venetia; she had garrisons in Naples, Piedmont, and the Romagna; and Rome was ruled according to her will. But there is always something fatally defective in the vigilance of a policeman; and in the very place which perhaps Austria thought it quite needless to guard, the restless and indomitable spirit of free thought entered. It was in Tuscany, a fief of the Holy Roman Empire, reigned over by a family set on the grand-ducal throne by Austria herself, and united to her Hapsburgs by many ties of blood and affection — in Tuscany, right under both noses of the double-headed eagle, as it were, that a new literary and political life began for Italy. The Leopoldine code was famously mild toward criminals, and the Lorrainese princes did not show themselves crueler than they could help toward poets, essayists, historians, philologists, and that class of malefactors. Indeed it was the philosophy of their family to let matters alone; and the grand duke restored after the fall of Napoleon was, as has been said, an absolute monarch, but he was also an honest man. This *galantuomo* had even a minister who successfully combated the Austrian influences, and so, though there were, of course, spies and a censorship in Florence, there was also indulgence; and if it was not altogether a pleasant place for literary men to live, it was at least tolerable, and there they gathered from their exile and their silence throughout Italy. Their point of union, and their means of affecting the popular mind, was for twelve years the critical journal entitled the *Antologia*, founded by that Vieusseux who also opened those delightful and beneficent reading-rooms whither we all rush, as soon as we reach Florence, to look at the newspapers and magazines of our native land. The Antologia had at last the misfortune to offend the Emperor of Russia, and to do that prince a pleasure the Tuscan government suppressed it: such being the international amenities when sovereigns really reigned in Europe. After the Antologia there came another review, published at Leghorn, but it was not so successful, and in fact the conditions of literature gradually grew more irksome in Tuscany, until the violent liberation came in '48, and a little later the violent reënslavement.

Giambattista Niccolini, like nearly all the poets of his time and country, was of noble birth, his father being a *cavaliere*, and holding a small government office at San Giuliano, near Pistoja. Here, in 1782, Niccolini was born to very decided penury. His father had only that little office, and his income died with him; the mother had nothing — possibly because she was descended from a poet, the famous Filicaja. From his mother, doubtless, Niccolini inherited his power, and perhaps his patriotism. But little or nothing is known of his early life. It is certain, merely, that after leaving school, he continued his studies in the University of Pisa, and that he very soon showed himself a poet. His first published effort was a sort of lamentation over an epidemic that desolated Tuscany in 1804, and this was followed by five or six pretty thoroughly forgotten tragedies in the classic or Alfierian manner. Of these, only the *Medea* is still played, but they all made a stir in their time; and for another he was crowned by the Accademia della Crusca, which I suppose does not mean a great deal. The fact that Niccolini early caught the attention and won the praises of Ugo Foscolo is more important. There grew up, indeed, between the two poets such esteem that the elder at this time dedicated one of his books to the younger, and their friendship continued through life.

When Elisa Bonaparte was made queen of Etruria by Napoleon, Niccolini became secretary of the Academy of Fine Arts, and professor of history and mythology. It is said that in the latter capacity he instilled into his hearers his own notions of liberty and civic virtue. He was, in truth, a democrat, and he suffered with the other Jacobins, as they were called in Italy, when the Napoleonic governments were overthrown. The benefits which the French Revolution conferred upon the people of their conquered provinces when not very doubtful were still such as they were not prepared to receive; and after the withdrawal of the French support, all the Italians through whom they had ruled fell a prey to the popular hate and contumely. In those days when dynasties, restored to their thrones after the lapse of a score of years, ignored the intervening period and treated all its events as if they had no bearing upon the future, it was thought the part of the true friends of order to resume the old fashions which went out with the old *régime*. The queue, or pigtail, had always been worn, when it was safe to wear it, by the supporters of religion and good government (from this fashion came the famous political nickname *codino*, pigtail-wearer, or conservative, which used to occur so often in Italian talk and literature), and now whoever appeared on the street without this emblem of loyalty and piety was in danger of public outrage. A great many Jacobins bowed their heads to the popular will, and had pigtails sewed on them — a device which the idle boys and other unemployed friends of legitimacy busied themselves in detecting. They laid rude hands on this ornament singing,

> If the queue remains in your hand,
> A true republican is he;
> Hurrah! hurrah! hurrah!
> Give him a kick for liberty.

It is related that the superficial and occasional character of Niccolini's conversation was discovered by this test, and that he underwent the apposite penalty. He rebelled against the treatment he received, and was arrested and imprisoned for his contumacy. When Ferdinando III. had returned and established his government on the let-alone principle to which I have alluded, the dramatist was made librarian of the Palatine Library at the Pitti Palace, but he could not endure the necessary attendance at court, where his politics were remembered against him by the courtiers, and he gave up the place. The grand duke was sorry, and said so, adding that he was perfectly contented. "Your Highness," answered the poet, "in this case it takes two to be contented."

II

THE first political tragedy of Niccolini was the *Nebuchadnezzar*, which was printed in London in 1819, and figured, under that Scriptural disguise, the career of Napoleon. After that came his *Antonio Foscarini*, in which the poet, who had heretofore been a classicist, tried to reconcile that school with the romantic by violating the sacred unities in a moderate manner. In his subsequent tragedies he seems not to have regarded them at all, and to have been romantic as the most romantic Lombard of them all could have asked. Of course, his defection gave exquisite pain to the lovers of Italian good taste, as the classicists called themselves, but these were finally silenced by the success of his tragedy. The reader of it nowadays, we suspect, will think its success not very expensively achieved, and it certainly has a main fault that makes it strangely disagreeable. When the past was chiefly the affair of fable, the storehouse of tradition, it was well enough for the poet to take historical events and figures, and fashion them in any way that served his purpose; but this will not do in our modern daylight, where a freedom with the truth is an offense against common knowledge, and does not charm the fancy, but painfully bewilders it at the best, and at the second best is impudent and ludicrous. In his tragedy, Niccolini takes two very familiar incidents of Venetian history: that of the Foscari, which Byron has used; and that of Antonio Foscarini, who was unjustly hanged more than a hundred years later for privity to a conspiracy against the state, whereas the attributive crime of Jacopo Foscari was the assassination of a fellow-patrician. The poet is then forced to make the Doge Foscari do duty throughout as the father of Foscarini, the only doge of whose name served out his term very peaceably, and died the author of an extremely dull official history of Venetian literature. Foscarini, who, up to the time of his hanging, was an honored servant of the state, and had been ambassador to France, is obliged, on his part, to undergo all of Jacopo Foscari's troubles; and I have not been able to see why the poet should have vexed himself to make all this confusion, and why the story of the Foscari was not sufficient for his purpose. In the tragedy there is much denunciation of the oligarchic oppression of the Ten in Venice, and it may be regarded as the first of Niccolini's dramatic appeals to the love of freedom and the manhood of the Italians.

It is much easier to understand the success of Niccolini's subsequent drama, *Lodovico il Moro*, which is in many respects a touching and effective tragedy, and the historical truth is better observed in it; though, as none of our race can ever love his country with that passionate and personal devotion which the Italians feel, we shall never relish the high patriotic flavor of the piece. The story is simply that of Giovan-Galeazzo Sforza, Duke of Milan, whose uncle, Lodovico, on pretense of relieving him of the cares of government, has usurped the sovereignty, and keeps Galeazzo and his wife in virtual imprisonment, the young duke wasting away with a slow but fatal malady. To further his ambitious schemes in Lombardy, Lodovico has called in Charles VIII. of France, who claims the crown of Naples against the Aragonese family, and pauses, on his way to Naples, at Milan. Isabella, wife of Galeazzo, appeals to Charles to liberate them, but reaches his presence in such an irregular way that she is suspected of treason both to her husband and to Charles. Yet the king is convinced of her innocence, and he places the sick duke under the protection of a French garrison, and continues his march on Naples. Lodovico has appeared to consent, but by seeming to favor the popular leaders has procured the citizens to insist upon his remaining in power; he has also secretly received the investiture from the Emperor of Germany, to be published upon the death of Galeazzo. He now, therefore, defies the French; Galeazzo, tormented by alternate hope and despair, dies suddenly; and Lodovico, throwing off the mask of a popular ruler, puts the republican leaders to death, and reigns the feudatory of the Emperor. The interest of the play is almost entirely political, and patriotism is the chief passion involved. The main personal attraction of the tragedy is in the love of Galeazzo and his wife, and in the character of the latter the dreamy languor of a hopeless invalid is delicately painted.

The *Giovanni da Procida* was a further advance in political literature. In this tragedy, abandoning the indirectly liberal teachings of the Foscarini, Niccolini set himself to the purpose of awakening a Tuscan hatred of foreign rule. The subject is the expulsion of the French from Sicily; and when the French ambassador complained to the Austrian that such a play should be tolerated by the Tuscan government, the Austrian answered, "The address is to the French, but the letter is for the Germans." The Giovanni da Procida was a further development of Niccolini's political purposes in literature, and at the time of its first representation it raised the Florentines to a frenzy of theater-going patriotism. The tragedy ends with the terrible Sicilian Vespers, but its main affair is with preceding events, largely imagined by the poet, and the persons are in great part fictitious; yet they all bear a certain relation to fact, and the historical persons are more or less historically painted. Giovanni da Procida, a great Sicilian nobleman, believed dead by the French, comes home to Palermo, after long exile, to stir up the Sicilians to rebellion, and finds that his daughter is married to the son of one of the French rulers, though neither this daughter Imelda nor her husband Tancredi knew the origin of the latter at the time of their marriage. Procida, in his all-absorbing hate of the oppressors, cannot forgive them; yet he seizes Tancredi, and imprisons him in his castle, in order to save his life from the impending massacre of the French; and in a scene with Imelda, he tells her that, while she was a babe, the father of Tancredi had abducted her mother and carried her to France. Years after, she returned heart-broken to die in her husband's arms, a secret which she tries to reveal perishing with her. While Imelda remains horror-struck by this history, Procida receives an intercepted letter from Eriberto, Tancredi's father, in which he tells the young man that he and Imelda are children of the same mother. Procida in pity of his daughter, the victim of this awful fatality, prepares to send her away to a convent in Pisa; but a French law forbids any ship to sail at that time, and Imelda is brought back and confronted in a public place with Tancredi, who has been rescued by the French.

He claims her as his wife, but she, filled with the horror of what she knows, declares that he is not her husband. It is the moment of the Vespers, and Tancredi falls among the first slain by the Sicilians. He implores Imelda for a last kiss, but wildly answering that they are brother and sister, she swoons away, while Tancredi dies in this climax of self-loathing and despair. The management of a plot so terrible is very simple. The feelings of the characters in the hideous maze which involves them are given only such expression as should come from those utterly broken by their calamity. Imelda swoons when she hears the letter of Eriberto declaring the fatal tie of blood that binds her to her husband, and forever separates her from him. When she is restored, she finds her father weeping over her, and says:

              Ah, thou dost look on me
And weep! At least this comfort I can feel
In the horror of my state: thou canst not hate
A woman so unhappy. . . . .
. . . . Oh, from all
Be hid the atrocity! to some holy shelter
Let me be taken far from hence. I feel
Naught can be more than my calamity,
Saving God's pity. I have no father now,
Nor child, nor husband (heavens, what do I say?
He is my brother now!. and well I know
I must not ask to see him more). I, living, lose
Everything death robs other women of,

By far the greater feeling and passion are shown in the passages describing the wrongs which the Sicilians have suffered from the French, and expressing the aspiration and hate of Procida and his fellow-patriots. Niccolini does not often use pathos, and he is on that account perhaps the more effective in the use of it. However this may be, I find it very touching when, after coming back from his long exile, Procida says to Imelda, who is trembling for the secret of her marriage amidst her joy in his return:

     Daughter, art thou still
So sad? I have not heard yet from thy lips
A word of the old love. . . . .
. . . . Ah, thou knowest not
What sweetness hath the natal spot, how many
The longings exile hath; how heavy 't is
To arrive at doors of homes where no one waits thee!
Imelda, thou may'st abandon thine own land,
But not forget her; I, a pilgrim, saw
Many a city; but none among them had
A memory that spoke unto my heart;
And fairer still than any other seemed
The country whither still my spirit turned.

In a vein as fierce and passionate as this is tender, Procida relates how, returning to Sicily when he was believed dead by the French, he passed in secret over the island and inflamed Italian hatred of the foreigners:

     I sought the pathless woods,
And drew the cowards thence and made them blush,
And then made fury follow on their shame.
I hailed the peasant in his fertile fields,
Where, 'neath the burden of the cruel tribute,
He dropped from famine 'midst the harvest sheaves,

With his starved brood: "Open thou with thy scythe
The breasts of Frenchmen; let the earth no more
Be fertile to our tyrants." I found my way
In palaces, in hovels; tranquil, I
Both great and lowly did make drunk with rage.
I knew the art to call forth cruel tears
In every eye, to wake in every heart
A love of slaughter, a ferocious need
Of blood. And in a thousand strong right hands
Glitter the arms I gave.

In the last act occurs one of those lyrical passages in which Niccolini excels, and two lines from this chorus are among the most famous in modern Italian poetry:

> Perchè tanto sorriso del cielo
> Sulla terra del vile dolor?

The scene is in a public place in Palermo, and the time is the moment before the massacre of the French begins. A chorus of Sicilian poets remind the people of their sorrows and degradation, and sing:

> The wind vexes the forest no longer,
>   In the sunshine the leaflets expand:
>   With barrenness cursed be the land
> That is bathed with the sweat of the slave!
>
> On the fields now the harvests are waving,
>   On the fields that our blood has made red;
>   Harvests grown for our enemy's bread
> From the bones of our children they wave!
>
> With a veil of black clouds would the tempest
>   Might the face of this Italy cover;
>   Why should Heaven smile so glorious over
> The land of our infamous woe?

All nature is suddenly wakened,
  Here in slumbers unending man sleeps;
  Dust trod evermore by the steps
Of ever-strange lords he lies low!

"With this tragedy," says an Italian biographer of Niccolini, " the poet potently touched all chords of the human heart, from the most impassioned love to the most implacable hate. . . . The enthusiasm rose to the greatest height, and for as many nights of the severe winter of 1830 as the tragedy was given, the theater was always thronged by the overflowing audience; the doors of the Cocomero were opened to the impatient people many hours before the spectacle began. Spectators thought themselves fortunate to secure a seat next the roof of the theater; even in the prompter's hole* places were sought to witness the admired work. . . . And whilst they wept over the ill-starred love of Imelda, and all hearts palpitated in the touching situation of the drama, — where the public and the personal interests so wonderfully blended, and the vengeance of a people mingled with that of a man outraged in the most sacred affections of the heart, — Procida rose terrible as the billows of his sea, imprecating before all the wrongs of their oppressed country, in whatever servitude inflicted, by whatever aliens, among all those that had trampled, derided, and martyred her, and raising the cry of

---

* On the Italian stage the prompter rises from a hole in the floor behind the foot-lights, and is hidden from the audience merely by a canvas shade.

GIAMBATTISTA NICCOLINI.

GIAMBATTISTA NICCOLINI.

resistance which stirred the heart of all Italy. At the picture of the abject sufferings of their common country, the whole audience rose and repeated with tears of rage:

> 'Why should heaven smile so glorious over
> The land of our infamous woe?'"

By the year 1837 had begun the singular illusion of the Italians, that their freedom and unity were to be accomplished through a liberal and patriotic Pope. Niccolini, however, never was cheated by it, though he was very much disgusted, and he retired, not only from the political agitation, but almost from the world. He was seldom seen upon the street, but to those who had access to him he did not fail to express all the contempt and distrust he felt. "A liberal Pope! a liberal Pope!" he said, with a scornful enjoyment of that contradiction in terms. He was thoroughly Florentine and Tuscan in his anti-papal spirit, and he was faithful in it to the tradition of Dante, Petrarch, Machiavelli, Guicciardini, and Alfieri, who all doubted and combated the papal influence as necessarily fatal to Italian hopes. In 1843 he published his great and principal tragedy, *Arnaldo da Brescia*, which was a response to the ideas of the papal school of patriots. In due time Pius IX. justified Niccolini, and all others that distrusted him, by turning his back upon the revolution, which belief in him, more than anything else, had excited.

The tragedies which succeeded the Arnaldo were the *Filippo Strozzi*, published in 1847; the *Beatrice*

Cenci, a version from the English of Shelley, and the *Mario e i Cimbri*.

A part of the Arnaldo da Brescia was performed in Florence in 1858, not long before the war which has finally established Italian freedom. The name of the Cocomero theater had been changed to the Teatro Niccolini, and, in spite of the governmental anxiety and opposition, the occasion was made a popular demonstration in favor of Niccolini's ideas as well as himself. His biographer says: "The audience now maintained a religious silence; now, moved by irresistible force, broke out into uproarious applause as the eloquent protests of the friar and the insolent responses of the Pope awakened their interest; for Italy then, like the unhappy martyr, had risen to proclaim the decline of that monstrous power which, in the name of a religion profaned by it, sanctifies its own illegitimate and feudal origin, its abuses, its pride, its vices, its crimes. It was a beautiful and affecting spectacle to see the illustrious poet receiving the warm congratulations of his fellow-citizens, who enthusiastically recognized in him the utterer of so many lofty truths and the prophet of Italy. That night Niccolini was accompanied to his house by the applauding multitude." And if all this was a good deal like the honors the Florentines were accustomed to pay to a very pretty *ballerina* or a successful *prima donna*, there is no doubt that a poet is much worthier the popular frenzy; and it is a pity that the forms of popular frenzy have to be so cheapened by frequent use. The two remaining years of Niccolini's life were spent in great retirement, and in a satisfaction with the fortunes of Italy which was only marred by the fact that the French still remained in Rome, and that the temporal power yet stood. He died in 1861.

III

The work of Niccolini in which he has poured out all the lifelong hatred and distrust he had felt for the temporal power of the popes is the Arnaldo da Brescia. This we shall best understand through a sketch of the life of Arnaldo, who is really one of the most heroic figures of the past, deserving to rank far above Savonarola, and with the leaders of the Reformation, though he preceded these nearly four hundred years. He was born in Brescia of Lombardy, about the year 1105, and was partly educated in France, in the school of the famous Abelard. He early embraced the ecclesiastical life, and, when he returned to his own country, entered a convent, but not to waste his time in idleness and the corruptions of his order. In fact, he began at once to preach against these, and against the usurpation of temporal power by all the great and little dignitaries of the Church. He thus identified himself with the democratic side in politics, which was then locally arrayed against the bishop aspiring to rule Brescia. Arnaldo denounced the political power of the Pope, as well as that of the prelates; and the bishop, making this known to the pontiff at Rome, had sufficient influence to procure a sentence against Arnaldo as a schismatic, and an order enjoining silence upon him. He was also banished from Italy; whereupon, retiring to France, he got himself into further trouble by aiding Abelard in the defense of his teachings, which had been attainted of heresy. Both Abelard and Arnaldo were at this time bitterly persecuted by St. Bernard, and Arnaldo took refuge in Switzerland, whence, after several years, he passed to Rome, and there began to assume an active part in the popular movements against the papal rule. He was an ardent republican, and was a useful and efficient partisan, teaching openly that, whilst the Pope was to be respected in all spiritual things, he was not to be recognized at all as a temporal prince. When the English monk, Nicholas Breakspear, became Pope Adrian IV., he excommunicated and banished Arnaldo; but Arnaldo, protected by the senate and certain powerful nobles, remained at Rome in spite of the Pope's decree, and disputed the lawfulness of the excommunication. Finally, the whole city was laid under interdict until Arnaldo should be driven out. Holy Week was drawing near; the people were eager to have their churches thrown open and to witness the usual shows and splendors, and they consented to the exile of their leader. The followers of a cardinal arrested him, but he was rescued by his friends, certain counts of the Campagna, who held him for a saint, and who now lodged him safely in one of their castles. The Emperor Frederick Barbarossa, coming to Rome to assume the imperial crown, was met by embassies from both parties in the city. He warmly favored that of the Pope, and not only received that of the people very coldly, but arrested one of the counts who had rescued Arnaldo, and forced him to name the castle in which the monk lay concealed. Arnaldo was then given into the hands of the cardinals, and these delivered him to the prefect of Rome, who caused him to be hanged, his body to be burned upon a spit, and his ashes to be scattered in the Tiber, that the people might not venerate his relics as those of a saint. "This happened," says the priest Giovanni Battista Guadagnini, of Brescia, whose Life, published in 1790, I have made use of—" this happened in the year 1155 before the 18th of June, previous to the coronation of Frederick, Arnaldo being, according to my thinking, fifty years of age. His eloquence," continues Guadagnini, "was celebrated by his enemies themselves; the exemplarity of his life was superior to their malignity, constraining them all to silence, although they were in such great number, and it received a splendid eulogy from St. Bernard, the luminary of that century, who, being strongly impressed against him, condemned him first as a schismatic, and then for the affair of the Council of Sens (the defense of Abelard), persecuted him as a heretic, and then had finally nothing to say against him. His courage and his zeal for the discipline of the Church have been sufficiently attested by the toils, the persecutions, and the death which he underwent for that cause."

IV

The scene of the first act of Niccolini's tragedy is near the Capitoline Hill, in Rome, where two rival leaders, Frangipani and Giordano Pierleone, are disputing in the midst of their adherents. The former is a supporter of the papal usurpations; the latter is a republican chief, who has been excommunicated for his politics, and is also under sentence of banishment; but who, like Arnaldo, remains in Rome in spite of Church and State. Giordano withdraws to the Campidôglio with his adherents, and there Arnaldo suddenly appears among them. When the people ask what cure there is for their troubles, Arnaldo answers, in denunciation of the papacy:

    Liberty and God.
A voice from the orient,
A voice from the occident,

A voice from thy deserts,
A voice of echoes from the open graves,
Accuses thee, thou shameless harlot! Drunk
Art thou with blood of saints, and thou hast lain
With all the kings of earth. Ah, you behold her!
She is clothed on with purple; gold and pearls
And gems are heaped upon her; and her vestments
Once white, the pleasure of her former spouse,
That now 's in heaven, she has dragged in dust.
Lo, is she full of names and blasphemies,
And on her brow is written *Mystery!*
Ah, nevermore you hear her voice console
The afflicted; all she threatens, and creates
With her perennial curse in trembling souls
Ineffable pangs; the unhappy — as we here
Are all of us — fly in their common sorrows
To embrace each other; she, the cruel one,
Sunders them in the name of Jesus; fathers
She kindles against sons, and wives she parts
From husbands, and she makes a war between
Harmonious brothers; of the Evangel she
Is cruel interpreter, and teaches hate
Out of the book of love. The years are come
Whereof the rapt Evangelist of Patmos
Did prophesy; and, to deceive the people,
Satan has broken the chains he bore of old;
And she, the cruel, on the infinite waters
Of tears that are poured out for her, sits throned.
The enemy of man two goblets places
Unto her shameless lips; and one is blood,
And gold is in the other; greedy and fierce
She drinks so from them both, the world knows not
If she of blood or gold have greater thirst. . . .
Lord, those that fled before thy scourge of old
No longer stand to barter offerings

About thy temple's borders, but within
Man's self is sold, and thine own blood is trafficked,
Thou son of God!

The people ask Arnaldo what he counsels them to do, and he advises them to restore the senate and the tribunes, appealing to the glorious memories of the place where they stand, the Capitoline Hill:

Where the earth calls at every step, "Oh, pause,
Thou treadest on a hero!"

They desire to make him a tribune, but he refuses, promising, however, that he will not withhold his counsel. Whilst he speaks, some cardinals, with nobles of the papal party, appear, and announce the election of the new Pope, Adrian. "What is his name?" the people demand; and a cardinal answers, "Breakspear, a Briton." Giordano exclaims:

Impious race! you've chosen Rome for shepherd
A cruel barbarian, and even his name
Tortures our ears.
 Arnaldo. I never care to ask
Where popes are born; and from long suffering,
You, Romans, before heaven, should have learnt
That priests can have no country. . . .
I know this man; his father was a thrall,
And he is fit to be a slave. He made
Friends with the Norman that enslaves his country;
A wandering beggar to Avignon's cloisters
He came in boyhood and was known to do
All abject services; there those false monks
He with astute humility cajoled;

He learned their arts, and 'mid intrigues and hates
He rose at last out of his native filth
A tyrant of the vile.

The cardinals, confounded by Arnaldo's presence and invectives, withdraw, but leave one of their party to work on the fears of the Romans, and make them return to their allegiance by pictures of the desolating war which Barbarossa, now approaching Rome to support Adrian, has waged upon the rebellious Lombards at Rosate and elsewhere. Arnaldo replies: —

                          Romans,
I will tell all the things that he has hid;
I know not how to cheat you. Yes, Rosate
A ruin is, from which the smoke ascends.
The bishop, lord of Monferrato, guided
The German arms against Chieri and Asti,
Now turned to dust; that shepherd pitiless
Did thus avenge his own offenses on
His flying flocks; himself with torches armed
The German hand; houses and churches saw
Destroyed, and gave his blessing on the flames.
This is the pardon that *you* may expect
From mitered tyrants. A heap of ashes now
Crowneth the hill where once Tortona stood;
And drunken with her wine and with her blood,
Fallen there amidst their spoil upon the dead,
Slept the wild beasts of Germany: like ghosts
Dim wandering through the darkness of the night,
Those that were left by famine and the sword,
Hidden within the heart of thy dim caverns,
Desolate city! rose and turned their steps
Noiselessly toward compassionate Milan.

There they have borne their swords and hopes: I see
A thousand heroes born from the example
Tortona gave. O city, if I could,
O sacred city! upon thy ruins fall
Reverently, and take them in my loving arms,
The relics of thy brave I 'd gather up
In precious urns, and from the altars here
In days of battle offer to be kissed!
Oh, praise be to the Lord! Men die no more
For chains and errors; martyrs now at last
Hast thou, O holy Freedom; and fain were I
Ashes for thee!—But I see you grow pale,
Ye Romans! Down, go down; this holy height
Is not for cowards. In the valley there
Your tyrant waits you; go and fall before him
And cover his haughty foot with tears and kisses.
He 'll tread you in the dust, and then absolve you.
 The People. The arms we have are strange and few.
  Our walls
Are fallen and ruinous.
 Arnaldo.   Their hearts are walls
Unto the brave. . . .
    And they shall rise again,
The walls that blood of freemen has baptized,
But among slaves their ruins are eternal.
 People. You outrage us, sir!
 Arnaldo.   Wherefore do ye tremble
Before the trumpet sounds? O thou that wast
Once the world's lord and first in Italy,
Wilt thou be now the last?
 People. No more! Cease, or thou diest!

Arnaldo, having roused the pride of the Romans, now tells them that two thousand Swiss have followed him from his exile; and the act closes with some lyrical passages leading to the fraternization of the people with these.

The second act of this curious tragedy, where there may be said to be scarcely any personal interest, but where we are aware of such an impassioned treatment of public interests as perhaps never was before, opens with a scene between the Pope Adrian and the Cardinal Guido. The character of both is finely studied by the poet; and Guido, the type of ecclesiastical submission, has not more faith in the sacredness and righteousness of Adrian, than Adrian, the type of ecclesiastical ambition, has in himself. The Pope tells Guido that he stands doubting between the cities of Lombardy leagued against Frederick, and Frederick, who is coming to Rome, not so much to befriend the papacy as to place himself in a better attitude to crush the Lombards. The German dreams of the restoration of Charlemagne's empire; he believes the Church corrupt; and he and Arnaldo would be friends, if it were not for Arnaldo's vain hope of reëstablishing the republican liberties of Rome. The Pope utters his ardent desire to bring Arnaldo back to his allegiance; and when Guido reminds him that Arnaldo has been condemned by a council of the Church, and that it is scarcely in his power to restore him, Adrian turns upon him:

What sayest thou?
I can do all. Dare the audacious members
Rebel against the head? Within these hands
Lie not the keys that once were given to Peter?
The heavens repeat as 't were the word of God,

My word that here has power to loose and bind.
Arnaldo did not dare so much. The kingdom
Of earth alone he did deny me. Thou
Art more outside the Church than he.
  Guido (kneeling at Adrian's feet). O God,
I erred; forgive! I rise not from thy feet
Till thou absolve me. My zeal blinded me.
I 'm clay before thee; shape me as thou wilt,
A vessel apt to glory or to shame.

 Guido then withdraws at the Pope's bidding, in order to send a messenger to Arnaldo, and Adrian utters this fine soliloquy:

At every step by which I 've hither climbed
I 've found a sorrow; but upon the summit
All sorrows are; and thorns more thickly spring
Around my chair than ever round a throne.
What weary toil to keep up from the dust
This mantle that 's weighed down the strongest limbs!
These splendid gems that blaze in my tiara,
They are a fire that burns the aching brow,
I lift with many tears, O Lord, to thee!
Yet I must fear not; He that did know how
To bear the cross, so heavy with the sins
Of all the world, will succor the weak servant
That represents his power here on earth.
O silences of the cloister, O ye mists
Of mine own isle that make the light o' the sun
Obscure as one day was my lot, amidst
The furious tumults of this guilty Rome,
Here, under the superb effulgency
Of burning skies, I think of you and weep!

 The Pope's messenger finds Arnaldo in the castle of Giordano, where these two are talking of the present fortunes and future chances of Rome. The patrician forebodes evil from the approach of the emperor, but Arnaldo encourages him, and, when the Pope's messenger appears, he is eager to go to Adrian, believing that good to their cause will come of it. Giordano in vain warns him against treachery, bidding him remember that Adrian will hold any falsehood sacred that is used with a heretic. It is observable throughout that Niccolini is always careful to make his rebellious priest a good Catholic; and now Arnaldo rebukes Giordano for some doubts of the spiritual authority of the Pope. When Giordano says:

These modern pharisees, upon the cross
Where Christ hung dying once, have nailed mankind,

Arnaldo answers:

He will know how to save that rose and conquered;

And Giordano replies:

> Yes, Christ arose; but Freedom cannot break
> The stone that shuts her ancient sepulcher,
> For on it stands the altar.

Adrian, when Arnaldo appears before him, bids him fall down and kiss his feet, and speak to him as to God; he will hear Arnaldo only as a penitent. Arnaldo answers:

     The feet
Of his disciples did that meek One kiss
Whom here thou representest. But I hear
Now from thy lips the voice of fiercest pride.

Repent, O Peter, that deniest him,
And near the temple art, but far from God!
. . . .

                      The name of king
Is never heard in Rome. And if thou art
The vicar of Christ on earth, well should'st thou know
That of thorns only was the crown he wore.
   Adrian. He gave to me the empire of the earth
When this great mantle I put on, and took
The Church's high seat I was chosen to;
The word of God did erst create the world,
And now mine guides it. Would'st thou that the soul
Should serve the body? Thou dost dream of freedom,
And makest war on him who sole on earth
Can shield man from his tyrants. O Arnaldo,
Be wise; believe me, all thy words are vain,
Vain sounds that perish or disperse themselves
Amidst the wilderness of Rome. I only
Can speak the words that the whole world repeats.
   Arnaldo. Thy words were never Freedom's; placed
      between
The people and their tyrants, still the Church.
With the weak cruel, with the mighty vile,
Has been, and crushed in pitiless embraces
That emperors and pontiffs have exchanged,
Man has been ever.
. . . .

Why seek'st thou empire here, and great on earth
Art mean in heaven? Ah! vainly in thy prayer
Thou criest, "Let the heart be lifted up!"
'T is ever bowed to earth.
. . . .

                Now, then, if thou wilt,
Put forth the power that thou dost vaunt; repress

The crimes of bishops, make the Church ashamed
To be a step-mother to the poor and lowly.
In all the Lombard cities every priest
Has grown a despot, in shrewd perfidy
Now siding with the Church, now with the Empire.
They have dainty food, magnificent apparel,
Lascivious joys, and on their altars cold
Gathers the dust, where lies the miter dropt,
Forgotten, from the haughty brow that wears
The helmet, and no longer bows itself
Before God's face in th' empty sanctuaries;
But upon the fields of slaughter, smoking still,
Bends o'er the fallen foe, and aims the blows
O' th' sacrilegious sword, with cruel triumph
Insulting o'er the prayers of dying men.
There the priest rides o'er breasts of fallen foes,
And stains with blood his courser's iron heel.
When comes a brief, false peace, and wearily
Amidst the havoc doth the priest sit down,
His pleasures are a crime, and after rapine
Luxury follows. Like a thief he climbs
Into the fold, and that desired by day
He dares amid the dark, and violence
Is the priest's marriage. Vainly did Rome hope
That they had thrown aside the burden vile
Of the desires that weigh down other men.
Theirs is the ungrateful lust of the wild beast,
That doth forget the mother nor knows the child.
. . . . On the altar of Christ,
Who is the prince of pardon and of peace,
Vows of revenge are registered, and torches
That are thrown into hearts of leaguered cities
Are lit from tapers burning before God.
Become thou king of sacrifice; ascend
The holy hill of God; on these perverse

Launch thou thy thunderbolts; and feared again
And great thou wilt be. Tell me, Adrian,
Must thou not bear a burden that were heavy
Even for angels? Wherefore wilt thou join
Death unto life, and make the word of God,
That says, "My kingdom is not of this world,"
A lie? Oh, follow Christ's example here
In Rome; it pleased both God and her
To abase the proud and to uplift the weak.
I 'll kiss the foot that treads on kings!
    Adrian.   Arnaldo,
I parley not, I rule; and I, become
On earth as God in heaven, am judge of all,
And none of me; I watch, and I dispense
Terrors and hopes, rewards and punishments,
To peoples and to kings; fountain and source
Of life am I, who make the Church of God
One and all-powerful. Many thrones and peoples
She has seen tost upon the madding waves
Of time, and broken on the immovable rock
Whereon she sits; and since one errless spirit
Rules in her evermore, she doth not rave
For changeful doctrine, but she keeps eternal
The grandeur of her will and purposes.
  . . . . Arnaldo,
Thou movest me to pity. In vain thou seek'st
To warm thy heart over these ruins, groping
Among the sepulchers of Rome. Thou 'lt find
No bones to which thou canst say, "Rise!" Ah, here
Remaineth not one hero's dust. Thou thinkest
That with old names old virtues shall return?
And thou desirest tribunes, senators,
Equestrian orders, Rome! A greater glory
Thy sovereign pontiff is who doth not guard
The rights uncertain of a crazy rabble;
But tribune of the world he sits in Rome,

And "I forbid," to kings and peoples cries.
I tell thee a greater than the impious power
That thou in vain endeavorest to renew
Here built the dying fisherman of Judea.
Out of his blood he made a fatherland
For all the nations, and this place, that once
A city was, became a world; the borders
That did divide the nations, by Christ's law
Are ta'en away, and this the kingdom is
For which he asked his Father in his prayer.
The Church has sons in every race; I rule,
An unseen king, and Rome is everywhere!
  Arnaldo. Thou errest, Adrian. Rome's thunderbolts
Wake little terror now, and reason shakes
The bonds that thou fain would'st were everlasting.
. . . . Christ calls to her
As of old to the sick man, "Rise and walk."
She 'll tread on you if you go not before.
The world has other truth besides the altar's.
It will not have a temple that hides heaven.
Thou wast a shepherd: be a father. The race
Of man is weary of being called a flock.

Adrian's final reply is, that if Arnaldo will renounce his false doctrine and leave Rome, the Pope will, through him, give the Lombard cities a liberty that shall not offend the Church. Arnaldo refuses, and quits Adrian's presence. It is quite needless to note the bold character of the thought here, or the nobility of the poetry, which Niccolini puts as well into the mouth of the Pope whom he hates as the monk whom he loves.

Following this scene is one of greater dramatic force, in which the Cardinal Guido, sent to the Campidôglio by the Pope to disperse the popular assembly, is stoned by the people and killed. He dies full of faith in the Church and the righteousness of his cause, and his body, taken up by the priests, is carried into the square before St. Peter's. A throng, including many women, has followed; and now Niccolini introduces a phase of the great Italian struggle which was perhaps the most perplexing of all. The subjection of the women to the priests is what has always greatly contributed to defeat Italian efforts for reform; it now helps to unnerve the Roman multitude; and the poet finally makes it the weakness through which Arnaldo is dealt his death. With a few strokes in the scene that follows the death of Guido, he indicates the remorse and dismay of the people when the Pope repels them from the church door and proclaims the interdict; and then follow some splendid lyrical passages, in which the Pope commands the pictures and images to be veiled and the relics to be concealed, and curses the enemies of the Church. I shall but poorly render this curse by a rhymeless translation, and yet I am tempted to give it:

The Pope. To-day let the perfidious
Learn at thy name to tremble,
Nor triumph o'er the ruinous
Place of thy vanished altars.
Oh, brief be their days and uncertain;
In the desert their wandering footsteps,
Every tremulous leaflet affright them!
 The Cardinals. Anathema, anathema, anathema!
Pope. May their widows sit down 'mid the ashes

On the hearths of their desolate houses,
With their little ones wailing around them.
 Cardinals. Anathema, anathema, anathema!
 Pope. May he who was born to the fury
Of heaven, afar from his country
Be lost in his ultimate anguish.
 Cardinals. Anathema, anathema, anathema!
 Pope. May he fly to the house of the alien oppressor
That is filled with the spoil of his brothers, with women
Destroyed by the pitiless hands that defiled them;
There in accents unknown and derided, abase him
At portals ne'er opened in mercy, imploring
A morsel of bread.
 Cardinals.   Be that morsel denied him!
 Pope. I hear the wicked cry: I from the Lord
Will fly away with swift and tireless feet;
His anger follows me upon the sea;
I'll seek the desert; who will give me wings?
In cloudy horror, who shall lead my steps?
The eye of God maketh the night as day.
   O brothers, fulfill then
    The terrible duty;
   Throw down from the altars
    The dim-burning tapers;
And be all joy, and be the love of God
In thankless hearts that know not Peter, quenched,
As is the little flame that falls and dies,
Here in these tapers trampled under foot.

In the first scene of the third act, which is a desolate place in the Campagna, near the sea, Arnaldo appears. He has been expelled from Rome by the people, eager for the opening of their churches, and he soliloquizes upon his fate in language that subtly hints all his passing moods, and paints the struggle of his soul. It appears to me that it is a wise thing to make him almost regret the cloister in the midst of his hatred of it, and then shrink from that regret with horror; and there is also a fine sense of night and loneliness in the scene:

> Like this sand
> Is life itself, and evermore each path
> Is traced in suffering, and one footprint still
> Obliterates another; and we are all
> Vain shadows here that seem a little while,
> And suffer, and pass. Let me not fight in vain,
> O Son of God, with thine immortal word,
> Yon tyrant of eternity and time,
> Who doth usurp thy place on earth, whose feet
> Are in the depths, whose head is in the clouds,
> Who thunders all abroad, *The world is mine!*
> Laws, virtues, liberty I have attempted
> To give thee, Rome. Ah! only where death is
> Abides thy glory. Here the laurel only
> Flourishes on the ruins and the tombs.
> I will repose upon this fallen column
> My weary limbs. Ah, lower than this ye lie,
> You Latin souls, and to your ancient height
> Who shall uplift you? I am all weighed down
> By the great trouble of the lofty hopes
> Of Italy still deluded, and I find
> Within my soul a drearer desert far
> Than this, where the air already darkens round,
> And the soft notes of distant convent bells
> Announce the coming night. . . . I cannot hear them
> Without a trembling wish that in my heart
> Wakens a memory that becomes remorse. . . .

Ah, Reason, soon thou languishest in us,
Accustomed to such outrage all our lives.
Thou know'st the cloister; thou a youth didst enter
That sepulcher of the living where is war,—
Remember it and shudder! The damp wind
Stirs this gray hair. I 'm near the sea. O night,
Thy silence is no more; sweet on the ear
Cometh the far-off murmur of the floods
In the vast desert; now no more the darkness
Imprisons wholly; now less gloomily
Lowers the sky that lately threatened storm.
Less thick the air is, and the trembling light
O' the stars among the breaking clouds appears.
Praise to the Lord! The eternal harmony
Of all his work I feel. Though these vague beams
Reveal to me here only fens and tombs,
My soul is not so heavily weighed down
By burdens that oppressed it. . . .
I rise to grander purposes: man's tents
Are here below, his city is in heaven.
I doubt no more; the terror of the cloister
No longer assails me.

Presently Giordano comes to join Arnaldo in this desolate place, and, in the sad colloquy which follows, tells him of the events of Rome, and the hopelessness of their cause, unless they have the aid and countenance of the Emperor. He implores Arnaldo to accompany the embassy which he is about to send to Frederick; but Arnaldo, with a melancholy disdain, refuses. He asks where are the Swiss who accompanied him to Rome, and he is answered by one of the Swiss captains, who at that moment appears. The Emperor has ordered them to return home, under penalty of the ban of the empire. He begs Arnaldo to return with them, but Arnaldo will not; and Giordano sends him under a strong escort to the castle of Ostasio. Arnaldo departs with much misgiving, for the wife of Ostasio is Adelasia, a bigoted papist, who has hitherto resisted the teaching to which her husband has been converted.

As the escort departs, the returning Swiss are seen. One of their leaders expresses the fear that moves them, when he says that the Germans will desolate their homes if they do not return to them. Moreover, the Italian sun, which destroys even those born under it, drains their life, and man and nature are leagued against them there. "What have you known here!" he asks, and his soldiers reply in chorus:

The pride of old names, the caprices of fate,
In vast desert spaces the silence of death,
Or in mist-hidden lowlands, his wandering fires;
No sweet song of birds, no heart-cheering sound,
But eternal memorials of ancient despair,
And ruins and tombs that waken dismay
At the moan of the pines that are stirred by the wind.
Full of dark and mysterious peril the woods;
No life-giving fountains, but only bare sands,
Or some deep-bedded river that silently moves,
With a wave that is livid and stagnant, between
Its margins ungladdened by grass or by flowers,
And in sterile sands vanishes wholly away.
Out of huts that by turns have been shambles and tombs,
All pallid and naked, and burned by their fevers,

The peasant folk suddenly stare as you pass,
With visages ghastly, and eyes full of hate,
Aroused by the accent that 's strange to their ears.
Oh, heavily hang the clouds here on the head!
Wan and sick is the earth, and the sun is a tyrant.

Then one of the Swiss soldiers speaks alone:

> The unconquerable love of our own land
> Draws us away till we behold again
> The eternal walls the Almighty builded there.
> Upon the arid ways of faithless lands
> I am tormented by a tender dream
> Of that sweet rill which runs before my cot.
> Oh, let me rest beside the smiling lake,
> And hear the music of familiar words,
> And on its lonely margin, wild and fair,
> Lie down and think of my belovèd ones.

There is no page of this tragedy which does not present some terrible or touching picture, which is not full of brave and robust thought, which has not also great dramatic power. But I am obliged to curtail the proof of this, and I feel that, after all, I shall not give a complete idea of the tragedy's grandeur, its subtlety, its vast scope and meaning.

There is a striking dialogue between a Roman partisan of Arnaldo, who, with his fancy oppressed by the heresy of his cause, is wavering in his allegiance, and a Brescian, whom the outrages of the priests have forever emancipated from faith in their power to bless or ban in the world to come. Then ensues a vivid scene, in which a fanatical and insolent monk of Arnaldo's order, leading a number of soldiers, arrests him by command of Adrian. Ostasio's soldiers approaching to rescue him, the monk orders him to be slain, but he is saved, and the act closes with the triumphal chorus of his friends. Here is fine occasion for the play of different passions, and the occasion is not lost.

With the fourth act is introduced the new interest of the German oppression; and as we have had hitherto almost wholly a study of the effect of the papal tyranny upon Italy, we are now confronted with the shame and woe which the empire has wrought her. Exiles from the different Lombard cities destroyed by Barbarossa meet on their way to seek redress from the Pope, and they pour out their sorrows in pathetic and passionate lyrics. To read these passages gives one a favorable notion of the liberality or the stupidity of the government which permitted the publication of the tragedy. The events alluded to were many centuries past, the empire had long ceased to be; but the Italian hatred of the Germans was one and indivisible for every moment of all times, and we may be sure that to each of Niccolini's readers these mediæval horrors were but masks for cruelties exercised by the Austrians in his own day, and that in those lyrical bursts of rage and grief there was full utterance for his smothered sense of present wrong. There is a great charm in these strophes; they add unspeakable pathos to a drama which is so largely concerned with political interests; and they make us feel that it is a beautiful and noble work of art, as well as grand appeal to the patriotism of the Italians and the justice of mankind.

When we are brought into the presence of Barbarossa, we find him awaiting the arrival of Adrian, who is to accompany him to Rome and crown him emperor, in return for the aid that Barbarossa shall give in reducing the rebellious citizens and delivering Arnaldo into the power of the papacy. Heralds come to announce Adrian's approach, and riding forth a little way, Frederick dismounts in order to go forward on foot and meet the Pope, who advances, preceded by his clergy, and attended by a multitude of his partisans. As Frederick perceives the Pope and quits his horse, he muses:

> I leave thee,
> O faithful comrade mine in many perils,
> Thou generous steed! and now, upon the ground
> That should have thundered under thine advance,
> With humble foot I silent steps must trace.
> But what do I behold? Toward us comes,
> With tranquil pride, the servant of the lowly,
> Upon a white horse docile to the rein
> As he would kings were; all about the path
> That Adrian moves on, warriors and people
> Of either sex, all ages, in blind homage,
> Mingle, press near and fall upon the ground,
> Or one upon another; and man, whom God
> Made to look up to heaven, becomes as dust
> Under the feet of pride; and they believe
> The gates of Paradise would be set aside
> To any one whom his steed crushed to death.
> With me thou never hast thine empire shared;

Thou alone hold'st the world! He will not turn
On me in sign of greeting that proud head,
Encircled by the tiara; and he sees,
Like God, all under him in murmured prayer
Or silence, blesses them, and passes on.
What wonder if he will not deign to touch
The earth I tread on with his haughty foot!
He gives it to be kissed of kings; I too
Must stoop to the vile act.

Since the time of Henry II. it had been the custom of the emperors to lead the Pope's horse by the bridle, and to hold his stirrup while he descended. Adrian waits in vain for this homage from Frederick, and then alights with the help of his ministers, and seats himself in his episcopal chair, while Frederick draws near, saying aside:

I read there in his face his insolent pride
Veiled by humility.

He bows before Adrian and kisses his foot, and then offers him the kiss of peace, which Adrian refuses, and haughtily reminds him of the fate of Henry. Frederick answers furiously that the thought of this fate has always filled him with hatred of the papacy; and Adrian, perceiving that he has pressed too far in this direction, turns and soothes the Emperor:

I am truth,
And thou art force, and if thou part'st from me,
Blind thou becomest, helpless I remain.
We are but one at last. . . .
Cæsar and Peter,

They are the heights of God; man from the earth
Contemplates them with awe, and never questions
Which thrusts its peak the higher into heaven.
Therefore be wise, and learn from the example
Of impious Arnaldo. He 's the foe
Of thrones who wars upon the altar.

But he strives in vain to persuade Frederick to the despised act of homage, and it is only at the intercession of the Emperor's kinsmen and the German princes that he consents to it. When it is done in the presence of all the army and the clerical retinue, Adrian mounts, and says to Frederick, with scarcely hidden irony:

     In truth thou art
An apt and ready squire, and thou hast held
My stirrup firmly. Take, then, O my son,
The kiss of peace, for thou hast well fulfilled
All of thy duties.

But Frederick, crying aloud, and fixing the sense of the multitude upon him, answers:

    Nay, not all, O Father!—
Princes and soldiers, hear! I have done homage
To Peter, not to him.

The Church and the Empire being now reconciled, Frederick receives the ambassadors of the Roman republic with scorn; he outrages all their pretensions to restore Rome to her old freedom and renown; insults their prayer that he will make her his capital, and heaps contempt upon the weakness and vileness of the people they represent. Giordano replies for them:

     When will you dream,
You Germans, in your thousand stolid dreams,—
The fume of drunkenness,—a future greater
Than our Rome's memories? Never be her banner
Usurped by you! In prison and in darkness
Was born your eagle, that did but descend
Upon the helpless prey of Roman dead,
But never dared to try the ways of heaven,
With its weak vision wounded by the sun.
Ye prate of Germany. The whole world conspired,
And even more in vain, to work us harm,
Before that day when, the world being conquered,
Rome slew herself.
 . . . . Of man's great brotherhood
Unworthy still, ye change not with the skies.
In Italy the German's fate was ever
To grow luxurious and continue cruel.

The soldiers of Barbarossa press upon Giordano to kill him, and Frederick saves the ambassadors with difficulty, and hurries them away.

In the first part of the fifth act, Niccolini deals again with the *rôle* which woman has played in the tragedy of Italian history, the hopes she has defeated, and the plans she has marred through those religious instincts which should have blest her country, but which through their perversion by priestcraft have been one of its greatest curses. Adrian is in the Vatican, after his triumphant return to Rome, when Adelasia, the wife of that Ostasio, Count of the Campagna, in whose castle Arnaldo is concealed, and who shares his excommunication, is ushered into the Pope's presence. She is half mad with terror at the penalties under which her husband has fallen, in days when the excommunicated were shunned like lepers, and to shelter them, or to eat and drink with them, even to salute them, was to incur privation of the sacraments; when a bier was placed at their door, and their houses were stoned; when King Robert of France, who fell under the anathema, was abandoned by all his courtiers and servants, and the beggars refused the meat that was left from his table—and she comes into Adrian's presence accusing herself as the greatest of sinners. The Pope asks:

                Hast thou betrayed
Thy husband, or from some yet greater crime
Cometh the terror that oppresses thee?
Hast slain him?
  Adelasia.   Haply I ought to slay him.
  Adrian.   What?
  Adelasia. I fain would hate him and I cannot.
  Adrian.   What
Hath his fault been?
  Ad.   Oh, the most horrible
Of all.
  Adr. And yet is he dear unto thee?
  Ad. I love him, yes, I love him, though he's changed
From that he was. Some gloomy cloud involves
That face one day so fair, and 'neath the feet,
Now grown deformed, the flowers wither away.
I know not if I sleep or if I wake,
If what I see be a vision or a dream.
But all is dreadful, and I cannot tell

The falsehood from the truth; for if I reason,
I fear to sin. I fly the happy bed
Where I became a mother, but return
In midnight's horror, where my husband lies
Wrapt in a sleep so deep it frightens me,
And question with my trembling hand his heart,
The fountain of his life, if it still beat.
Then a cold kiss I give him, then embrace him
With shuddering joy, and then I fly again,—
For I do fear his love,—and to the place
Where sleep my little ones I hurl myself,
And wake them with my moans, and drag them forth
Before an old miraculous shrine of her,
The Queen of Heaven, to whom I 've consecrated,
With never-ceasing vigils, burning lamps.
There naked, stretched upon the hard earth, weep
My pretty babes, and each of them repeats
The name of Mary whom I call upon;
And I would swear that she looks down and weeps.
Then I cry out, "Have pity on my children!
Thou wast a mother, and the good obtain
Forgiveness for the guilty."

Adrian has little trouble to draw from the distracted woman the fact that her husband is a heretic—that heretic, indeed, in whose castle Arnaldo is concealed. On his promise that he will save her husband, she tells him the name of the castle. He summons Frederick, who claims Ostasio as his vassal, and declares that he shall die, and his children shall be carried to Germany. Adrian, after coldly asking the Emperor to spare him, feigns himself helpless, and Adelasia too late awakens to a knowledge of his perfidy. She falls at his feet:

I clasp thy knees once more, and I do hope
Thou hast not cheated me! .... Ah, now I see
Thy wicked arts! Because thou knewest well
My husband was a vassal of the empire,
That pardon which it was not thine to give
Thou didst pretend to promise me. O priest,
Is this thy pity? Sorrow gives me back
My wandering reason, and I waken on
The brink of an abyss; and from this wretch
The mask that did so hide his face drops down
And shows it in its naked hideousness
Unto the light of truth.

Frederick sends his soldiers to secure Arnaldo, but as to Ostasio and his children he relents somewhat, being touched by the anguish of Adelasia. Adrian rebukes his weakness, saying that he learned in the cloister to subdue these compassionate impulses. In the next scene, which is on the Capitoline Hill, the Roman Senate resolves to defend the city against the Germans to the last, and then we have Arnaldo a prisoner in a cell of the Castle of St. Angelo. The Prefect of Rome vainly entreats him to recant his heresy, and then leaves him with the announcement that he is to die before the following day. As to the soliloquy which follows, Niccolini says: "I have feigned in Arnaldo in the solemn hour of death these doubts, and I believe them exceedingly probable in a disciple of Abelard. This struggle between reason and faith is found more or less in the intellect of every one, and constitutes a sublime torment in the life of those who, like the Brescian monk, have devoted themselves from an early age to the study of philosophy and religion. None of the ideas which I attribute to Arnaldo were unknown to him, and, according to Müller, he believed that God was all, and that the whole creation was but one of his thoughts. His other conceptions in regard to divinity are found in one of his contemporaries." The soliloquy is as follows:

> Aforetime thou hast said, O King of heaven,
> That in the world thou wilt not power or riches.
> And can he be divided from the Church
> Who keeps his faith in thine immortal word,
> The light of souls? To remain in the truth
> It only needs that I confess to thee
> All sins of mine. O thou eternal priest,
> Thou read'st my heart, and that which I can scarce
> Express thou seest. A great mystery
> Is man unto himself, conscience a deep
> Which only thou canst sound. What storm is there
> Of guilty thoughts! Oh, pardon my rebellion!
> Evil springs up within the mind of man,
> As in its native soil, since that day Adam
> Abused thy great gift, and created guilt.
> And if each thought of ours became a deed,
> Who would be innocent? I did once defend
> The cause of Abelard, and at the decree
> Imposing silence on him I, too, ceased.
> What fault in me? Bernard in vain inspired
> The potentates of Europe to defend
> The sepulcher of God. Mankind, his temple,
> I sought to liberate, and upon the earth
> Desired the triumph of the love divine,
> And life, and liberty, and progress. This,
> This was my doctrine, and God only knows
> How reason struggles with the faith in me

For the supremacy of my spirit. Oh,
Forgive me, Lord. These in their war are like
The rivers twain of heaven, till they return
To their eternal origin, and the truth
Is seen in thee, and God denies not God.
I ought to pray. Thinking on thee, I pray.
Yet how thy substance by three persons shared,
Each equal with the other, one remains,
I cannot comprehend, nor give in thee
Bounds to the infinite and human names.
Father of the world, that which thou here revealest
Perchance is but a thought of thine; or this
Movable veil that covers here below
All thy creation is eternal illusion
That hides God from us. Where to rest itself
The mind hath not. It palpitates uncertain
In infinite darkness, and denies more wisely
Than it affirms. O God omnipotent!
I know not what thou art, or, if I know,
How can I utter thee? The tongue has not
Words for thee, and it falters with my thought
That wrongs thee by its effort. Soon I go
Out of the last doubt unto the first truth.
What did I say? The intellect is soothed
To faith in Christ, and therein it reposes
As in the bosom of a tender mother
Her son. Arnaldo, that which thou art seeking
With sterile torment, thy great teacher sought
Long time in vain, and at the cross's foot
His weary reason cast itself at last.
Follow his great example, and with tears
Wash out thy sins.

We leave Arnaldo in his prison, and it is supposed that he is put to death during the combat that follows between the Germans and Romans immediately after the coronation of Frederick. As the forces stand opposed to each other, two beautiful choruses are introduced — one of Romans and one of Germans. And, just before the onset, Adelasia appears and confesses that she has betrayed Arnaldo, and that he is now in the power of the papacy. At the same time the clergy are heard chanting Frederick's coronation hymn, and then the battle begins. The Romans are beaten by the number and discipline of their enemies, and their leaders are driven out. The Germans appear before Frederic and Adrian with two hundred prisoners, and ask mercy for them. Adrian delivers them to his prefect, and it is implied that they are put to death. Then turning to Frederick, Adrian says:

> Art thou content? for I have given to thee
> More than the crown. My words have consecrated
> Thy power. So let the Church and Empire be
> Now at last reconciled. The mystery
> That holds three persons in one substance, nor
> Confounds them, may it make us here on earth
> To reign forever, image of itself,
> In unity which is like to that of God.

V

So ENDS the tragedy, and so was accomplished the union which rested so heavily ever after upon the hearts and hopes, not only of Italians, but of all Christian men. So was confirmed that temporal power of the popes, whose destruction will be known in history as infinitely the greatest event of our greatly eventful time, and will free from the doubt and dread of many one of the most powerful agencies for good in the world; namely, the Catholic Church.

I have tried to give an idea of the magnificence and scope of this mighty tragedy of Niccolini's, and I do not know that I can now add anything which will make this clearer. If we think of the grandeur of its plan, and how it employs for its effect the evil and the perverted good of the time in which the scene was laid, how it accords perfect sincerity to all the great actors,— to the Pope as well as to Arnaldo, to the Emperor as well as to the leaders of the people,— we must perceive that its conception is that of a very great artist. It seems to me that the execution is no less admirable. We cannot judge it by the narrow rule which the tragedies of the stage must obey; we must look at it with the generosity and the liberal imagination with which we can alone enjoy a great fiction. Then the patience, the subtlety, the strength, with which each character, individual and typical, is evolved; the picturesqueness with which every event is presented; the lyrical sweetness and beauty with which so many passages are enriched, will all be apparent to us, and we shall feel the æsthetic sublimity of the work as well as its moral force and its political significance.

GIACOMO LEOPARDI

I

In the year 1798, at Recanati, a little mountain town of Tuscany, was born, noble and miserable, the poet Giacomo Leopardi, who began even in childhood to suffer the malice of that strange conspiracy of ills which consumed him. His constitution was very fragile, and it early felt the effect of the passionate ardor with which the sickly boy dedicated his life to literature. From the first he seems to have had little or no direction in his own studies, and hardly any instruction. He literally lived among his books, rarely leaving his own room except to pass into his father's library; his research and erudition were marvelous, and at the age of sixteen he presented his father a Latin translation and comment on Plotinus, of which Sainte-Beuve said that "one who had studied Plotinus his whole life could find something useful in this work of a boy." At that age Leopardi already knew all Greek and Latin literature; he knew French, Spanish, and English; he knew Hebrew, and disputed in that tongue with the rabbis of Ancona.

The poet's father was Count Monaldo Leopardi, who had written little books of a religious and political character; the religion very bigoted, the politics very reactionary. His library was the largest anywhere in that region, but he seems not to have learned wisdom in it; and, though otherwise a blameless man, he used his son, who grew to manhood differing from him in all his opinions, with a rigor that was scarcely less than cruel. He was bitterly opposed to what was called progress, to religious and civil liberty; he was devoted to what was called order, which meant merely the existing order of things, the divinely appointed prince, the infallible priest. He had a mediæval taste, and he made his palace at Recanati as much like a feudal castle as he could, with all sorts of baronial bric-à-brac. An armed vassal at his gate was out of the question, but at the door of his own chamber stood an effigy in rusty armor, bearing a tarnished halberd. He abhorred the fashions of our century, and wore those of an earlier epoch; his wife, who shared his prejudices and opinions, fantastically appareled herself to look like the portrait of some gentlewoman of as remote a date. Halls hung in damask, vast mirrors in carven frames, and stately furniture of antique form attested throughout the palace "the splendor of a race which, if its fortunes had somewhat declined, still knew how to maintain its ancient state."

In this home passed the youth and early manhood of a poet who no sooner began to think for himself than he began to think things most discordant with his father's principles and ideas. He believed in neither the religion nor the politics of his race; he cherished with the desire of literary achievement that vague faith in humanity, in freedom, in the future, against which the Count Monaldo had so sternly set his face; he chafed under the restraints of his father's authority, and longed for some escape into the world. The Italians sometimes write of Leopardi's unhappiness with passionate condemnation of his father; but neither was Count Monaldo's part an enviable one, and it was certainly not at this period that he had all the wrong in his differences with his son. Nevertheless, it is pathetic to read how the heartsick, frail, ambitious boy, when he found some article in a newspaper that greatly pleased him, would write to the author and ask his friendship. When these journalists, who were possibly not always the wisest publicists of their time, so far responded to the young scholar's advances as to give him their personal acquaintance as well as their friendship, the old count received them with a courteous tolerance, which had no kindness in it for their progressive ideas. He lived in dread of his son's becoming involved in some of the many plots then hatching against order and religion, and he repressed with all his strength Leopardi's revolutionary tendencies, which must always have been mere matters of sentiment, and not deserving of great rigor.

He seems not so much to have loved Italy as to have hated Recanati. It is a small village high up in the Apennines, between Loreto and Macerata, and is chiefly accessible in ox-carts. Small towns everywhere are dull, and perhaps are not more deadly so in Italy than they are elsewhere, but there they have a peculiarly obscure, narrow life indoors. Outdoors there is a little lounging about the *caffè*, a little stir on holidays among the lower classes and the neighboring peasants, a great deal of gossip at all times, and hardly anything more. The local nobleman, perhaps, cultivates literature as Leopardi's father did; there is always some abbate mousing about in the local archives and writing pamphlets on disputed points of the local history; and there is the parish priest, to help form the polite society of the place. As if this social barrenness were not enough, Recanati was physically hurtful to Leopardi: the climate was very fickle; the harsh, damp air was cruel to his nerves. He says it seems to him a den where no good or beautiful thing ever comes; he bewails the common ignorance; in Recanati there is no love for letters, for the humanizing arts; nobody frequents his father's great library, nobody buys books, nobody reads the newspapers. Yet this forlorn and detestable little town has one good thing. It has a preëminently good Italian accent, better even, he thinks, than the Roman,— which would be a greater consolation to an Italian than we can well understand. Nevertheless it was not society, and it did not make his fellow-townsmen endurable to him. He recoiled from them more and more, and the solitude in which he lived among his books filled him with a black melancholy, which he describes as a poison, corroding the life of body and soul alike. To a friend who tries to reconcile him to Recanati, he writes: "It is very well to tell me that Plutarch and Alfieri loved Chæronea and Asti; they loved them, but they left them; and so shall I love my native place when I am away from it. Now I say I hate it because I am in it. To recall the spot where one's childhood days were passed is dear and sweet; it is a fine saying, 'Here you were born, and here Providence wills you to stay.' All very fine! Say to the sick man striving to be well that he is flying in the face of Providence; tell the poor man struggling to advance himself that he is defying heaven; bid the Turk beware of baptism, for God has made him a Turk!" So Leopardi wrote when he was in comparative health and able to continue his studies. But there were long periods when his ailments denied him his sole consolation of work. Then he rose late, and walked listlessly about without opening his lips or looking at a book the whole day. As soon as he might, he returned to his studies; when he must, he abandoned them again. At such a time he once wrote to a friend who understood and loved him: "I have not energy enough to conceive a single desire, not even for death; not because I fear death, but because I cannot see any difference between that and my present life. For the first time *ennui* not merely oppresses and wearies me, but it also agonizes and lacerates me, like a cruel pain. I am overwhelmed with a sense

GIACOMO LEOPARDI.

of the vanity of all things and the condition of men. My passions are dead, my very despair seems nonentity. As to my studies, which you urge me to continue, for the last eight months I have not known what study means; the nerves of my eyes and of my whole head are so weakened and disordered that I cannot read or listen to reading, nor can I fix my mind upon any subject."

At Recanati Leopardi suffered not merely solitude, but the contact of people whom he despised, and whose vulgarity was all the greater oppression when it showed itself in a sort of stupid compassionate tenderness for him. He had already suffered one of those disappointments which are the rule rather than the exception, and his first love had ended as first love always does when it ends fortunately — in disappointment. He scarcely knew the object of his passion, a young girl of humble lot, whom he used to hear singing at her loom in the house opposite his father's palace. Count Monaldo promptly interfered, and not long afterward the young girl died. But the sensitive boy, and his biographers after him, made the most of this sorrow; and doubtless it helped to render life under his father's roof yet heavier and harder to bear. Such as it was, it seems to have been the only love that Leopardi ever really felt, and the young girl's memory passed into the melancholy of his life and poetry.

But he did not summon courage to abandon Recanati before his twenty-fourth year, and then he did not go with his father's entire good-will.

The count wished him to become a priest, but Leopardi shrank from the idea with horror, and there remained between him and his father not only the difference of their religious and political opinions, but an unkindness which must be remembered against the judgment, if not the heart, of the latter. He gave his son so meager an allowance that it scarcely kept him above want, and obliged him to labors and subjected him to cares which his frail health was not able bear.

From Recanati Leopardi first went to Rome; but he carried Recanati everywhere with him, and he was as solitary and as wretched in the capital of the world as in the little village of the Apennines. He despised the Romans, as they deserved, upon very short acquaintance, and he declared that his dullest fellow-villager had a greater share of good sense than the best of them. Their frivolity was incredible; the men moved him to rage and pity; the women, high and low, to loathing. In one of his letters to his brother Carlo, he says of Rome, as he found it: "I have spoken to you only about the women, because I am at a loss what to say to you about literature. Horrors upon horrors! The most sacred names profaned, the most absurd follies praised to the skies, the greatest spirits of the century trampled under foot as inferior to the smallest literary man in Rome. Philosophy despised; genius, imagination, feeling, names — I do not say things, but even names — unknown and alien to these professional poets and poetesses! Antiquarianism placed at the summit of human learning, and considered invariably and universally as the only true study of man!" This was Rome in 1822. "I do not exaggerate," he writes, "because it is impossible, and I do not even say enough." One of the things that moved him to the greatest disgust in the childish and insipid society of a city where he had fondly hoped to find a response to his high thoughts was the sensation caused throughout Rome by the dress and theatrical effectiveness with which a certain prelate said mass. All Rome talked of it, cardinals and noble ladies complimented the performer as if he were a ballet-dancer, and the flattered prelate used to rehearse his part, and expatiate upon his methods of study for it, to private audiences of admirers. In fact, society had then touched almost the lowest depth of degradation where society had always been corrupt and dissolute, and the reader of Massimo d'Azeglio's memoirs may learn particulars (given with shame and regret, indeed, and yet with perfect Italian frankness) which it is not necessary to repeat here.

There were, however, many foreigners living at Rome in whose company Leopardi took great pleasure. They were chiefly Germans, and first among them was Niebuhr, who says of his first meeting with the poet: "Conceive of my astonishment when I saw standing before me in the poor little chamber a mere youth, pale and shy, frail in person, and obviously in ill health, who was by far the first, in fact the only, Greek philologist in Italy, the author of critical comments and observations which would have won honor for the first philologist in Germany, and yet only twenty-two years old! He had become thus profoundly learned without school, without instructor, without help, without encouragement, in his father's house. I understand, too, that he is one of the first of the rising poets of Italy. What a nobly gifted people!"

Niebuhr offered to procure him a professorship of Greek philosophy in Berlin, but Leopardi would not consent to leave his own country; and then Niebuhr unsuccessfully used his influence to get him some employment from the papal government,— compliments and good wishes it gave him, but no employment and no pay.

From Rome Leopardi went to Milan, where he earned something — very little — as editor of a comment upon Petrarch. A little later he went to Bologna, where a generous and sympathetic nobleman made him tutor in his family; but Leopardi returned not long after to Recanati, where he probably found no greater content than he left there. Presently we find him at Pisa, and then at Florence, eking out the allowance from his father by such literary work as he could find to do. In the latter place it is somewhat dimly established that he again fell in love, though he despised the Florentine women almost as much as the Romans, for their extreme ignorance, folly, and pride. This love also was unhappy. There is no reason to believe that Leopardi, who inspired tender and ardent friendships in men, ever moved any woman to love. The Florentine ladies are darkly accused by one of his biographers of having laughed at the poor young pessimist, and it is very possible; but that need not make us think the worse of him, or of them either, for that matter. He is supposed to have figured the lady of his latest love under the name of Aspasia, in one of his poems, as he did his first love under that of Sylvia, in the poem so called. Doubtless the experience further embittered a life already sufficiently miserable. He left Florence, but after a brief sojourn at Rome he returned thither, where his friend Antonio Ranieri watched with a heavy heart the gradual decay of his forces, and persuaded him finally to seek the milder air of Naples. Ranieri's father was, like Leopardi's, of reactionary opinions, and the Neapolitan, dreading the effect of their discord, did not take his friend to his own house, but hired a villa at Capodimonte, where he lived four years in fraternal intimacy with Leopardi, and where the poet died in 1837.

Ranieri has in some sort made himself the champion of Leopardi's fame. He has edited his poems, and has written a touching and beautiful sketch of his life. Their friendship, which was of the greatest tenderness, began when Leopardi sorely needed it; and Ranieri devoted himself to the hapless poet like a lover, as if to console him for the many years in which he had known neither reverence nor love. He indulged all the eccentricities of his guest, who for a sick man had certain strange habits, often not rising till evening, dining at midnight, and going to bed at dawn. Ranieri's sister Paolina kept house for the friends, and shared all her brother's compassion for Leopardi, whose family appears to have willingly left him to the care of these friends. How far the old unkindness between him and his father continued, it is hard to say. His last letter was written to his mother in May, 1837, some two weeks before his death; he thanks her for a present of ten dollars,— one may imagine from the gift and the gratitude that he was still held in a strict and parsimonious tutelage,— and begs her prayers and his father's, for after he has seen them again, he shall not have long to live.

He did not see them again, but he continued to smile at the anxieties of his friends, who had too great reason to think that the end was much nearer than Leopardi himself supposed. On the night of the 14th of June, while they were waiting for the carriage which was to take them into the country, where they intended to pass the time together and sup at daybreak, Leopardi felt so great a difficulty of breathing — he called it asthma, but it was dropsy of the heart — that he begged them to send for a doctor. The doctor on seeing the sick man took Ranieri apart, and bade him fetch a priest without delay, and while they waited the coming of the friar, Leopardi spoke now and then with them, but sank rapidly. Finally, says Ranieri, "Leopardi opened his eyes, now larger even than their wont, and looked at me more fixedly than before. 'I can't see you,' he said, with a kind of sigh. And he ceased to breathe, and his pulse and heart beat no more; and at the same moment the Friar Felice of the barefoot order of St. Augustine entered the chamber, while I, quite beside myself, called with a loud voice on him who had been my friend, my brother, my father, and who answered me nothing, and yet seemed to gaze upon me. . . . His death was inconceivable to me; the others were dismayed and mute; there arose between the good friar and myself the most cruel and painful dispute, . . . I madly contending that my friend was still alive, and beseeching him with tears to accompany with the offices of religion the passing of that great soul. But he, touching again and again the pulse and the heart, continually answered that the spirit had taken flight. At last, a spontaneous and solemn silence fell upon all in the room; the friar knelt beside the dead, and we all followed his example. Then after long and profound meditation he prayed, and we prayed with him."

In another place Ranieri says: "The malady of Leopardi was indefinable, for having its spring in the most secret sources of life, it was like life itself, inexplicable. The bones softened and dissolved away, refusing their frail support to the flesh that covered them. The flesh itself grew thinner and more lifeless every day, for the organs of nutrition denied their office of assimilation. The lungs, cramped into a space too narrow, and not sound themselves, expanded with difficulty. With difficulty the heart freed itself from the lymph with which a slow absorption burdened it. The blood, which ill renewed itself in the hard and painful respiration, returned cold, pale, and sluggish to the enfeebled veins. And in fine, the whole mysterious circle of life, moving with such great effort, seemed from moment to moment about to pause forever. Perhaps the great cerebral sponge, beginning and end of that mysterious circle, had prepotently sucked up all the vital forces, and itself consumed in a brief time all that was meant to suffice the whole system for a long period. However it may be, the life of Leopardi was not a course, as in most men, but truly a precipitation toward death."

Some years before he died, Leopardi had a presentiment of his death, and his end was perhaps hastened by the nervous shock of the terror produced by the cholera, which was then raging in Naples. At that time the body of a Neapolitan minister of state who had died of cholera was cast into the common burial-pit at Naples — such was the fear of contagion, and so rapidly were the dead hurried to the grave. A heavy bribe secured the remains of Leopardi from this fate, and his dust now reposes in a little church on the road to Pozzuoli.

II

"In the years of boyhood," says the Neapolitan critic, Francesco de Sanctis, "Leopardi saw his youth vanish forever; he lived obscure, and achieved posthumous envy and renown; he was rich and noble, and he suffered from want and despite; no woman's love ever smiled upon him, the solitary lover of his own mind, to which he gave the names of Sylvia, Aspasia, and Nerina. Therefore, with a precocious and bitter penetration, he held what we call happiness for illusions and deceits of fancy; the objects of our desire he called idols, our labors idleness, and everything vanity. Thus he saw nothing here below equal to his own intellect, or that was worthy the throb of his heart; and inertia, rust, as it were, even more than pain consumed his life, alone in what he called this formidable desert of the world. In such solitude life becomes a dialogue of man with his own soul, and the internal colloquies render more bitter and intense the affections which have returned to the heart for want of nourishment in the world. Mournful colloquies and yet pleasing, where man is the suicidal vulture perpetually preying upon himself, and caressing the wound that drags him to the grave. . . . The first cause of his sorrow is Recanati: the intellect, capable of the universe, feels itself oppressed in an obscure village, cruel to the body and deadly to the spirit. . . . He leaves Recanati; he arrives in Rome; we believe him content at last, and he too believes it.

Brief illusion! Rome, Bologna, Milan, Florence, Naples, are all different places, where he forever meets the same man, himself. Read the first letter that he writes from Rome: 'In the great things I see I do not feel the least pleasure, for I know that they are marvelous, but I do not feel it, and I assure you that their multitude and grandeur wearied me after the first day.' . . . To Leopardi it is rarely given to interest himself in any spectacle of nature, and he never does it without a sudden and agonized return to himself. . . . Malign and heartless men have pretended that Leopardi was a misanthrope, a fierce hater and enemy of the human race! . . . Love, inexhaustible and almost ideal, was the supreme craving of that angelic heart, and never left it during life. 'Love me, for God's sake,' he beseeches his brother Carlo; 'I have need of love, love, love, fire, enthusiasm, life.' And in truth it may be said that pain and love form the twofold poetry of his life."

Leopardi lived in Italy during the long contest between the Classic and Romantic schools, and it may be said that in him many of the leading ideas of both parties were reconciled. His literary form was as severe and sculpturesque as that of Alfieri himself, whilst the most subjective and introspective of the Romantic poets did not so much color the world with his own mental and spiritual hue as Leopardi. It is not plain whether he ever declared himself for one theory or the other. He was a contributor to the literary journal which the partisans of the Romantic School founded at Florence;

but he was a man so weighed upon by his own sense of the futility and vanity of all things that he could have had little spirit for mere literary contentions. His admirers try hard to make out that he was positively and actively patriotic; and it is certain that in his earlier youth he disagreed with his father's conservative opinions, and despised the existing state of things; but later in life he satirized the aspirations and purposes of progress, though without sympathizing with those of reaction.

The poem which his chief claim to classification with the poets militant of his time rests upon is that addressed "To Italy." Those who have read even only a little of Leopardi have read it; and I must ask their patience with a version which drops the irregular rhyme of the piece for the sake of keeping its peculiar rhythm and measure.

My native land, I see the walls and arches,
The columns and the statues, and the lonely
Towers of our ancestors,
But not their glory, not
The laurel and the steel that of old time
Our great forefathers bore. Disarmèd now,
Naked thou showest thy forehead and thy breast!
O me, how many wounds,
What bruises and what blood! How do I see thee,
Thou loveliest Lady! Unto Heaven I cry,
And to the world: "Say, say,
Who brought her unto this?" To this and worse,
For both her arms are loaded down with chains,
So that, unveiled and with disheveled hair,

She crouches all forgotten and forlorn,
Hiding her beautiful face
Between her knees, and weeps.
Weep, weep, for well thou may'st, my Italy!
Born, as thou wert, to conquest,
Alike in evil and in prosperous sort!
  If thy sweet eyes were each a living stream,
Thou could'st not weep enough
For all thy sorrow and for all thy shame.
For thou wast queen, and now thou art a slave.
Who speaks of thee or writes,
That thinking on thy glory in the past
But says, "She was great once, but is no more."
Wherefore, oh, wherefore? Where is the ancient
    strength,
The valor and the arms, and constancy?
Who rent the sword from thee?
Who hath betrayed thee? What art, or what toil,
Or what o'erwhelming force,
Hath stripped thy robe and golden wreath from thee?
How did'st thou fall, and when,
From such a height unto a depth so low?
Doth no one fight for thee, no one defend thee,
None of thy own? Arms, arms! For I alone
Will fight and fall for thee.
Grant me, O Heaven, my blood
Shall be as fire unto Italian hearts!
  Where are thy sons? I hear the sound of arms,
Of wheels, of voices, and of drums;
In foreign fields afar
Thy children fight and fall.
Wait, Italy, wait! I see, or seem to see,
A tumult as of infantry and horse,
And smoke and dust, and the swift flash of swords
Like lightning among clouds.

Wilt thou not hope? Wilt thou not lift and turn
Thy trembling eyes upon the doubtful close?
For what, in yonder fields,
Combats Italian youth? O gods, ye gods,
For other lands Italian swords are drawn!
Oh, misery for him who dies in war,
Not for his native shores and his beloved,
His wife and children dear,
But by the foes of others
For others' cause, and cannot dying say,
"Dear land of mine,
The life thou gavest me I give thee back."

This suffers, of course, in translation, but I confess that in the original it wears something of the same perfunctory air. His patriotism was the fever-flame of the sick man's blood; his real country was the land beyond the grave, and there is a far truer note in this address to Death.

And thou, that ever from my life's beginning
I have invoked and honored,
Beautiful Death! who only
Of all our earthly sorrows knowest pity:
If ever celebrated
Thou wast by me; if ever I attempted
To recompense the insult
That vulgar terror offers
Thy lofty state, delay no more, but listen
To prayers so rarely uttered:
Shut to the light forever,
Sovereign of time, these eyes of weary anguish!

I suppose that Italian criticism of the present day would not give Leopardi nearly so high a place among the poets as his friend Ranieri claims for him and his contemporaries accorded. He seems to have been the poet of a national mood; he was the final expression of that long, hopeless apathy in which Italy lay bound for thirty years after the fall of Napoleon and his governments, and the reëstablishment of all the little despots, native and foreign, throughout the peninsula. In this time there was unrest enough, and revolt enough of a desultory and unorganized sort, but every struggle, apparently every aspiration, for a free political and religious life ended in a more solid confirmation of the leaden misrule which weighed down the hearts of the people. To such an apathy the pensive monotone of this sick poet's song might well seem the only truth; and one who beheld the universe with the invalid's loath eyes, and reasoned from his own irremediable ills to a malign mystery presiding over all human affairs, and ordering a sad destiny from which there could be no defense but death, might have the authority of a prophet among those who could find no promise of better things in their earthly lot.

Leopardi's malady was such that when he did not positively suffer he had still the memory of pain, and he was oppressed with a dreary ennui, from which he could not escape. Death, oblivion, annihilation, are the thoughts upon which he broods, and which fill his verse. The passing color of other men's minds is the prevailing cast of his, and he, probably with far more sincerity than any other poet, nursed his despair in such utterances as this:

TO HIMSELF.

Now thou shalt rest forever,
O weary heart! The last deceit is ended,
For I believed myself immortal. Cherished
Hopes, and beloved delusions,
And longings to be deluded,—all are perished!
Rest thee forever! Oh, greatly,
Heart, hast thou palpitated. There is nothing
Worthy to move thee more, nor is earth worthy
Thy sighs. For life is only
Bitterness and vexation; earth is only
A heap of dust. So rest thee!
Despair for the last time. To our race Fortune
Never gave any gift but death. Disdain, then,
Thyself and Nature and the Power
Occultly reigning to the common ruin:
Scorn, heart, the infinite emptiness of all things!

Nature was so cruel a stepmother to this man that he could see nothing but harm even in her apparent beneficence, and his verse repeats again and again his dark mistrust of the very loveliness which so keenly delights his sense. One of his early poems, called "The Quiet after the Storm," strikes the key in which nearly all his songs are pitched. The observation of nature is very sweet and honest, and I cannot see that the philosophy in its perversion of the relations of physical and spiritual facts is less mature than that of his later work: it is a philosophy of which the first conception cannot well differ from the final expression.

. . . . See yon blue sky that breaks
The clouds above the mountain in the west!

The fields disclose themselves,
And in the valley bright the river runs.
All hearts are glad; on every side
Arise the happy sounds
Of toil begun anew.
The workman, singing, to the threshold comes,
With work in hand, to judge the sky,
Still humid, and the damsel next,
On his report, comes forth to brim her pail
With the fresh-fallen rain.
The noisy fruiterers
From lane to lane resume
Their customary cry.
The sun looks out again, and smiles upon
The houses and the hills. Windows and doors
Are opened wide; and on the far-off road
You hear the tinkling bells and rattling wheels
Of travelers that set out upon their journey.

Every heart is glad;
So grateful and so sweet
When is our life as now?
. . . .
O Pleasure, child of Pain,
Vain joy which is the fruit
Of bygone suffering overshadowèd
And wrung with cruel fears
Of death, whom life abhors;
Wherein, in long suspense,
Silent and cold and pale,
Man sat, and shook and shuddered to behold
Lightnings and clouds and winds,
Furious in his offense!
Beneficent Nature, these,
These are thy bounteous gifts;

These, these are the delights
Thou offerest unto mortals! To escape
From pain is bliss to us;
Anguish thou scatterest broadcast, and our woes
Spring up spontaneous, and that little joy
Born sometimes, for a miracle and show,
Of terror is our mightiest gain. O man,
Dear to the gods, count thyself fortunate
If now and then relief
Thou hast from pain, and blest
When death shall come to heal thee of all pain!

"The bodily deformities which humiliated Leopardi, and the cruel infirmities that agonized him his whole life long, wrought in his heart an invincible disgust, which made him invoke death as the sole relief. His songs, while they express discontent, the discord of the world, the conviction of the nullity of human things, are exquisite in style; they breathe a perpetual melancholy, which is often sublime, and they relax and pain your soul like the music of a single chord, while their strange sweetness wins you to them again and again." This is the language of an Italian critic who wrote after Leopardi's death, when already it had begun to be doubted whether he was the greatest Italian poet since Dante. A still later critic finds Leopardi's style, "without relief, without lyric flight, without the great art of contrasts, without poetic leaven," hard to read. "Despoil those verses of their masterly polish," he says, "reduce those thoughts to prose, and you will see how little they are akin to poetry."

I have a feeling that my versions apply some such test to Leopardi's work, and that the reader sees it in them at much of the disadvantage which this critic desires for it. Yet, after doing my worst, I am not wholly able to agree with him. It seems to me that there is the indestructible charm in it which, wherever we find it, we must call poetry. It is true that "its strange sweetness wins you again and again," and that this "lonely pipe of death" thrills and solemnly delights as no other stop has done. Let us hear it again, as the poet sounds it, figuring himself a Syrian shepherd, guarding his flock by night, and weaving his song under the Eastern moon:

> O flock that liest at rest, O blessèd thou
> That knowest not thy fate, however hard,
> How utterly I envy thee!
> Not merely that thou goest almost free
> Of all this weary pain,—
> That every misery and every toil
> And every fear thou straightway dost forget,—
> But most because thou knowest not ennui
> When on the grass thou liest in the shade.
> I see thee tranquil and content,
> And great part of thy years
> Untroubled by ennui thou passest thus.
> I likewise in the shadow, on the grass,
> Lie, and a dull disgust beclouds
> My soul, and I am goaded with a spur,
> So that, reposing, I am farthest still
> From finding peace or place.
> And yet I want for naught,
> And have not had till now a cause for tears.

What is thy bliss, how much,
I cannot tell; but thou art fortunate.

. . . .

Or, it may be, my thought
Errs, running thus to others' destiny;
May be, to everything,
Wherever born, in cradle or in fold,
That day is terrible when it was born.

It is the same note, the same voice; the theme does not change, but perhaps it is deepened in this ode:

ON THE LIKENESS OF A BEAUTIFUL WOMAN CARVEN UPON HER TOMB.

Such wast thou: now under earth
A skeleton and dust. O'er dust and bones
Immovably and vainly set, and mute,
Looking upon the flight of centuries,
Sole keeper of memory
And of regret is this fair counterfeit
Of loveliness now vanished. That sweet look,
Which made men tremble when it fell on them,
As now it falls on me; that lip, which once,
Like some full vase of sweets,
Ran over with delight; that fair neck, clasped
By longing, and that soft and amorous hand,
Which often did impart
An icy thrill unto the hand it touched;
That breast, which visibly
Blanched with its beauty him who looked on it—
All these things were, and now
Dust art thou, filth, a fell
And hideous sight hidden beneath a stone.

Thus fate hath wrought its will
Upon the semblance that to us did seem
Heaven's vividest image! Eternal mystery
Of mortal being! To-day the ineffable
Fountain of thoughts and feelings vast and high,
Beauty reigns sovereign, and seems
Like splendor thrown afar
From some immortal essence on these sands,
To give our mortal state
A sign and hope secure of destinies
Higher than human, and of fortunate realms,
And golden worlds unknown.
To-morrow, at a touch,
Loathsome to see, abominable, abject,
Becomes the thing that was
All but angelical before;
And from men's memories
All that its loveliness
Inspired forever faints and fades away.

Ineffable desires
And visions high and pure
Rise in the happy soul,
Lulled by the sound of cunning harmonies
Whereon the spirit floats,
As at his pleasure floats
Some fearless swimmer over the deep sea;
But if a discord strike
The wounded sense, to naught
All that fair paradise in an instant falls.

Mortality! if thou
Be wholly frail and vile,
Be only dust and shadow, how canst thou
So deeply feel? And if thou be

In part divine, how can thy will and thought
By things so poor and base
So easily be awakenèd and quenched?

Let us touch for the last time this pensive chord, and listen to its response of hopeless love. This poem, in which he turns to address the spirit of the poor child whom he loved boyishly at Recanati, is pathetic with the fact that possibly she alone ever reciprocated the tenderness with which his heart was filled.

TO SYLVIA.

Sylvia, dost thou remember
In this that season of thy mortal being
When from thine eyes shone beauty,
In thy shy glances fugitive and smiling,
And joyously and pensively the borders
Of childhood thou did'st traverse?

All day the quiet chambers
And the ways near resounded
To thy perpetual singing,
When thou, intent upon some girlish labor,
Sat'st utterly contented,
With the fair future brightening in thy vision.
It was the fragrant month of May, and ever
Thus thou thy days beguiledst.

I, leaving my fair studies,
Leaving my manuscripts and toil-stained volumes,
Wherein I spent the better
Part of myself and of my young existence,
Leaned sometimes idly from my father's windows,
And listened to the music of thy singing,

And to thy hand, that fleetly
Ran o'er the threads of webs that thou wast weaving.
I looked to the calm heavens,
Unto the golden lanes and orchards,
And unto the far sea and to the mountains:
No mortal tongue may utter
What in my heart I felt then.

O Sylvia mine, what visions,
What hopes, what hearts, we had in that far season!
How fair and good before us
Seemed human life and fortune!
When I remember hope so great, belovèd,
An utter desolation
And bitterness o'erwhelm me,
And I return to mourn my evil fortune.
O Nature, faithless Nature,
Wherefore dost thou not give us
That which thou promisest? Wherefore deceivest,
With so great guile, thy children?

Thou, ere the freshness of thy spring was withered,
Stricken by thy fell malady, and vanquished,
Did'st perish, O my darling! and the blossom
Of thy years never sawest;
Thy heart was never melted
At the sweet praise, now of thy raven tresses,
Now of thy glances amorous and bashful;
Never with thee the holiday-free maidens
Reasoned of love and loving.

Ah! briefly perished, likewise,
My own sweet hope; and destiny denied me
Youth, even in my childhood!
Alas, alas, belovèd,

Companion of my childhood!
Alas, my mournèd hope! how art thou vanished
Out of my place forever!
This is that world? the pleasures,
The love, the labors, the events, we talked of,
These, when we prattled long ago together?
Is this the fortune of our race, O Heaven?
At the truth's joyless dawning,
Thou fellest, sad one, with thy pale hand pointing
Unto cold death, and an unknown and naked
Sepulcher in the distance.

III

THESE pieces fairly indicate the range of Leopardi, and I confess that they and the rest that I have read leave me somewhat puzzled in the presence of his reputation. This, to be sure, is largely based upon his prose writings — his dialogues, full of irony and sarcasm — and his unquestionable scholarship. But the poetry is the heart of his fame, and is it enough to justify it? I suppose that such poetry owes very much of its peculiar influence to that awful love we all have of hovering about the idea of death — of playing with the great catastrophe of our several tragedies and farces, and of marveling what it can be. There are moods which the languid despair of Leopardi's poetry can always evoke, and in which it seems that the most life can do is to leave us, and let us lie down and cease. But I fancy we all agree that these are not very wise or healthful moods, and that their indulgence does not fit us particularly well for the duties of life, though I never heard that they interfered with its pleasures; on the contrary, they add a sort of zest to enjoyment. Of course the whole transaction is illogical, but if a poet will end every pensive strain with an appeal or apostrophe to death — not the real death, that comes with a sharp, quick agony, or "after long lying in bed," after many days or many years of squalid misery and slowly dying hopes and medicines that cease even to relieve at last; not this death, that comes in all the horror of undertaking, but a picturesque and impressive abstraction, whose business it is to relieve us in the most effective way of all our troubles, and at the same time to avenge us somehow upon the indefinitely ungrateful and unworthy world we abandon — if a poet will do this, we are very apt to like him. There is little doubt that Leopardi was sincere, and there is little reason why he should not have been so, for life could give him nothing but pain.

De Sanctis, whom I have quoted already, and who speaks, I believe, with rather more authority than any other modern Italian critic, and certainly with great clearness and acuteness, does not commit himself to specific praise of Leopardi's work. But he seems to regard him as an important expression, if not force or influence, and he has some words about him, at the close of his "History

of Italian Literature," which have interested me,
not only for the estimate of Leopardi which they
embody, but for the singularly distinct statement
which they make of the modern literary attitude.
I should not, myself, have felt that Leopardi represented this, but I am willing that the reader
should feel it, if he can. De Sanctis has been
speaking of the Romantic period in Italy, when he
says:

"Giacomo Leopardi marks the close of this
period. Metaphysics at war with theology had
ended in this attempt at reconciliation. The multiplicity of systems had discredited science itself.
Metaphysics was regarded as a revival of theology. The Idea seemed a substitute for providence.
Those philosophies of history, of religion, of humanity, had the air of poetical inventions. . . .
That reconciliation between the old and new, tolerated as a temporary political necessity, seemed
at bottom a profanation of science, a moral weakness. . . . Faith in revelation had been wanting;
faith in philosophy itself was now wanting. Mystery re-appeared. The philosopher knew as much
as the peasant. Of this mystery, Giacomo Leopardi was the echo in the solitude of his thought
and his pain. His skepticism announced the dissolution of this theologico-metaphysical world, and
inaugurated the reign of the arid True, of the
Real. His songs are the most profound and occult
voices of that laborious transition called the nineteenth century. That which has importance is
not the brilliant exterior of that century of prog-

ress, and it is not without irony that he speaks of the progressive destinies of mankind. That which has importance is the exploration of one's own breast, the inner world, virtue, liberty, love, all the ideals of religion, of science, and of poetry — shadows and illusions in the presence of reason, yet which warm the heart, and will not die. Mystery destroys the intellectual world; it leaves the moral world intact. This tenacious life of the inner world, despite the fall of all theological and metaphysical worlds, is the originality of Leopardi, and gives his skepticism a religious stamp. . . . Every one feels in it a new creation. The instrument of this renovation is criticism. . . . The sense of the real continues to develop itself; the positive sciences come to the top, and cast out all the ideal and systematic constructions. New dogmas lose credit. Criticism remains intact. The patient labor of analysis begins again. . . . Socialism re-appears in the political order, positivism in the intellectual order. The word is no longer liberty, but justice. . . . Literature also undergoes transformation. It rejects classes, distinctions, privileges. The ugly stands beside the beautiful; or rather, there is no longer ugly or beautiful, neither ideal nor real, neither infinite nor finite. . . . There is but one thing only, the Living."

GIUSEPPE GIUSTI

I

GIUSEPPE GIUSTI, who is the greatest Italian satirist of this century, and is in some respects the greatest Italian poet, was born in 1809 at Mossummano in Tuscany, of parentage noble and otherwise distinguished; one of his paternal ancestors had assisted the liberal Grand Duke Pietro Leopoldo to compile his famous code, and his mother's father had been a republican in 1799. There was also an hereditary taste for literature in the family; and Giusti says, in one of his charming letters, that almost as soon as he had learned to speak, his father taught him the ballad of Count Ugolino, and he adds, "I have always had a passion for song, a passion for verses, and more than a passion for Dante." His education passed later into the hands of a priest, who had spent much time as a teacher in Vienna, and was impetuous, choleric, and thoroughly German in principle. "I was given him to be taught," says Giusti, "but he undertook to tame me"; and he remembered reading with him a Plutarch for youth, and the "Lives of the Saints," but chiefly was, as he says, so "caned, contraried, and martyred" by him, that, when the priest wept at their final parting, the boy could by no means account for the burst of tenderness. Giusti was then going to Florence to be placed in a school where he had the immeasurable good fortune to fall into the hands of one whose gentleness and wisdom he remembered through life. "Drea Francioni," he says, "had not time to finish his work, but he was the first and the only one to put into my heart the need and love of study. Oh, better far than stuffing the head with Latin, with histories and with fables! Endear study, even if you teach nothing; this is the great task!" And he afterward dedicated his book on Tuscan proverbs, which he thought one of his best performances, to this beloved teacher.

He had learned to love study, yet from this school, and from others to which he was afterward sent, he came away with little Latin and no Greek; but, what is more important, he began life about this time as a poet—by stealing a sonnet. His theft was suspected, but could not be proved. "And so," he says of his teacher and himself, "we remained, he in his doubt and I in my lie. Who would have thought from this ugly beginning that I should really have gone on to make sonnets of my own? . . . The Muses once known, the vice grew upon me, and from my twelfth to my fifteenth year I rasped, and rasped, and rasped, until finally I came out with a sonnet to Italy, represented in the usual fashion, by the usual matron weeping as usual over her highly estimable misfortunes. In school, under certain priests who were more Chinese than Italian, and without knowing whether Italy were round or square, long or short, how that sonnet to Italy should get into my head I don't know. I only know that it was found beautiful, and I was advised to hide it,"—that being the proper thing to do with patriotic poetry in those days.

After leaving school, Giusti passed three idle years with his family, and then went to study the humanities at Pisa, where he found the *café* better adapted to their pursuit than the University, since he could there unite with it the pursuit of the exact science of billiards. He represents himself in his letters and verses to have led just the life at Pisa which was most agreeable to former governments of Italy,—a life of sensual gayety, abounding in the small excitements which turn the thought from the real interests of the time, and weaken at once the moral and intellectual fiber. But how far a man can be credited to his own disgrace is one of the unsettled questions: the repentant and the unrepentant are so apt to over-accuse themselves. It is very wisely conjectured by some of Giusti's biographers that he did not waste himself so much as he says in the dissipations of student life at Pisa. At any rate, it is certain that he began there to make those sarcastic poems upon political events which are so much less agreeable to a paternal despotism than almost any sort of love-songs. He is said to have begun by writing in the manner of Béranger, and several critics have labored to prove the similarity of their genius, with scarcely more effect, it seems to us, than those who would make him out the Heinrich Heine of Italy, as they call him. He was a political satirist, whose success was due to his genius, but who can never be thoroughly appreciated by a foreigner, or even an Italian not intimately acquainted with the affairs of his times; and his reputation must inevitably diminish with the waning interest of men in the obsolete politics of those vanished kingdoms and duchies. How mean and little were all their concerns is scarcely credible; but Giusti tells an adventure of his, at the period, which throws light upon some of the springs of action in Tuscany. He had been arrested for a supposed share in applause supposed revolutionary at the theater; he boldly denied that he had been at the play. "If you were not at the theater, how came your name on the list of the accused?" demanded the logical commissary. "Perhaps," answered Giusti, "the spies have me so much in mind that they see me where I am not. . . . Here," he continues, "the commissary fell into a rage, but I remained firm, and cited the Count Mastiani in proof, with whom the man often dined,"—Mastiani being governor in Pisa and the head of society. "At the name of Mastiani there seemed to pass before the commissary a long array of stewed and roast, eaten and to be eaten, so that he instantly turned and said to me, 'Go, and at any rate take this summons for a paternal admonition.'"

Ever since the French Revolution of 1830, and the sympathetic movements in Italy, Giusti had written political satires which passed from hand to hand in manuscript copies, the possession of which was rendered all the more eager and relishing by the pleasure of concealing them from spies; so that for a defective copy a person by no means rich would give as much as ten scudi. When a Swiss printed edition appeared in 1844, half the delight in them was gone; the violation of the law being naturally so dear to the human heart that, when combined with patriotism, it is almost a rapture.

But, in the midst of his political satirizing, Giusti felt the sting of one who is himself a greater satirist than any, when he will, though he is commonly known for a sentimentalist. The poet fell in love very seriously and, it proved, very unhappily, as he has recorded in three or four poems of great sweetness and grace, but no very characteristic merit. This passion is improbably believed to have had a disastrous effect upon Giusti's health, and ultimately to have shortened his life; but then the Italians always like to have their poets *agonizzanti*, at least. Like a true humorist, Giusti has himself taken both sides of the question; professing himself properly heart-broken in the poems referred to, and in a letter written late in life, after he had encountered his faded love at his own home in Pescia, making a jest of any reconciliation or renewal of the old passion between them.

"Apropos of the heart," says Giusti in this letter, "you ask me about a certain person who once had mine, whole and sound, roots and all. I saw her this morning in passing, out of the corner of my eye, and I know that she is well and enjoying herself. As to our coming together again, the case, if it were once remote, is now impossible;

for you can well imagine that, all things considered,
I could never be such a donkey as to tempt her to
a comparison of me with myself. I am certain
that, after having tolerated me for a day or two for
simple appearance' sake, she would find some good
excuse for planting me a yard outside the door.
In many, obstinacy increases with the ails and
wrinkles; but in me, thank Heaven, there comes a
meekness, a resignation, not to be expressed. Perhaps it has not happened otherwise with her. In
that case we could accommodate ourselves, and
talk as long as the evening lasted of magnesia, of
quinine, and of nervines; lament, not the rising
and sinking of the heart, but of the barometer;
talk, not of the theater and all the rest, but whether
it is better to crawl out into the sun like lizards,
or stay at home behind battened windows. 'Good-
evening, my dear, how have you been to-day?'
'Eh! you know, my love, the usual rheumatism;
but for the rest I don't complain.' 'Did you sleep
well last night?' 'Not so bad; and you?' 'O,
little or none at all; and I got up feeling as if all
my bones were broken.' 'My idol, take a little
laudanum. Think that when you are not well I
suffer with you. And your appetite, how is it?'
'O, don't speak of it! I can't get anything down.'
'My soul, if you don't eat you'll not be able to
keep up.' 'But, my heart, what would you do if
the mouthfuls stuck in your throat?' 'Take a little
quassia; . . . but, dost thou remember, once—?'
"Yes, I remember; but once was once,' . . . and
so forth, and so forth. Then some evening, if a

GIUSEPPE GIUSTI.

priest came in, we could take a hand at whist with a dummy, and so live on to the age of crutches in a passion whose phases are confided to the apothecary rather than to the confessor."

Giusti's first political poems had been inspired by the revolutionary events of 1830 in France; and he continued part of that literary force which, quite as much as the policy of Cavour, has educated Italians for freedom and independence. When the French revolution of 1848 took place, and the responsive outbreaks followed all over Europe, Tuscany drove out her Grand Duke, as France drove out her king, and, still emulous of that wise exemplar, put the novelist Guerrazzi at the head of her affairs, as the next best thing to such a poet as Lamartine, which she had not. The affair ended in the most natural way; the Florentines under the supposed popular government became very tired of themselves, and called back their Grand Duke, who came again with Austrian bayonets to support him in the affections of his subjects, where he remained secure until the persuasive bayonets disappeared before Garibaldi ten years later.

Throughout these occurrences the voice of Giusti was heard whenever that of good sense and a temperate zeal for liberty could be made audible. He was an aristocrat by birth and at heart, and he looked upon the democratic shows of the time with distrust, if not dislike, though he never lost faith in the capacity of the Italians for an independent national government. His broken health would not let him join the Tuscan volunteers who marched to encounter the Austrians in Lombardy; and though he was once elected member of the representative body from Pescia, he did not shine in it, and refused to be chosen a second time. His letters of this period afford the liveliest and truest record of feeling in Tuscany during that memorable time of alternating hopes and fears, generous impulses, and mean derelictions, and they strike me as among the best letters in any language.

Giusti supported the Grand Duke's return philosophically, with a sarcastic serenity of spirit, and something also of the indifference of mortal sickness. His health was rapidly breaking, and in March, 1850, he died very suddenly of a hemorrhage of the lungs.

II

In noticing Giusti's poetry I have a difficulty already hinted, for if I presented some of the pieces which gave him his greatest fame among his contemporaries, I should be doing, as far as my present purpose is concerned, a very unprofitable thing. The greatest part of his poetry was inspired by the political events or passions of the time at which it was written, and, except some five or six pieces, it is all of a political cast. These events are now many of them grown unimportant and obscure, and the passions are, for the most part, quite extinct; so that it would be useless to give certain of his most popular pieces as historical, while others do not represent him at his best as a poet. Some degree of social satire is involved; but the poems are principally light, brilliant mockeries of transient aspects of politics, or outcries against forgotten wrongs, or appeals for long-since-accomplished or defeated purposes. We know how dreary this sort of poetry generally is in our own language, after the occasion is once past, and how nothing but the enforced privacy of a desolate island could induce us to read, however ardent our sympathies may have been, the lyrics about slavery or the war, except in very rare cases. The truth is, the Muse, for a lady who has seen so much of life and the ways of the world, is an excessively jealous personification, and is apt to punish with oblivion a mixed devotion at her shrine. The poet who desires to improve and exalt his time must make up his mind to a double martyrdom,— first, to be execrated by vast numbers of respectable people, and then to be forgotten by all. It is a great pity, but it cannot be helped. It is chiefly your

Rogue of canzonets and serenades

who survives. Anacreon lives; but the poets who appealed to their Ionian fellow-citizens as men and brethren, and lectured them upon their servility and their habits of wine-bibbing and of basking away the dearest rights of humanity in the sun, who ever heard of them? I do not mean to say that Giusti ever lectured his generation; he was too good an artist for that; but at least one Italian critic forebodes that the figure he made in the patriotic imagination must diminish rapidly with the establishment of the very conditions he labored to bring about. The wit of much that he said must grow dim with the fading remembrance of what provoked it; the sting lie pointless and painless in the dust of those who writhed under it,— so much of the poet's virtue perishing in their death. We can only judge of all this vaguely and for a great part from the outside, for we cannot pretend to taste the finest flavor of the poetry which is sealed to a foreigner in the local phrases and racy Florentine words which Giusti used; but I think posterity in Italy will stand in much the same attitude toward him that we do now. Not much of the social life of his time is preserved in his poetry, and he will not be resorted to as that satirist of the period to whom historians are fond of alluding in support of conjectures relative to society in the past. Now and then he touches upon some prevailing intellectual or literary affectation, as in the poem describing the dandified, desperate young poet of fashion, who,

> Immersed in suppers and balls,
> A martyr in yellow gloves,

sings of Italy, of the people, of progress, with the rhetoricalities of the modern Arcadians; and he has a poem called "The Ball," which must fairly, as it certainly does wittily, represent one of those anomalous entertainments which rich foreigners give in Italy, and to which all sorts of irregular aliens resort, something of the local aristocracy appearing also in a ghostly and bewildered way. Yet even in this poem there is a political lesson.

I suppose, in fine, that I shall most interest my readers in Giusti, if I translate here the pieces that have most interested me. Of all, I like best the poem which he calls "St. Ambrose," and I think the reader will agree with me about it. It seems not only very perfect as a bit of art, with its subtly intended and apparently capricious mingling of satirical and pathetic sentiment, but valuable for its vivid expression of Italian feeling toward the Austrians. These the Italians hated as part of a stupid and brutal oppression; they despised them somewhat as a torpid-witted folk, but individually liked them for their amiability and good nature, and in their better moments they pitied them as the victims of a common tyranny. I will not be so adventurous as to say how far the beautiful military music of the Austrians tended to lighten the burden of a German garrison in an Italian city; but certainly whoever has heard that music must have felt, for one base and shameful moment, that the noise of so much of a free press as opposed his own opinions might be advantageously exchanged for it. The poem of "St. Ambrose," written in 1846, when the Germans seemed so firmly fixed in Milan, is impersonally addressed to some Italian holding office under the Austrian government, and, therefore, in the German interest.

ST. AMBROSE.

Your Excellency is not pleased with me
  Because of certain jests I made of late,
And, for my putting rogues in pillory,
  Accuse me of being anti-German. Wait,
And hear a thing that happened recently:
  When wandering here and there one day as fate
Led me, by some odd accident I ran
On the old church St. Ambrose, at Milan.

My comrade of the moment was, by chance,
  The young son of one Sandro*—one of those
Troublesome heads—an author of romance—
  Promessi Sposi—your Excellency knows
The book, perhaps?—has given it a glance?
  Ah, no? I see! God give your brain repose;
With graver interests occupied, your head
To all such stuff as literature is dead.

I enter, and the church is full of troops:
  Of northern soldiers, of Croatians, say,
And of Bohemians, standing there in groups
  As stiff as dry poles stuck in vineyards,—nay,
As stiff as if impaled, and no one stoops
  Out of the plumb of soldierly array;
All stand, with whiskers and mustache of tow,
Before their God like spindles in a row.

        *Alessandro Manzoni.

I started back: I cannot well deny
   That being rained down, as it were, and thrust
Into that herd of human cattle, I
   Could not suppress a feeling of disgust
Unknown, I fancy, to your Excellency,
   By reason of your office. Pardon! I must
Say the church stank of heated grease, and that
The very altar-candles seemed of fat.

But when the priest had risen to devote
   The mystic wafer, from the band that stood
About the altar came a sudden note
   Of sweetness over my disdainful mood;
A voice that, speaking from the brazen throat
   Of warlike trumpets, came like the subdued
Moan of a people bound in sore distress,
And thinking on lost hopes and happiness.

'T was Verdi's tender chorus rose aloof,—
   That song the Lombards there, dying of thirst,
Send up to God, "Lord, from the native roof."
   O'er countless thrilling hearts the song has burst,
And here I, whom its magic put to proof,
   Beginning to be no longer I, immersed
Myself amidst those tallowy fellow-men
As if they had been of my land and kin.

What would your Excellency? The piece was fine,
   And ours, and played, too, as it should be played;
It drives old grudges out when such divine
   Music as that mounts up into your head!
But when the piece was done, back to my line
   I crept again, and there I should have staid,
But that just then, to give me another turn,
From those mole-mouths a hymn began to yearn:

A German anthem, that to heaven went
  On unseen wings, up from the holy fane;
It was a prayer, and seemed like a lament,
  Of such a pensive, grave, pathetic strain
That in my soul it never shall be spent;
  And how such heavenly harmony in the brain
Of those thick-skulled barbarians should dwell
I must confess it passes me to tell.

In that sad hymn, I felt the bitter sweet
  Of the songs heard in childhood, which the soul
Learns from beloved voices, to repeat
  To its own anguish in the days of dole;
A thought of the dear mother, a regret,
  A longing for repose and love,—the whole
Anguish of distant exile seemed to run
Over my heart and leave it all undone:

When the strain ceased, it left me pondering
  Tenderer thoughts and stronger and more clear;
These men, I mused, the self-same despot king,
  Who rules in Slavic and Italian fear,
Tears from their homes and arms that round them cling,
  And drives them slaves thence, to keep us slaves here;
From their familiar fields afar they pass
Like herds to winter in some strange morass.

To a hard life, to a hard discipline,
  Derided, solitary, dumb, they go;
Blind instruments of many-eyed Rapíne
  And purposes they share not, and scarce know;
And this fell hate that makes a gulf between
  The Lombard and the German, aids the foe
Who tramples both divided, and whose bane
Is in the love and brotherhood of men.

Poor souls! far off from all that they hold dear,
　And in a land that hates them! Who shall say
That at the bottom of their hearts they bear
　Love for our tyrant? I should like to lay
They 've our hate for him in their pockets! Here,
　But that I turned in haste and broke away,
I should have kissed a corporal, stiff and tall,
And like a scarecrow stuck against the wall.

I could not well praise this poem enough, without praising it too much. It depicts a whole order of things, and it brings vividly before us the scene described; while its deep feeling is so lightly and effortlessly expressed, that one does not know which to like best, the exquisite manner or the excellent sense. To prove that Giusti was really a fine poet, I need give nothing more, for this alone would imply poetic power; not perhaps of the high epic sort, but of the kind that gives far more comfort to the heart of mankind, amusing and consoling it. "Giusti composed satires, but no poems," says a French critic; but I think most will not, after reading this piece, agree with him. There are satires and satires, and some are fierce enough and brutal enough; but when a satire can breathe so much tenderness, such generous humanity, such pity for the means, at the same time with such hatred of the source of wrong, and all with an air of such smiling pathos, I say, if it is not poetry, it is something better, and by all means let us have it instead of poetry. It is humor, in its best sense; and, after religion, there is nothing in the world can make men so conscious, thoughtful, and modest.

A certain pensiveness very perceptible in "St. Ambrose" is the prevailing sentiment of another poem of Giusti's, which I like very much, because it is more intelligible than his political satires, and because it places the reader in immediate sympathy with a man who had not only the subtlety to depict the faults of the time, but the sad wisdom to know that he was no better himself merely for seeing them. The poem was written in 1844, and addressed to Gino Capponi, the life-long friend in whose house Giusti died, and the descendant of the great Gino Capponi who threatened the threatening Frenchmen when Charles VIII. occupied Florence: "If you sound your trumpets," as a call to arms against the Florentines, "we will ring our bells," he said.

Giusti speaks of the part which he bears as a spectator and critic of passing events, and then apostrophizes himself:

Who art thou that a scourge so keen dost bear
And pitilessly dost the truth proclaim,
And that so loath of praise for good and fair,
So eager art with bitter songs of blame?
Hast thou achieved, in thine ideal's pursuit,
The secret and the ministry of art?
Did'st thou seek first to kill and to uproot
All pride and folly out of thine own heart
Ere turning to teach other men their part?
. . . . .
O wretched scorn! from which alone I sing,
Thou weariest and saddenest my soul!
O butterfly that joyest on thy wing,

Pausing from bloom to bloom, without a goal —
And thou, that singing of love for evermore,
Fond nightingale! from wood to wood dost go,
My life is as a never-ending war
Of doubts, when likened to the peace ye know,
And wears what seems a smile and is a throe!

There is another famous poem of Giusti's in quite a different mood. It is called "Instructions to an Emissary," sent down into Italy to excite a revolution, and give Austria a pretext for interference, and the supposed speaker is an Austrian minister. It is done with excellent sarcasm, and it is useful as light upon a state of things which, whether it existed wholly in fact or partly in the suspicion of the Italians, is equally interesting and curious. The poem was written in 1847, when the Italians were everywhere aspiring to a national independence and self-government, and their rulers were conceding privileges while secretly leaguing with Austria to continue the old order of an Italy divided among many small tyrants. The reader will readily believe that my English is not as good as the Italian.

INSTRUCTIONS TO AN EMISSARY.

You will go into Italy; you have here
   Your passport and your letters of exchange;
You travel as a count, it would appear,
   Going for pleasure and a little change;
Once there, you play the rodomont, the queer
   Crack-brain good fellow, idle gamester, strange
Spendthrift and madcap. Give yourself full swing;
People are taken with that kind of thing.

When you behold — and it will happen so —
  The birds flock down about the net, be wary;
Talk from a warm and open heart, and show
  Yourself with everybody bold and merry.
The North's a dungeon, say, a waste of snow,
  The very house and home of January,
Compared with that fair garden of the earth,
Beautiful, free, and full of life and mirth.

And throwing in your discourse this word *free*,
  Just to fill up, and as by accident,
Look round among your listeners, and see
  If it has had at all the effect you meant;
Beat a retreat if it fails, carelessly
  Talking of this and that; but in the event
Some one is taken with it, never fear,
Push boldly forward, for the road is clear.

Be bold and shrewd; and do not be too quick,
  As some are, and plunge headlong on your prey
When, if the snare shall happen not to stick,
  Your uproar frightens all the rest away;
To take your hare by carriage is the trick;
  Make a wide circle, do not mind delay;
Experiment and work in silence; scheme
With that wise prudence that shall folly seem.

The minister bids the emissary, "Turn me into a jest; say I 'm sleepy and begin to dote; invent what lies you will, I give you *carte-blanche.*"

Of governments down yonder say this, too,
  At the cafés and theaters; indeed
For this, I 've made a little sign for you
  Upon your passport that the wise will read
For an express command to let you do
  Whatever you think best, and take no heed.

Then the emissary is instructed to make himself center of the party of extremes, and in different companies to pity the country, to laugh at moderate progress as a sham, and to say that the concessions of the local governments are merely *ruses* to pacify and delude the people,—as in great part they were, though Giusti and his party did not believe so. The instructions to the emissary conclude with the charge to

Scatter republican ideas, and say
    That all the rich and all the well-to-do
Use common people hardly better, nay,
    Worse, than their dogs; and add some hard words, too:
Declare that *bread* 's the question of the day,
    And that the communists alone are true;
And that the foes of the agrarian cause
Waste more than half of all by wicked laws.

Then, he tells him, when the storm begins to blow, and the pockets of the people feel its effect, and the mob grows hungry, to contrive that there shall be some sort of outbreak, with a bit of pillage,—

    So that the kings down there, pushed to the wall,
    For congresses and bayonets shall call.

If you should have occasion to spend, spend,
    The money won't be wasted; there must be
Policemen in retirement, spies without end,
    Shameless and penniless; buy, you are free.
If destiny should be so much your friend
    That you could shake a throne or two for me,
Pour me out treasures. I shall be content;
My gains will be at least seven cent. per cent.

Or, in the event the inconstant goddess frown,
  Let me know instantly when you are caught;
A thunderbolt shall burst upon your crown,
  And you become a martyr on the spot.
As minister I turn all upside down,
  Our government disowns you as it ought.
And so the cake is turned upon the fire,
And we can use you next as we desire.

In order not to awaken any fear
  In the post-office, 't is my plan that you
Shall always correspond with liberals here;
  Don't doubt but I shall hear of all you do.
. . . . 's a Republican known far and near;
  I have n't another spy that 's *half* as true!
You understand, and I need say no more;
Lucky for you if you get me up a war!

We get the flavor of this, at least the literary flavor, the satire, and the irony, but it inevitably falls somewhat cold upon us, because it had its origin in a condition of things which, though historical, are so opposed to all our own experience that they are hard to be imagined. Yet we can fancy the effect such a poem must have had, at the time when it was written, upon a people who felt in the midst of their aspirations some disturbing element from without, and believed this to be espionage and Austrian interference. If the poem had also to be passed about secretly from one hand to another, its enjoyment must have been still keener; but strip it of all these costly and melancholy advantages, and it is still a piece of subtle and polished satire.

Most of Giusti's poems, however, are written in moods and manners very different from this; there is sparkle and dash in the movement, as well as the thought, which I cannot reproduce, and in giving another poem I can only hope to show something of his varying manner. Some foreigner, Lamartine, I think, called Italy the Land of the Dead,— whereupon Giusti responded with a poem of that title, addressed to his friend Gino Capponi:

THE LAND OF THE DEAD.

'Mongst us phantoms of Italians,—
  Mummies even from our birth,—
The very babies' nurses
  Help to put them under earth.

'T is a waste of holy water
  When we 're taken to the font:
They that make us pay for burial
  Swindle us to that amount.

In appearance we 're constructed
  Much like Adam's other sons,—
Seem of flesh and blood, but really
  We are nothing but dry bones.

O deluded apparitions,
  What do *you* do among men?
Be resigned to fate, and vanish
  Back into the past again!

Ah! of a perished people
  What boots now the brilliant story?
Why should skeletons be bothering
  About liberty and glory?

> Why deck this funeral service
>   With such pomp of torch and flower?
> Let us, without more palaver,
>   Growl this requiem of ours.

And so the poet recounts the Italian names distinguished in modern literature, and describes the intellectual activity that prevails in this Land of the Dead. Then he turns to the innumerable visitors of Italy:

> O you people hailed down on us
>   From the living, overhead,
> With what face can you confront us,
>   Seeking health among us dead?
>
> Soon or late this pestilential
>   Clime shall work you harm—beware!
> Even you shall likewise find it
>   Foul and poisonous grave-yard air.
>
> O ye grim, sepulchral friars,
>   Ye inquisitorial ghouls,
> Lay down, lay down forever,
>   The ignorant censor's tools.
>
> This wretched gift of thinking,
>   O ye donkeys, is our doom;
> Do you care to expurgate us,
>   Positively, in the tomb?
>
> Why plant this bayonet forest
>   On our sepulchers? what dread
> Causes you to place such jealous
>   Custody upon the dead?

Well, the mighty book of Nature
    Chapter first and last must have;
Yours is now the light of heaven,
    Ours the darkness of the grave.

But, then, if you ask it,
    We lived greatly in our turn;
We were grand and glorious, Gino,
    Ere our friends up there were born!

O majestic mausoleums,
    City walls outworn with time,
To our eyes are even your ruins
    Apotheosis sublime!

O barbarian unquiet,
    Raze each storied sepulcher!
With their memories and their beauty
    All the lifeless ashes stir.

O'er these monuments in vigil
    Cloudless the sun flames and glows
In the wind for funeral torches,—
    And the violet, and the rose,

And the grape, the fig, the olive,
    Are the emblems fit of grieving;
'T is, in fact, a cemetery
    To strike envy in the living.

Well, in fine, O brother corpses,
    Let them pipe on as they like;
Let us see on whom hereafter
    Such a death as ours shall strike!

> 'Mongst the anthems of the function.
> Is not *Dies Iræ?* Nay,
> In all the days to come yet,
> Shall there be no Judgment Day?

In a vein of like irony, the greater part of Giusti's political poems are written, and none of them is wanting in point and bitterness, even to a foreigner who must necessarily lose something of their point and the *tang* of their local expressions. It was the habit of the satirist, who at least loved the people's quaintness and originality — and perhaps this is as much democracy as we ought to demand of a poet — it was Giusti's habit to replenish his vocabulary from the fountains of the popular speech. By this means he gave his satires a racy local flavor; and though he cannot be said to have written dialect, since Tuscan is the Italian language, he gained by these words and phrases the frankness and fineness of dialect.

But Giusti had so much gentleness, sweetness, and meekness in his heart, that I do not like to leave the impression of him as a satirist last upon the reader. Rather let me close these meager notices with the beautiful little poem, said to be the last he wrote, as he passed his days in the slow death of the consumptive. It is called

A PRAYER.

> For the spirit confused
> With misgiving and with sorrow,
> Let me, my Saviour, borrow
> The light of faith from thee.

O lift from it the burden
That bows it down before thee.
With sighs and with weeping
I commend myself to thee;
My faded life, thou knowest,
Little by little is wasted
Like wax before the fire,
Like snow-wreaths in the sun.
And for the soul that panteth
For its refuge in thy bosom,
Break, thou, the ties, my Saviour,
That hinder it from thee.

FRANCESCO DALL' ONGARO.

I

IN the month of March, 1848, news came to Rome of the insurrection in Vienna, and a multitude of the citizens assembled to bear the tidings to the Austrian Ambassador, who resided in the ancient palace of the Venetian Republic. The throng swept down the Corso, gathering numbers as it went, and paused in the open space before the Palazzo di Venezia. At its summons, the ambassador abandoned his quarters, and fled without waiting to hear the details of the intelligence from Vienna. The people, incited by a number of Venetian exiles, tore down the double-headed eagle from the portal, and carried it for a more solemn and impressive destruction to the Piazza del Popolo, while a young poet erased the inscription asserting the Austrian claim to the palace, and wrote in its stead the words, " Palazzo della Dieta Italiana."

The sentiment of national unity expressed in this legend had been the ruling motive of the young poet Francesco Dall' Ongaro's life, and had already made his name famous through the patriotic songs that were sung all over Italy. Garibaldi had chanted one of his Stornelli when embarking from Montevideo in the spring of 1848 to take part in the Italian revolutions, of which these little ballads had become the rallying-cries; and if the voice of the people is in fact inspired, this poet could certainly have claimed the poet's long-lost honors of prophecy, for it was he who had shaped their utterance. He had ceased to assume any other sacred authority, though educated a priest, and at the time when he devoted the Palazzo di Venezia to the idea of united Italy, there was probably no person in Rome less sacerdotal than he.

Francesco Dall' Ongaro was born in 1808, at an obscure hamlet in the district of Oderzo in the Friuli, of parents who were small freeholders. They removed with their son in his tenth year to Venice, and there he began his education for the Church in the Seminary of the Madonna della Salute. The tourist who desires to see the Titians and Tintorettos in the sacristy of this superb church, or to wonder at the cold splendors of the interior of the temple, is sometimes obliged to seek admittance through the seminary; and it has doubtless happened to more than one of my readers to behold many little sedate old men in their teens, lounging up and down the cool, humid courts there, and trailing their black priestly robes over the springing mold. The sun seldom strikes into that sad close, and when the boys form into long files, two by two, and march out for recreation, they have a torpid and melancholy aspect, upon which the daylight seems to smile in vain. They march solemnly up the long Zattere, with a pale young father at their head, and then march solemnly back again, sweet, genteel, pathetic specters of childhood, and reënter their common tomb, doubtless unenvied by the hungriest and raggedest street boy, who asks charity of them as they pass, and hoarsely whispers "Raven!" when their leader is beyond hearing. There is no reason to suppose that a boy, born poet among the mountains, and full of the wild and free romance of his native scenes, could love the life led at the Seminary of the Salute, even though it included the study of literature and philosophy. From his childhood Dall' Ongaro had given proofs of his poetic gift, and the reverend ravens of the seminary were unconsciously hatching a bird as little like themselves as might be. Nevertheless, Dall' Ongaro left their school to enter the University of Padua as student of theology, and after graduating took orders, and went to Este, where he lived some time as teacher of belles-lettres.

At Este his life was without scope, and he was restless and unhappy, full of ardent and patriotic impulses, and doubly restricted by his narrow field and his priestly vocation. In no long time he had trouble with the Bishop of Padua, and, abandoning Este, seems also to have abandoned the Church forever. The chief fruit of his sojourn in that quaint and ancient village was a poem entitled Il Venerdì Santo, in which he celebrated some incidents of the life of Lord Byron, somewhat as Byron would have done. Dall' Ongaro's poems, however, confess the influence of the English poet less than those of other modern Italians, whom Byron infected so much more than his own nation.

From Este, Dall' Ongaro went to Trieste, where he taught literature and philosophy, wrote for the theater, and established a journal in which, for ten years, he labored to educate the people in his ideas of Italian unity and progress. That these did not coincide with the ideas of most Italian dreamers and politicians of the time may be inferred from the fact that he began in 1846 a course of lectures on Dante, in which he combated the clerical tendencies of Gioberti and Balbo, and criticised the first acts of Pius IX. He had as profound doubt of Papal liberality as Niccolini, at a time when other patriots were fondly cherishing the hope of a united Italy under an Italian pontiff; and at Rome, two years later, he sought to direct popular feeling from the man to the end, in one of the earliest of his graceful Stornelli.

PIO NONO.

Pio Nono is a name, and not the man
   Who saws the air from yonder Bishop's seat;
Pio Nono is the offspring of our brain,
   The idol of our hearts, a vision sweet;
Pio Nono is a banner, a refrain,
   A name that sounds well sung upon the street.

Who calls, "Long live Pio Nono!" means to call,
Long live our country, and good-will to all!
And country and good-will, these signify
That it is well for Italy to die;
But not to die for a vain dream or hope,
Not to die for a throne and for a Pope!

During these years at Trieste, however, Dall' Ongaro seems to have been also much occupied with pure literature, and to have given a great deal of study to the sources of national poetry, as he discovered them in the popular life and legends. He had been touched with the prevailing romanticism; he had written hymns like Manzoni, and, like Carrer, he sought to poetize the traditions and superstitions of his countrymen. He found a richer and deeper vein than the Venetian poet among his native hills and the neighboring mountains of Slavonia, but I cannot say that he wrought it to much better effect. The two volumes which he published in 1840 contain many ballads which are very graceful and musical, but which lack the fresh spirit of songs springing from the popular heart, while they also want the airy and delicate beauty of the modern German ballads. Among the best of them are two which Dall' Ongaro built up from mere lines and fragments of lines current among the people, as in later years he more successfully restored us two plays of Menander from the plots and a dozen verses of each. "One may imitate," he says, "more or less fortunately, Manzoni, Byron, or any other poet, but not the simple inspirations of the people. And 'The Pilgrim who comes from Rome,' and the 'Rosettina,' if one could have them complete as they once were, would probably make me blush for my elaborate variations." But study which was so well directed, and yet so conscious of its limitations, could not but be of great value; and Dall' Ongaro, no doubt, owed to it his gift of speaking so authentically for the popular heart.

That which he did later showed that he studied the people's thought and expression *con amore*, and in no vain sentiment of dilettanteism, or antiquarian research, or literary patronage.

It is not to be supposed that Dall' Ongaro's literary life had at this period an altogether objective tendency. In the volumes mentioned, there is abundant evidence that he was of the same humor as all men of poetic feeling must be at a certain time of life. Here are pretty verses of occasion, upon weddings and betrothals, such as people write in Italy; here are stanzas from albums, such as people used to write everywhere; here are didactic lines; here are bursts of mere sentiment and emotion. In the volume of Fantasie, published at Florence in 1866, Dall' Ongaro collected some of the ballads from his early works, but left out the more subjective effusions.

I give one of these in which, under a fantastic name and in a fantastic form, the poet expresses the tragic and pathetic interest of the life to which he was himself vowed.

THE SISTER OF THE MOON.

Shine, moon, ah shine! and let thy pensive light
    Be faithful unto me:
I have a sister in the lonely night
    When I commune with thee.

Alone and friendless in the world am I,
    Sorrow's forgotten maid,
Like some poor dove abandonèd to die
    By her first love unwed.

Like some poor floweret in a desert land
    I pass my days alone;
In vain upon the air its leaves expand,
    In vain its sweets are blown.

No loving hand shall save it from the waste,
    And wear the lonely thing;
My heart shall throb upon no loving breast
    In my neglected spring.

That trouble which consumes my weary soul
    No cunning can relieve,
No wisdom understand the secret dole
    Of the sad sighs I heave.

My fond heart cherished once a hope, a vow,
    The leaf of autumn gales!
In convent gloom, a dim lamp burning low,
    My spirit lacks and fails.

I shall have prayers and hymns like some dead saint
    Painted upon a shrine,
But in love's blessed power to fall and faint,
    It never shall be mine.

Born to entwine my life with others, born
    To love and to be wed,
Apart from all I lead my life forlorn,
    Sorrow's forgotten maid.

Shine, moon, ah shine! and let thy tender light
    Be faithful unto me:
Speak to me of the life beyond the night
    I shall enjoy with thee.

II

It will here satisfy the strongest love of contrasts to turn from Dall' Ongaro the sentimental poet to Dall' Ongaro the politician, and find him on his feet and making a speech at a public dinner given to Richard Cobden at Trieste, in 1847. Cobden was then, as always, the advocate of free trade, and Dall' Ongaro was then, as always, the advocate of free government. He saw in the union of the Italians under a customs-bond the hope of their political union, and in their emancipation from oppressive imposts their final escape from yet more galling oppression. He expressed something of this, and, though repeatedly interrupted by the police, he succeeded in saying so much as to secure his expulsion from Trieste.

Italy was already in a ferment, and insurrections were preparing in Venice, Milan, Florence, and Rome; and Dall' Ongaro, consulting with the Venetian leaders Manin and Tommaseo, retired to Tuscany, and took part in the movements which wrung a constitution from the Grand Duke, and preceded the flight of that prince. In December he went to Rome, where he joined himself with the Venetian refugees and with other Italian patriots, like D'Azeglio and Durando, who were striving to direct the popular mind toward Italian unity. The following March he was, as we have seen, one of the exiles who led the people against the Palazzo di Venezia. In the mean time the insurrection of the glorious Five Days had taken place at Milan, and the Lombard cities, rising one after another, had driven out the Austrian garrisons. Dall' Ongaro went from Rome to Milan, and thence, by advice of the revolutionary leaders, to animate the defense against the Austrians in Friuli; one of his brothers was killed at Palmanuova, and another severely wounded. Treviso, whither he had retired, falling into the hands of the Germans, he went to Venice, then a republic under the presidency of Manin; and here he established a popular journal, which opposed the union of the struggling republic with Piedmont under Carlo Alberto. Dall' Ongaro was finally expelled and passed next to Ravenna, where he found Garibaldi, who had been banished by the Roman government, and was in doubt as to how he might employ his sword on behalf of his country. In those days the Pope's moderately liberal minister, Rossi, was stabbed, and Count Pompeo Campello, an old literary friend and acquaintance of Dall' Ongaro, was appointed minister of war. With Garibaldi's consent the poet went to Rome, and used his influence to such effect that Garibaldi was authorized to raise a legion of volunteers, and was appointed general of those forces which took so glorious a part in the cause of Italian Independence. Soon after, when the Pope fled to Gaeta, and the Republic was proclaimed, Dall' Ongaro and Garibaldi were chosen representatives of the people. Then followed events of which it is still a pang keen to read: the troops of the French Republic marched upon Rome, and, after a defense more splendid and heroic than any

FRANCESCO DALL' ONGARA.

victory, the city fell. The Pope returned, and all who loved Italy and freedom turned in exile from Rome. The cities of the Romagna, Tuscany, Lombardy, and Venetia had fallen again under the Pope, the Grand Duke, and the Austrians, and Dall' Ongaro took refuge in Switzerland.

Without presuming to say whether Dall' Ongaro was mistaken in his political ideas, we may safely admit that he was no wiser a politician than Dante or Petrarch. He was an anti-Papist, as these were, and like these he opposed an Italy of little principalities and little republics. But his dream, unlike theirs, was of a great Italian democracy, and in 1848–49 he opposed the union of the Italian patriots under Carlo Alberto, because this would have tended to the monarchy.

III

But it is not so much with Dall' Ongaro's political opinions that we have to do as with his poetry of the revolutionary period of 1848, as we find in it the little collection of lyrics which he calls "Stornelli." These commemorate nearly all the interesting aspects of that epoch; and in their wit and enthusiasm and aspiration, we feel the spirit of a race at once the most intellectual and the most emotional in the world, whose poets write as passionately of politics as of love. Arnaud awards Dall' Ongaro the highest praise, and declares him "the first to formulate in the common language of Italy patriotic songs which, current on the tongues of the people, should also remain the patrimony of the national literature. . . . In his popular songs," continues this critic, "Dall' Ongaro has given all that constitutes true, good, and — not the least merit — novel poetry. Meter and rhythm second the expression, imbue the thought with harmony, and develop its symmetry. . . . How enviable is that perspicuity which does not oblige you to re-read a single line to evolve therefrom the latent idea!" And we shall have no less to admire the perfect art which, never passing the intelligence of the people, is never ignoble in sentiment or idea, but always as refined as it is natural.

I do not know how I could better approach our poet than by first offering this lyric, written when, in 1847, the people of Leghorn rose in arms to repel a threatened invasion of the Austrians.

THE WOMAN OF LEGHORN.

Adieu, Livorno! adieu, paternal walls!
  Perchance I never shall behold you more!
On father's and mother's grave the shadow falls.
  My love has gone under our flag to war;
And I will follow him where fortune calls;
  I have had a rifle in my hands before.

The ball intended for my lover's breast,
Before he knows it my heart shall arrest;

And over his dead comrade's visage he
　　Shall pitying stoop, and look whom it can be.
　.Then he shall see and know that it is I:
　　Poor boy! how bitterly my love will cry!

The Italian editor of the "Stornelli" does not give the closing lines too great praise when he declares that "they say more than all the lament of Tancred over Clorinda." In this little flight of song, we pass over more tragedy than Messer Torquato could have dreamed in the conquest of many Jerusalems; for, after all, there is nothing so tragic as fact. The poem is full at once of the grand national impulse, and of purely personal and tender devotion; and that fluttering, vehement purpose, thrilling and faltering in alternate lines, and breaking into a sob at last, is in every syllable the utterance of a woman's spirit and a woman's nature.

Quite as womanly, though entirely different, is this lament, which the poet attributes to his sister for their brother, who fell at Palmanuova, May 14, 1848.

THE SISTER.
(Palma, May 14, 1848.)

And he, my brother, to the fort had gone,
　　And the grenade, it struck him in the breast;
He fought for liberty, and death he won,
　　For country here, and found in heaven rest.

And now only to follow him I sigh;
A new desire has taken me to die,—
To follow him where is no enemy,
Where every one lives happy and is free.

All hope and purpose are gone from this woman's heart, for whom Italy died in her brother, and who has only these artless, half-bewildered words of regret to speak, and speaks them as if to some tender and sympathetic friend acquainted with all the history going before their abrupt beginning. I think it most pathetic and natural, also, that even in her grief and her aspiration for heaven, her words should have the tint of her time, and she should count freedom among the joys of eternity.

Quite as womanly again, and quite as different once more, is the lyric which the reader will better appreciate when I remind him how the Austrians massacred the unarmed people in Milan, in January, 1848, and how, later, during the Five Days, they murdered their Italian prisoners, sparing neither sex nor age.*

THE LOMBARD WOMAN.
(Milan, January, 1848.)

Here, take these gaudy robes and put them by;
I will go dress me black as widowhood;
I have seen blood run, I have heard the cry
  Of him that struck and him that vainly sued.
Henceforth no other ornament will I
  But on my breast a ribbon red as blood.

---

* "Many foreigners," says Emilio Dandolo, in his restrained and temperate history of "I Volontarii e Bersaglieri Lombardi," "have cast a doubt upon the incredible ferocity of the Austrians during the Five Days, and especially before evacuating the city. But, alas! the witnesses are too many to be doubted. A Croat was seen carrying a babe transfixed upon his bayonet. All know of those women's hands and ears

And when they ask what dyed the silk so red,
I 'll say, The life-blood of my brothers dead.
And when they ask how it may cleanséd be,
I 'll say, O, not in river nor in sea;
Dishonor passes not in wave nor flood;
My ribbon ye must wash in German blood.

The repressed horror in the lines,

> I have seen blood run, I have heard the cry
> Of him that struck and him that vainly sued,

is the sentiment of a picture that presents the scene to the reader's eye as this shuddering woman saw it; and the heart of woman's fierceness and hate is in that fragment of drama with which the brief poem closes. It is the history of an epoch. That epoch is now past, however; so long and so irrevocably past, that Dall' Ongaro commented in a note upon the poem: "The word 'German' is left as a key to the opinions of the time. Human brotherhood has been greatly promoted since 1848. German is now no longer synonymous with enemy. Italy has made peace with the peoples, and is leagued with them all against their common oppressors."

found in the haversacks of the prisoners; of those twelve unhappy men burnt alive at Porta Tosa; of those nineteen buried in a lime-pit at the Castello, whose scorched bodies we found. I myself, ordered with a detachment, after the departure of the enemy, to examine the Castello and neighborhood, was horror-struck at the sight of a babe nailed to a post."

There is still another of these songs, in which the heart of womanhood speaks, though this time with a voice of pride and happiness.

THE DECORATION.

My love looks well under his helmet's crest;
  He went to war, and did not let them see
His back, and so his wound is in the breast:
  For one he got, he struck and gave them three.
When he came back, I loved him, hurt so, best;
  He married me and loves me tenderly.

When he goes by, and people give him way,
  I thank God for my fortune every day;
When he goes by he seems more grand and fair
  Than any crossed and ribboned cavalier:
The cavalier grew up with his cross on,
  And I know how my darling's cross was won!

This poem, like that of La Livornese and La Donna Lombarda, is a vivid picture: it is a liberated city, and the streets are filled with jubilant people; the first victorious combats have taken place, and it is a wounded hero who passes with his ribbon on his breast. As the fond crowd gives way to him, his young wife looks on him from her window with an exultant love, unshadowed by any possibility of harm:

    Mi menò a moglie e mi vuol tanto bene!

This is country and freedom to her,—this is strength which despots cannot break,—this is joy to which defeat and ruin can never come nigh!

It might be any one of the sarcastic and quick-witted people talking politics in the streets of Rome in 1847, who sees the newly elected Senator — the head of the Roman municipality, and the legitimate mediator between Pope and people — as he passes, and speaks to him in these lines the dominant feeling of the moment:

THE CARDINALS.

O Senator of Rome! if true and well
   You are reckoned honest, in the Vatican,
Let it be yours His Holiness to tell,
   There are many Cardinals, and not one man.

They are made like lobsters, and, when they are dead,
Like lobsters change their colors and turn red;
And while they are living, with their backward gait
Displace and tangle good Saint Peter's net.

An impulse of the time is strong again in the following Stornello, — a cry of reproach that seems to follow some recreant from a beleaguered camp of true comrades, and to utter the feeling of men who marched to battle through defection, and were strong chiefly in their just cause. It bears the date of that fatal hour when the king of Naples, after a brief show of liberality, recalled his troops from Bologna, where they had been acting against Austria with the confederated forces of the other Italian states, and when every man lost to Italy was as an ebbing drop of her life's blood.

THE DESERTER.

(Bologna, May, 1848.)

Never did grain grow out of frozen earth;
  From the dead branch never did blossom start:
If thou lovest not the land that gave thee birth,
  Within thy breast thou bear'st a frozen heart;
If thou lovest not this land of ancient worth,
  To love aught else, say, traitor, how thou art!

To thine own land thou could'st not faithful be, —
Woe to the woman that puts faith in thee!
To him that trusteth in the recreant, woe!
Never from frozen earth did harvest grow:
To her that trusteth a deserter, shame!
Out of the dead branch never blossom came.

And this song, so fine in its picturesque and its dramatic qualities, is not less true to the hope of the Venetians when they rose in 1848, and intrusted their destinies to Daniele Manin.

THE RING OF THE LAST DOGE.

I saw the widowed Lady of the Sea
  Crownéd with corals and sea-weed and shells,
Who her long anguish and adversity
  Had seemed to drown in plays and festivals.

I said: "Where is thine ancient fealty fled? —
Where is the ring with which Manin did wed
His bride?" With tearful visage she:
"An eagle with two beaks tore it from me.
Suddenly I arose, and how it came
I know not, but I heard my bridegroom's name."
Poor widow! 't is not he. Yet he may bring —
Who knows? — back to the bride her long-lost ring.

The Venetians of that day dreamed that San Marco might live again, and the fineness and significance of the poem could not have been lost on the humblest in Venice, where all were quick to beauty and vividly remembered that the last Doge who wedded the sea was named, like the new President, Manin.

I think the Stornelli of the revolutionary period of 1848 have a peculiar value, because they embody, in forms of artistic perfection, the evanescent as well as the enduring qualities of popular feeling. They give us what had otherwise been lost, in the passing humor of the time. They do not celebrate the battles or the great political occurrences. If they deal with events at all, is it with events that express some belief or longing,— rather with what people hoped or dreamed than with what they did. They sing the Friulan volunteers, who bore the laurel instead of the olive during Holy Week, in token that the patriotic war had become a religion; they remind us that the first fruits of Italian longing for unity were the cannons sent to the Romans by the Genoese; they tell us that the tricolor was placed in the hand of the statue of Marcus Aurelius at the Capitol, to signify that Rome was no more, and that Italy was to be. But the Stornelli touch with most effect those yet more intimate ties between national and individual life that vibrate in the hearts of the Livornese and the Lombard woman, of the lover who sees his bride in the patriotic colors, of the maiden who will be a sister of charity that she may follow her lover through all perils, of the mother who names her new-born babe Costanza in the very hour of the Venetian republic's fall. And I like the Stornelli all the better because they preserve the generous ardor of the time, even in its fondness and excess.

After the fall of Rome, the poet did not long remain unmolested even in his Swiss retreat. In 1852 the Federal Council yielded to the instances of the Austrian government, and expelled Dall' Ongaro from the Republic. He retired with his sister and nephew to Brussels, where he resumed the lectures upon Dante, interrupted by his exile from Trieste in 1847, and thus supported his family. Three years later he gained permission to enter France, and up to the spring-time of 1859 he remained in Paris, busying himself with literature, and watching events with all an exile's eagerness. The war with Austria broke out, and the poet seized the long-coveted opportunity to return to Italy, whither he went as the correspondent of a French newspaper. On the conclusion of peace at Villafranca, this journal changed its tone, and being no longer in sympathy with Dall' Ongaro's opinions, he left it. Baron Ricasoli, to induce him to make Tuscany his home, instituted a chair of comparative dramatic literature in connection with the University of Pisa, and offered it to Dall' Ongaro, whose wide general learning and special dramatic studies peculiarly qualified him to hold it. He therefore took up his abode at Florence, dedicating his main industry to a comparative course of ancient and modern dramatic literature, and writing his wonderful restorations of Menander's "Phasma" and "Treasure." He was well known to the local American and English Society, and was mourned by many friends when he died there, some ten years ago.

As with Dall' Ongaro literature had always been but an instrument for the redemption of Italy, even after his appointment to a university professorship he did not forget this prime object. In nearly all that he afterwards wrote, he kept the great aim of his life in view, and few of the events or hopes of that dreary period of suspense and abortive effort between the conclusion of peace at Villafranca and the acquisition of Venice went unsung by him. Indeed, some of his most characteristic "Stornelli" belong to this epoch. After Savoy and Nice had been betrayed to France, and while the Italians waited in angry suspicion for the next demand of their hated ally, which might be the surrender of the island of Sardinia or the sacrifice of the Genoese province, but which no one could guess in the impervious Napoleonic silence, our poet wrote:

THE IMPERIAL EGG.

(Milan, 1862.)

Who knows what hidden devil it may be
  Under yon mute, grim bird that looks our way? —
Yon silent bird of evil omen,— he
  That, wanting peace, breathes discord and dismay.
Quick, quick, and change his egg, my Italy,
  Before there hatch from it some bird of prey,—

Before some beak of rapine be set free,
That, after the mountains, shall infest the sea;
Before some ravenous eaglet shall be sent
After our isles to gorge the continent.
I 'd rather a goose even from yon egg should come,—
If only of the breed that once saved Rome!

 The flight of the Grand Duke from Florence in 1859, and his conciliatory address to his late subjects after Villafranca, in which by fair promises he hoped to win them back to their allegiance; the union of Tuscany with the kingdom of Italy; the removal of the Austrian flags from Milan; Garibaldi's crusade in Sicily; the movement upon Rome in 1862; Aspromonte,—all these events, with the shifting phases of public feeling throughout that time, the alternate hopes and fears of the Italian nation, are celebrated in the later Stornelli of Dall' Ongaro. Venice has long since fallen to Italy; and Rome has become the capital of the nation. But the unification was not accomplished till Garibaldi, who had done so much for Italy, had been wounded by her king's troops in his impatient attempt to expel the French at Aspromonte.

TO MY SONGS.

Fly, O my songs, to Varignano, fly!
 Like some lost flock of swallows homeward flying,
And hail me Rome's Dictator, who there doth lie
 Broken with wounds, but conquered not, nor dying;
Bid him think on the April that is nigh,
 Month of the flowers and ventures fear-defying.

Or if it is not nigh, it soon shall come,
As shall the swallow to his last year's home,
As on its naked stem the rose shall burn,
As to the empty sky the stars return,
As hope comes back to hearts crushed by regret;—
Nay, say not this to his heart ne'er crushed yet!

Let us conclude these notices with one of the Stornelli which is non-political, but which I think we wont find the less agreeable for that reason. I like it because it says a pretty thing or two very daintily, and is interfused with a certain arch and playful spirit which is not so common but we ought to be glad to recognize it.

If you are good as you are fair, indeed,
  Keep to yourself those sweet eyes, I implore!
A little flame burns under either lid
  That might in old age kindle youth once more:
I am like a hermit in his cavern hid,
  But can I look on you and not adore?

Fair, if you do not mean my misery
Those lovely eyes lift upward to the sky;
I shall believe you some saint shrined above,
And may adore you if I may not love;
I shall believe you some bright soul in bliss,
And may look on you and not look amiss.

I have already noted the more obvious merits of the Stornelli, and I need not greatly insist upon them. Their defects are equally plain; one sees that their simplicity all but ceases to be a virtue at times, and that at times their feeling is too much

14*

intellectualized. Yet for all this we must recognize their excellence, and the skill as well as the truth of the poet. It is very notable with what directness he expresses his thought, and with what discretion he leaves it when expressed. The form is always most graceful, and the success with which dramatic, picturesque, and didactic qualities are blent, for a sole effect, in the brief compass of the poems, is not too highly praised in the epithet of novelty. Nothing is lost for the sake of attitude; the actor is absent from the most dramatic touches, the painter is not visible in lines which are each a picture, the teacher does not appear for the purpose of enforcing the moral. It is not the grandest poetry, but is true feeling, admirable art.

GIOVANNI PRATI

I

THE Italian poet who most resembles in theme and treatment the German romanticists of the second period was nearest them geographically in his origin. Giovanni Prati was born at Dasindo, a mountain village of the Trentino, and his boyhood was passed amidst the wild scenes of that picturesque region, whose dark valleys and snowy, cloud-capped heights, foaming torrents and rolling mists, lend their gloom and splendor to so much of his verse. His family was poor, but it was noble, and he received, through whatever sacrifice of those who remained at home, the education of a gentleman, as the Italians understand it. He went to school in Trent, and won some early laurels by his Latin poems, which the good priests who kept the *collegio* gathered and piously preserved in an album for the admiration and emulation of future scholars; when in due time he matriculated at the University of Padua as student of law, he again shone as a poet, and there he wrote his "Edmenegarda," a poem that gave him instant popularity throughout Italy. When he quitted the university he visited different parts of the country, "having the need" of frequent change of scenes and impressions; but everywhere he poured out songs, ballads, and romances, and was already a voluminous poet in 1840, when, in his thirtieth year, he began to abandon his Teutonic phantoms and hectic maidens, and to make Italy in various disguises the heroine of his song. Whether Austria penetrated these disguises or not, he was a little later ordered to leave Milan. He took refuge in Piedmont, whose brave king, in spite of diplomatic remonstrances from his neighbors, made Prati his *poeta cesareo,* or poet laureate. This was in 1843; and five years later he took an active part in inciting with his verse the patriotic revolts which broke out all over Italy. But he was supposed by virtue of his office to be monarchical in his sympathies, and when he ventured to Florence, the novelist Guerrezzi, who was at the head of the revolutionary government there, sent the poet back across the border in charge of a carbineer. In 1851 he had the misfortune to write a poem in censure of Orsini's attempt upon the life of Napoleon III., and to take money for it from the gratified emperor. He seems to have remained up to his death in the enjoyment of his office at Turin. His latest poem, if one may venture to speak of any as the last among poems poured out with such bewildering rapidity, was "Satan and the Graces," which De Sanctis made himself very merry over.

II

The Edmenegarda, which first won him repute, was perhaps not more youthful, but it was a subject that appealed peculiarly to the heart of youth, and was sufficiently mawkish. All the characters of the Edmenegarda were living at the time of its publication, and were instantly recognized; yet there seems to have been no complaint against the poet on their part, nor any reproach on the part of criticism. Indeed, at least one of the characters was flattered by the celebrity given him. "So great," says Prati's biographer, in the *Galleria Nazionale*, " was the enthusiasm awakened everywhere, and in every heart, by the Edmenegarda, that the young man portrayed in it, under the name of Leoni, imagining himself to have become, through Prati's merit, an eminently poetical subject, presented himself to the poet in the Caffè Pedrocchi at Padua, and returned him his warmest thanks. Prati also made the acquaintance, at the Caffè Nazionale in Turin, of his Edmenegarda, but after the wrinkles had seamed the visage of his ideal, and canceled perhaps from her soul the memory of anguish suffered." If we are to believe this writer, the story of a wife's betrayal, abandonment by her lover, and repudiation by her husband, produced effects upon the Italian public as various as profound. "In this pathetic story of an unhappy love was found so much truth of passion, so much naturalness of sentiment, and so much power, that every sad heart was filled with love for the young poet, so compassionate toward innocent misfortune, so sympathetic in form, in thought, in sentiment. From that moment Prati became the poet of suffering youth; in every corner of Italy the tender verses of the Edmenegarda were read with love, and sometimes frenzied passion; the political prisoners of Rome, of Naples, and Palermo found them a grateful solace amid the privations and heavy tedium of incarceration; many sundered lovers were reconjoined indissolubly in the kiss of peace; more than one desperate girl was restrained from the folly of suicide; and even the students in the ecclesiastical seminaries at Milan revolted, as it were, against their rector, and petitioned the Archbishop of Gaisruk that they might be permitted to read the fantastic romance."

What he was at first, Prati seems always to have remained in character and in ideals. "Would you know the poet in ordinary of the king of Sardinia?" says Marc-Monnier. "Go up the great street of the Po, under the arcades to the left, around the Caffè Florio, which is the center of Turin. If you meet a great youngster of forty years, with brown hair, wandering eyes, long visage, lengthened by the imperial, prominent nose, diminished by the mustache,—good head, in fine, and proclaiming the artist at first glance, say to yourself that this is he, give him your hand, and he will give you his. He is the openest of Italians, and the best fellow in the world. It is here that he lives, under the arcades. Do not look for his dwelling; he does not dwell, he promenades. Life for

GIOVANNI PRATI.

him is not a combat nor a journey; it is a saunter (*flânerie*), cigar in mouth, eyes to the wind; a comrade whom he meets, and passes a pleasant word with; a group of men who talk politics, and leave you to read the newspapers; *puis cà et là, par hasard, une bonne fortune;* a woman or an artist who understands you, and who listens while you talk of art or repeat your verses. Prati lives so the whole year round. From time to time he disappears for a week or two. Where is he? Nobody knows. You grow uneasy; you ask his address: he has none. Some say he is ill; others, he is dead; but some fine morning, cheerful as ever, he re-appears under the arcades. He has come from the bottom of a wood or the top of a mountain, and he has made two thousand verses. . . . He is hardly forty-one years old, and he has already written a million lines. I have read seven volumes of his, and I have not read all."

I have not myself had the patience here boasted by M. Marc-Monnier; but three or four volumes of Prati's have sufficed to teach me the spirit and purpose of his poetry. Born in 1815, and breathing his first inspirations from that sense of romance blowing into Italy with every northern gale,— a son of the Italian Tyrol, the region where the fire meets the snow,— he has some excuse, if not a perfect reason, for being half-German in his feeling. It is natural that Prati should love the ballad form above all, and should pour into its easy verse the wild legends heard during a boyhood passed among mountains and mountaineers. As I read his poetic tales, with a little heart-break, more or less fictitious, in each, I seem to have found again the sweet German songs that fluttered away out of my memory long ago. There is a tender light on the pages; a mistier passion than that of the south breathes through the dejected lines; and in the ballads we see all our old acquaintance once more,— the dying girls, the galloping horsemen, the moonbeams, the familiar, inconsequent phantoms,— scarcely changed in the least, and only betraying now and then that they have been at times in the bad company of Lara, and Medora, and other dissipated and vulgar people. The following poem will give some proof of all this, and will not unfairly witness of the quality of Prati in most of the poetry he has written:

THE MIDNIGHT RIDE.

I.

Ruello, Ruello, devour the way!
  On your breath bear us with you, O winds, as ye swell!
My darling, she lies near her death to-day,—
  Gallop, gallop, gallop, Ruel!

That my spurs have torn open thy flanks, alas!
  With thy long, sad neighing, thou need'st not tell;
We have many a league yet of desert to pass,—
  Gallop, gallop, gallop, Ruel!

Hear'st that mocking laugh overhead in space?
  Hear'st the shriek of the storm, as it drives, swift and fell?
A scent as of graves is blown into my face,—
  Gallop, gallop, gallop, Ruel!

Ah, God! and if that be the sound I hear
  Of the mourner's song and the passing-bell!
O heaven! What see I? The cross and the bier?—
  Gallop, gallop, gallop, Ruel!

Thou falt'rest, Ruello? Oh, courage, my steed!
  Wilt fail me, O traitor I trusted so well?
The tempest roars over us,—halt not, nor heed!—
  Gallop, gallop, gallop, Ruel!

Gallop, Ruello, oh, faster yet!
  Good God, that flash! O God! I am chill,—
Something hangs on my eyelids heavy as death,—
  Gallop, gallop, gallop, Ruel!

II.

Smitten with the lightning stroke,
  From his seat the cavalier
Fell, and forth the charger broke,
  Rider-free and mad with fear,—
Through the tempest and the night,
Like a wingèd thing in flight.

In the wind his mane blown back,
  With a frantic plunge and neigh,—
In the shadow a shadow black,
  Ever wilder he flies away,—
Through the tempest and the night,
Like a wingèd thing in flight.

From his throbbing flanks arise
  Smokes of fever and of sweat,—
Over him the pebble flies
  From his swift feet swifter yet,—
Through the tempest and the night,
Like a wingèd thing in flight.

From the cliff unto the wood,
　　Twenty leagues he passed in all;
Soaked with bloody foam and blood,
　　Blind he struck against the wall:
Death is in the seat; no more
Stirs the steed that flew before.

III.

And the while, upon the colorless,
　　Death-white visage of the dying
Maiden, still and faint and fair,
　　Rosy lights arise and wane;
And her weakness lifting tremulous
　　From the couch where she was lying
Her long, beautiful, loose hair
　　Strives she to adorn in vain.

"Mother, what it is has startled me
　　From my sleep I cannot tell thee:
Only, rise and deck me well
　　In my fairest robes again.
For, last night, in the thick silences,—
　　I know not how it befell me,—
But the gallop of Ruel,
　　More than once I heard it plain.

"Look, O mother, through yon shadowy
　　Trees, beyond their gloomy cover:
Canst thou not an atom see
　　Toward us from the distance start?
Seest thou not the dust rise cloudily,
　　And above the highway hover?
Come at last! 'T is he! 't is he!
　　Mother, something breaks my heart."

Ah, poor child! she raises wearily
  Her dim eyes, and, turning slowly,
Seeks the sun, and leaves this strife
  With a loved name in her breath.
Ah, poor child! in vain she waited him.
  In the grave they made her lowly
Bridal bed. And thou, O life!
  Hast no hopes that know not death?

Among Prati's patriotic poems, I have read one which seems to me rather vivid, and which because it reflects yet another phase of that great Italian resurrection, as well as represents Prati in one of his best moods, I will give here:

THE SPY.

With ears intent, with eyes abased,
Like a shadow still my steps thou hast chased;
If I whisper aught to my friend, I feel
Thee follow quickly upon my heel.
Poor wretch, thou fill'st me with loathing; fly!
      Thou art a spy!

When thou eatest the bread that thou dost win
With the filthy wages of thy sin,
The hideous face of treason anear
Dost thou not see? dost thou not fear?
Poor wretch, thou fill'st me with loathing; fly!
      Thou art a spy!

The thief may sometimes my pity claim;
Sometimes the harlot for her shame;

Even the murderer in his chains
A hidden fear from me constrains;
But thou only fill'st me with loathing; fly!
   Thou art a spy!

Fly, poor villain; draw thy hat down,
Close be thy mantle about thee thrown;
And if ever my words weigh on thy heart,
Betake thyself to some church apart;
There, "Lord, have mercy!" weep and cry:
   "I am a spy!"

Forgiveness for thy great sin alone
Thou may'st hope to find before his throne.
Dismayed by thy snares that all abhor,
Brothers on earth thou hast no more;
Poor wretch, thou fill'st me with loathing; fly!
   Thou art a spy!

ALEARDO ALEARDI

I

IN the first quarter of the century was born a poet, in the village of San Giorgio, near Verona, of parents who endowed their son with the magnificent name of Aleardo Aleardi. His father was one of those small proprietors numerous in the Veneto, and, though not indigent, was by no means a rich man. He lived on his farm, and loved it, and tried to improve the condition of his tenants. Aleardo's childhood was spent in the country,— a happy fortune for a boy anywhere, the happiest fortune if that country be Italy, and its scenes the grand and beautiful scenes of the valley of the Adige. Here he learned to love nature with the passion that declares itself everywhere in his verse; and hence he was in due time taken and placed at school in the Collegio* of Sant' Anastasia, in Verona, according to the Italian system, now fallen into disuse, of fitting a boy for the world by giving him the training of a cloister. It is not greatly to Aleardi's discredit that he seemed to learn nothing

---

* Not a college in the American sense, but a private school of a high grade.

there, and that he drove his reverend preceptors to the desperate course of advising his removal. They told his father he would make a good farmer, but a scholar, never. They nicknamed him the *mole*, for his dullness; but, in the mean time, he was making underground progress of his own, and he came to the surface one day, a mole no longer, to everybody's amazement, but a thing of such flight and song as they had never seen before,—in fine, a poet. He was rather a scapegrace, after he ceased to be a mole, at school; but when he went to the University at Padua, he became conspicuous among the idle, dissolute students of that day for temperate life and severe study. There he studied law, and learned patriotism; political poetry and interviews with the police were the consequence, but no serious trouble.

One of the offensive poems, which he says he and his friends had the audacity to call an ode, was this:

> Sing we our country. 'T is a desolate
>   And frozen cemetery;
>   Over its portals undulates
>   A banner black and yellow;
>   And within it throng the myriad
>   Phantoms of slaves and kings:
>
> A man on a worn-out, tottering
>   Throne watches o'er the tombs:
>   The pallid lord of consciences,
>   The despot of ideas.
>   Tricoronate he vaunts himself
>   And without crown is he.

In this poem the yellow and black flag is, of course, the Austrian, and the enthroned man is the pope, of whose temporal power our poet was always the enemy. "The Austrian police," says Aleardi's biographer, "like an affectionate mother, anxious about everything, came into possession of these verses; and the author was admonished, in the way of maternal counsel, not to touch such topics, if he would not lose the favor of the police, and be looked on as a prodigal son." He had already been admonished for carrying a cane on the top of which was an old Italian pound, or lira, with the inscription, Kingdom of Italy,—for it was an offense to have such words about one in any way, so trivial and petty was the cruel government that once reigned over the Italians.

In due time he took that garland of paper laurel and gilt pasteboard with which the graduates of Padua are sublimely crowned, and returned to Verona, where he entered the office of an advocate to learn the practical workings of the law. These disgusted him, naturally enough; and it was doubtless far less to the hurt of his feelings than of his fortune that the government always refused him the post of advocate.

In this time he wrote his first long poem, Arnaldo, which was published at Milan in 1842, and which won him immediate applause. It was followed by the tragedy of Bragadino; and in the year 1845 he wrote Le Prime Storie, which he suffered to lie unpublished for twelve years. It appeared in Verona in 1857, a year after the publication of his Monte Circellio, written in 1846.

The revolution of 1848 took place; the Austrians retired from the dominion of Venice, and a provisional republican government, under the presidency of Daniele Manin, was established, and Aleardi was sent as one of its plenipotentiaries to Paris, where he learnt how many fine speeches the friends of a struggling nation can make when they do not mean to help it. The young Venetian republic fell. Aleardi left Paris, and, after assisting at the ceremony of being bombarded in Bologna, retired to Genoa. He later returned to Verona, and there passed several years of tranquil study. In 1852, for the part he had taken in the revolution, he was arrested and imprisoned in the fortress at Mantua, thus fulfilling the destiny of an Italian poet of those times.

All the circumstances and facts of this arrest and imprisonment are so characteristic of the Austrian method of governing Italy, that I do not think it out of place to give them with some fullness. In the year named, the Austrians were still avenging themselves upon the patriots who had driven them out of Venetia in 1848, and their courts were sitting in Mantua for the trial of political prisoners, many of whom were exiled, sentenced to long imprisonment, or put to death. Aleardi was first confined in the military prison at Verona, but was soon removed to Mantua, whither several of his friends had already been sent. All the other prisons being full, he was thrust into a place which

ALEARDO ALEARDI.

till now had seemed too horrible for use. It was a narrow room, dark, and reeking with the dampness of the great dead lagoon which surrounds Mantua. A broken window, guarded by several gratings, let in a little light from above; the day in that cell lasted six hours, the night eighteen. A mattress on the floor, and a can of water for drinking, were the furniture. In the morning they brought him two pieces of hard, black bread; at ten o'clock a thick soup of rice and potatoes; and nothing else throughout the day. In this dungeon he remained sixty days, without books, without pen or paper, without any means of relieving the terrible gloom and solitude. At the end of this time, he was summoned to the hall above to see his sister, whom he tenderly loved. The light blinded him so that for a while he could not perceive her, but he talked to her calmly and even cheerfully, that she might not know what he had suffered. Then he was remanded to his cell, where, as her retreating footsteps ceased upon his ear, he cast himself upon the ground in a passion of despair. Three months passed, and he had never seen the face of judge or accuser, though once the prison inspector, with threats and promises, tried to entrap him into a confession. One night his sleep was broken by a continued hammering; in the morning half a score of his friends were hanged upon the gallows which had been built outside his cell.

By this time his punishment had been so far mitigated that he had been allowed a German grammar and dictionary, and for the first time studied that language, on the literature of which he afterward lectured in Florence. He had, like most of the young Venetians of his day, hated the language, together with those who spoke it, until then.

At last, one morning at dawn, a few days after the execution of his friends, Aleardi and others were thrust into carriages and driven to the castle. There the roll of the prisoners was called; to several names none answered, for those who had borne them were dead. Were the survivors now to be shot, or sentenced to some prison in Bohemia or Hungary? They grimly jested among themselves as to their fate. They were marched out into the piazza, under the heavy rain, and there these men who had not only not been tried for any crime, but had not even been accused of any, received the grace of the imperial pardon.

Aleardi returned to Verona and to his books, publishing another poem in 1856, called Le Città Italiane Marinare e Commercianti. His next publication was, in 1857, Rafaello e la Fornarina; then followed Un' Ora della mia Giovinezza, Le Tre Fiume, and Le Tre Fanciulle, in 1858.

The war of 1859 broke out between Austria and France and Italy. Aleardi spent the brief period of the campaign in a military prison at Verona, where his sympathies were given an ounce of prevention. He had committed no offense, but at midnight the police appeared, examined his papers, found nothing, and bade him rise and go to prison. After the peace of Villafranca he was liberated, and left the Austrian states, retiring first to Brescia, and then to Florence. His publications since 1859 have been a Canto Politico and I Sette Soldati. He was condemned for his voluntary exile, by the Austrian courts, and I remember reading in the newspapers the official invitation given him to come back to Verona and be punished. But, oddly enough, he declined to do so.

II

THE first considerable work of Aleardi was Le Prime Storie (Primal Histories), in which he traces the course of the human race through the Scriptural story of its creation, its fall, and its destruction by the deluge, through the Greek and Latin days, through the darkness and glory of the feudal times, down to our own,—following it from Eden to Babylon and Tyre, from Tyre and Babylon to Athens and Rome, from Florence and Genoa to the shores of the New World, full of shadowy tradition and the promise of a peaceful and happy future.

He takes this fruitful theme, because he feels it to be alive with eternal interest, and rejects the well-worn classic fables, because

> Under the bushes of the odorous mint
> The Dryads are buried, and the placid Dian
> Guides now no longer through the nights below

Th' invulnerable hinds and pearly car,
To bless the Carian shepherd's dreams. No more
The valley echoes to the stolen kisses,
Or to the twanging bow, or to the bay
Of the immortal hounds, or to the Fauns'
Plebeian laughter. From the golden rim
Of shells, dewy with pearl, in ocean's depths
The snowy loveliness of Galatea
Has fallen; and with her, their endless sleep
In coral sepulchers the Nereids
Forgotten sleep in peace.

The poet cannot turn to his theme, however, without a sad and scornful apostrophe to his own land, where he figures himself sitting by the way, and craving of the frivolous, heartless, luxurious Italian throngs that pass the charity of love for Italy. They pass him by unheeded, and he cries:

Hast thou seen
In the deep circle of the valley of Siddim,
Under the shining skies of Palestine,
The sinister glitter of the Lake of Asphalt?
Those coasts, strewn thick with ashes of damnation,
Forever foe to every living thing,
Where rings the cry of the lost wandering bird
That, on the shore of the perfidious sea,
Athirsting dies,— that watery sepulcher
Of the five cities of iniquity,
Where even the tempest, when its clouds hang low,
Passes in silence, and the lightning dies,—
If thou hast seen them, bitterly hath been
Thy heart wrung with the misery and despair
Of that dread vision!

> Yet there is on earth
> A woe more desperate and miserable,—
> A spectacle wherein the wrath of God
> Avenges him more terribly. It is
> A vain, weak people of faint-heart old men,
> That, for three hundred years of dull repose,
> Has lain perpetual dreamer, folded in
> The ragged purple of its ancestors,
> Stretching its limbs wide in its country's sun,
> To warm them; drinking the soft airs of autumn
> Forgetful, on the fields where its forefathers
> Like lions fought! From overflowing hands,
> Strew we with hellebore and poppies thick
> The way.

But the throngs have passed by, and the poet takes up his theme. Abel sits before an altar upon the borders of Eden, and looks with an exile's longing toward the Paradise of his father, where, high above all the other trees, he beholds,

> Lording it proudly in the garden's midst,
> The guilty apple with its fatal beauty.

He weeps; and Cain, furiously returning from the unaccepted labor of the fields, lifts his hand against his brother.

> It was at sunset;
> The air was severed with a mother's shriek,
> And stretched beside the o'erturned altar's foot
> Lay the first corse.
>
> Ah! that primal stain
> Of blood that made earth hideous, did forebode
> To all the nations of mankind to come

The cruel household stripes, and the relentless
Battles of civil wars, the poisoned cup,
The gleam of axes lifted up to strike
The prone necks on the block.

                The fratricide
Beheld that blood amazed, and from on high
He heard the awful voice of cursing leap,
And in the middle of his forehead felt
God's lightning strike. . . .

           . . . . And there from out the heart
All stained with guiltiness emerged the coward
Religion that is born of loveless fears.

And, moved and shaken like a conscious thing,
The tree of sin dilated horribly
Its frondage over all the land and sea,
And with its poisonous shadow followed far
The flight of Cain. . . .

           . . . . And he who first
By th' arduous solitudes and by the heights
And labyrinths of the virgin earth conducted
This ever-wandering, lost Humanity
Was the Accursed.

Cain passes away, and his children fill the world, and the joy of guiltless labor brightens the poet's somber verse.

The murmur of the works of man arose
Up from the plains; the caves reverberated
The blows of restless hammers that revealed,
Deep in the bowels of the fruitful hills,
The iron and the faithless gold, with rays

Of evil charm. And all the cliffs repeated
The beetle's fall, and the unceasing leap
Of waters on the paddles of the wheel
Volubly busy; and with heavy strokes
Upon the borders of the inviolate woods
The ax was heard descending on the trees,
Upon the odorous bark of mighty pines.
Over the imminent upland's utmost brink
The blonde wild-goat stretched forth his neck to meet
The unknown sound, and, caught with sudden fear,
Down the steep bounded, and the arrow cut
Midway the flight of his aërial foot.

So all the wild earth was tamed to the hand of man, and the wisdom of the stars began to reveal itself to the shepherds,

> Who, in the leisure of the argent nights,
> Leading their flocks upon a sea of meadows,

turned their eyes upon the heavenly bodies, and questioned them in their courses. But a taint of guilt was in all the blood of Cain, which the deluge alone could purge.

And beautiful beyond all utterance
Were the earth's first-born daughters. Phantasms these
That now enamor us decrepit, by
The light of that prime beauty! And the glance
Those ardent sinners darted had beguiled
God's angels even, so that the Lord's command
Was weaker than the bidding of their eyes.
And there were seen, descending from on high,
His messengers, and in the tepid eves
Gathering their flight about the secret founts

Where came the virgins wandering sole to stretch
The nude pomp of their perfect loveliness.
Caught by some sudden flash of light afar,
The shepherd looked, and deemed that he beheld
A fallen star, and knew not that he saw
A fallen angel, whose distended wings,
All tremulous with voluptuous delight,
Strove vainly to lift him to the skies again.
The earth with her malign embraces blest
The heavenly-born, and they straightway forgot
The joys of God's eternal paradise
For the brief rapture of a guilty love.
And from these nuptials, violent and strange,
A strange and violent race of giants rose;
A chain of sin had linked the earth to heaven;
And God repented him of his own work.

  The destroying rains descended,

      And the ocean rose,
And on the cities and the villages
The terror fell apace. There was a strife
Of suppliants at the altars; blasphemy
Launched at the impotent idols and the kings;
There were embraces desperate and dear,
And news of suddenest forgivenesses,
And a relinquishment of all sweet things;
And, guided onward by the pallid prophets,
The people climbed, with lamentable cries,
In pilgrimage up the mountains.

      But in vain;
For swifter than they climbed the ocean rose,
And hid the palms, and buried the sepulchers
Far underneath the buried pyramids;

And the victorious billow swelled and beat
At eagles' Alpine nests, extinguishing
All lingering breath of life; and dreadfuller
Than the yell rising from the battle-field
Seemèd the hush of every human sound.

On the high solitude of the waters naught
Was seen but here and there unfrequently
A frail raft, heaped with languid men that fought
Weakly with one another for the grass
Hanging about a cliff not yet submerged,
And here and there a drowned man's head, and here
And there a file of birds, that beat the air
With weary wings.

After the deluge, the race of Noah repeoples the empty world, and the history of mankind begins anew in the Orient. Rome is built, and the Christian era dawns, and Rome falls under the feet of the barbarians. Then the enthusiasm of Christendom sweeps toward the East, in the repeated Crusades; and then, "after long years of twilight," Dante, the sun of Italian civilization, rises; and at last comes the dream of another world, unknown to the eyes of elder times.

But between that and our shore roared diffuse
Abysmal seas and fabulous hurricanes
Which, thought on, blanched the faces of the bold;
For the dread secret of the heavens was then
The Western world. Yet on the Italian coasts
A boy grew into manhood, in whose soul
The instinct of the unknown continent burned.
He saw in his prophetic mind depicted

15*

The opposite visage of the earth, and, turning
With joyful defiance to the ocean, sailed
Forth with two secret pilots, God and Genius.
Last of the prophets, he returned in chains
And glory.

In the New World are the traces, as in the Old, of a restless humanity, wandering from coast to coast, growing, building cities, and utterly vanishing. There are graves and ruins everywhere; and the poet's thought returns from these scenes of unstoried desolation, to follow again the course of man in the Old World annals. But here, also, he is lost in the confusion of man's advance and retirement, and he muses:

How many were the peoples? Where the trace
Of their lost steps? Wherë the funereal fields
In which they sleep? Go, ask the clouds of heaven
How many bolts are hidden in their breasts,
And when they shall be launched; and ask the path
That they shall keep in the unfurrowed air.
The peoples passed. Obscure as destiny,
Forever stirred by secret hope, forever
Waiting upon the promised mysteries,
Unknowing God, that urged them, turning still
To some kind star,—they swept o'er the sea-weed
In unknown waters, fearless swam the course
Of nameless rivers, wrote with flying feet
The mountain pass on pathless snows; impatient
Of rest, for aye, from Babylon to Memphis,
From the Acropolis to Rome, they hurried.

And with them passed their guardian household gods,
And faithful wisdom of their ancestors,

And the seed sown in mother fields, and gathered,
A fruitful harvest in their happier years.
And, 'companying the order of their steps
Upon the way, they sung the choruses
And sacred burdens of their country's songs,
And, sitting down by hospitable gates,
They told the histories of their far-off cities.
And sometimes in the lonely darknesses
Upon the ambiguous way they found a light,—
The deathless lamp of some great truth, that Heaven
Sent in compassionate answer to their prayers.

But not to all was given it to endure
That ceaseless pilgrimage, and not on all
Did the heavens smile perennity of life
Revirginate with never-ceasing change;
And when it had completed the great work
Which God had destined for its race to do,
Sometimes a weary people laid them down
To rest them, like a weary man, and left
Their nude bones in a vale of expiation,
And passed away as utterly forever
As mist that snows itself into the sea.

The poet views this growth of nations from youth to decrepitude, and, coming back at last to himself and to his own land and time, breaks forth into a lament of grave and touching beauty:

Muse of an aged people, in the eve
Of fading civilization, I was born
Of kindred that have greatly expiated
And greatly wept. For me the ambrosial fingers
Of Graces never wove the laurel crown,
But the Fates shadowed, from my youngest days,

My brow with passion-flowers, and I have lived
Unknown to my dear land. Oh, fortunate
My sisters that in the heroic dawn
Of races sung! To them did destiny give
The virgin fire and chaste ingenuousness
Of their land's speech; and, reverenced, their hands
Ran over potent strings. To me, the hopes
Turbid with hate; to me, the senile rage;
To me, the painted fancies clothed by art
Degenerate; to me, the desperate wish,
Not in my soul to nurse ungenerous dreams,
But to contend, and with the sword of song
To fight my battles too.

Such is the spirit, such is the manner, of the Prime Storie of Aleardi. The merits of the poem are so obvious, that it seems scarcely profitable to comment upon its picturesqueness, upon the clearness and ease of its style, upon the art which quickens its frequent descriptions of nature with a human interest. The defects of the poem are quite as plain, and I have again to acknowledge the critical acuteness of Arnaud, who says of Aleardi: "Instead of synthetizing his conceptions, and giving relief to the principal lines, the poet lingers caressingly upon the particulars, preferring the descriptive to the dramatic element. From this results poetry of beautiful arabesques and exquisite fragments, of harmonious verse and brilliant diction."

Nevertheless, the same critic confesses that the poetry of Aleardi "is not academically common," and pleases by the originality of its very mannerism.

III

Like Primal Histories, the Hour of my Youth is a contemplative poem, to which frequency of episode gives life and movement; but its scope is less grand, and the poet, recalling his early days, remembers chiefly the events of defeated revolution which give such heroic sadness and splendor to the history of the first third of this century. The work is characterized by the same opulence of diction, and the same luxury of epithet and imagery, as the Primal Histories, but it somehow fails to win our interest in equal degree: perhaps because the patriot now begins to overshadow the poet, and appeal is often made rather to the sympathies than the imagination. It is certain that art ceases to be less, and country more, in the poetry of Aleardi from this time. It could scarcely be otherwise; and had it been otherwise, the poet would have become despicable, not great, in the eyes of his countrymen.

The Hour of my Youth opens with a picture, where, for once at least, all the brilliant effects are synthetized; the poet has ordered here the whole Northern world, and you can dream of nothing grand or beautiful in those lonely regions which you do not behold in it.

> Ere yet upon the unhappy Arctic lands,
> In dying autumn, Erebus descends
> With the night's thousand hours, along the verge
> Of the horizon, like a fugitive,

Through the long days wanders the weary sun;
And when at last under the wave is quenched
The last gleam of its golden countenance,
Interminable twilight land and sea
Discolors, and the north-wind covers deep
All things in snow, as in their sepulchers
The dead are buried. In the distances
The shock of warring Cyclades of ice
Makes music as of wild and strange lament;
And up in heaven now tardily are lit
The solitary polar star and seven
Lamps of the Bear. And now the warlike race
Of swans gather their hosts upon the breast
Of some far gulf, and, bidding their farewell
To the white cliffs, and slender junipers,
And sea-weed bridal-beds, intone the song
Of parting, and a sad metallic clang
Send through the mists. Upon their southward way
They greet the beryl-tinted icebergs; greet
Flamy volcanoes, and the seething founts
Of Geysers, and the melancholy yellow
Of the Icelandic fields; and, wearying,
Their lily wings amid the boreal lights,
Journey away unto the joyous shores
Of morning.

In a strain of equal nobility, but of more personal and subjective effect, the thought is completed:

So likewise, my own soul, from these obscure
Days without glory, wings its flight afar
Backward, and journeys to the years of youth
And morning. Oh, give me back once more,
Oh, give me, Lord, one hour of youth again!

For in that time I was serene and bold,
And uncontaminate, and enraptured with
The universe. I did not know the pangs
Of the proud mind, nor the sweet miseries
Of love; and I had never gathered yet,
After those fires so sweet in burning, bitter
Handfuls of ashes, that, with tardy tears
Sprinkled, at last have nourished into bloom
The solitary flower of penitence.
The baseness of the many was unknown,
And civic woes had not yet sown with salt
Life's narrow field. Ah! then the infinite
Voices that Nature sends her worshipers
From land, from sea, and from the cloudy depths
Of heaven smote the echoing soul of youth
To music. And at the first morning sigh
Of the poor wood-lark,— at the measured bell
Of homeward flocks, and at the opaline wings
Of dragon-flies in their aërial dances
Above the gorgeous carpets of the marsh,—
At the wind's moan, and at the sudden gleam
Of lamps lighting in some far town by night,—
And at the dash of rain that April shoots
Through the air odorous with the smitten dust,—
My spirits rose, and glad and swift my thought
Over the sea of being sped all-sails.

There is a description of a battle, in the Hour of my Youth, which I cannot help quoting before I leave the poem. The battle took place between the Austrians and the French on the 14th of January, 1797, in the Chiusa, a narrow valley near Verona, and the fiercest part of the fight was for the possession of the hill of Rivoli.

                    Clouds of smoke
Floated along the heights; and, with her wild,
Incessant echo, Chiusa still repeated
The harmony of the muskets. Rival hosts
Contended for the poverty of a hill
That scarce could give their number sepulcher;
But from that hill-crest waved the glorious locks
Of Victory. And round its bloody spurs,
Taken and lost with fierce vicissitude,
Serried and splendid, swept and tempested
Long-haired dragoons, together with the might
Of the Homeric foot, delirious
With fury; and the horses with their teeth
Tore one another, or, tossing wild their manes,
Fled with their helpless riders up the crags,
By strait and imminent paths of rock, till down,
Like angels thunder-smitten, to the depths
Of that abyss the riders fell. With slain
Was heaped the dreadful amphitheater;
The rocks dropped blood; and if with gasping breath
Some wounded swimmer beat away the waves
Weakly between him and the other shore,
The merciless riflemen from the cliffs above,
With their inexorable aim, beneath
The waters sunk him.

The Monte Circellio is part of a poem in four cantos, dispersed, it is said, to avoid the researches of the police, in which the poet recounts in picturesque verse the glories and events of the Italian land and history through which he passes. A slender but potent cord of common feeling unites the episodes, and the lament for the present fate of Italy rises into hope for her future. More than half of the poem is given to a description of the geological growth of the earth, in which the imagination of the poet has unbridled range, and in which there is a success unknown to most other attempts to poetize the facts of science. The epochs of darkness and inundation, of the monstrous races of bats and lizards, of the mammoths and the gigantic vegetation, pass, and, after thousands of years, the earth is tempered and purified to the use of man by fire; and that

> Paradise of land and sea, forever
> Stirred by great hopes and by volcanic fires,
> Called Italy,

takes shape: its burning mountains rise, its valleys sink, its plains extend, its streams run. But first of all, the hills of Rome lifted themselves from the waters, that day when the spirit of God dwelling upon their face

> Saw a fierce group of seven enkindled hills,
> In number like the mystic candles lighted
> Within his future temple. Then he bent
> Upon that mystic pleiades of flame
> His luminous regard, and spoke to it:
> "Thou art to be my Rome." The harmony
> Of that note to the nebulous heights supreme,
> And to the bounds of the created world,
> Rolled like the voice of myriad organ-stops,
> And sank, and ceased. The heavenly orbs resumed
> Their daily dance and their unending journey;
> A mighty rush of plumes disturbed the rest
> Of the vast silence; here and there like stars

About the sky, flashed the immortal eyes
Of choral angels following after him.

The opening lines of Monte Circellio are scarcely less beautiful than the first part of Un' Ora della mia Giovinezza, but I must content myself with only one other extract from the poem, leaving the rest to the reader of the original. The fact that every summer the Roman hospitals are filled with the unhappy peasants who descend from the hills of the Abruzzi to snatch its harvests from the feverish Campagna will help us to understand all the meaning of the following passage, though nothing could add to its pathos, unless, perhaps, the story given by Aleardi in a note at the foot of his page: "How do you live here?" asked a traveler of one of the peasants who reap the Campagna. The Abruzzese answered, "Signor, we die."

What time,
In hours of summer, sad with so much light,
The sun beats ceaselessly upon the fields,
The harvesters, as famine urges them,
Draw hither in thousands, and they wear
The look of those that dolorously go
In exile, and already their brown eyes
Are heavy with the poison of the air.
Here never note of amorous bird consoles
Their drooping hearts; here never the gay songs
Of their Abruzzi sound to gladden these
Pathetic hands. But taciturn they toil,
Reaping the harvest for their unknown lords;
And when the weary labor is performed,
Taciturn they retire; and not till then

Their bagpipes crown the joys of the return,
Swelling the heart with their familiar strain.
Alas! not all return, for there is one
That dying in the furrow sits, and seeks
With his last look some faithful kinsman out,
To give his life's wage, that he carry it
Unto his trembling mother, with the last
Words of her son that comes no more. And dying,
Deserted and alone, far off he hears
His comrades going, with their pipes in time
Joyfully measuring their homeward steps.
And when in after years an orphan comes
To reap the harvest here, and feels his blade
Go quivering through the swaths of falling grain,
He weeps and thinks: haply these heavy stalks
Ripened on his unburied father's bones.

In the poem called The Marine and Commercial Cities of Italy (Le Città Italiane Marinare e Commercianti), Aleardi recounts the glorious rise, the jealousies, the fratricidal wars, and the ignoble fall of Venice, Florence, Pisa, and Genoa, in strains of grandeur and pathos; he has pride in the wealth and freedom of those old queens of traffic, and scorn and lamentation for the blind selfishness that kept them Venetian, Florentine, Pisan, and Genoese, and never suffered them to be Italian. I take from this poem the prophetic vision of the greatness of Venice, which, according to the patriotic tradition of Sabellico, Saint Mark beheld five hundred years before the foundation of the city, when one day, journeying toward Aquileja, his ship lost her course among the islands of the lagoons. The saint looked out over those melancholy swamps, and saw the phantom of a Byzantine cathedral rest upon the reeds, while a multitudinous voice broke the silence with the Venetian battle-cry, "Viva San Marco!" The lines that follow illustrate the pride and splendor of Venetian story, and are notable, I think, for a certain lofty grace of movement and opulence of diction.

There thou shalt lie, O Saint![*] but compassed round
Thickly by shining groves
Of pillars; on thy regal portico,
Lifting their glittering and impatient hooves,
Corinth's fierce steeds shall be bound;[†]
And at thy name, the hymn of future wars,
From their funereal caves
The bandits of the waves
Shall fly in exile;[‡] brought from bloody fields
Hard won and lost in far-off Palestine,
The glimmer of a thousand Arab moons
Shall fill thy broad lagoons;
And on the false Byzantine's towers shall climb
A blind old man sublime,[§]
Whom victory shall behold
Amidst his enemies with thy sacred flag,
All battle-rent, unrolled.

[*] The bones of St. Mark repose in his church at Venice.

[†] The famous bronze horses of St. Mark's still shine with the gold that once covered them.

[‡] Venice early swept the Adriatic of the pirates who infested it.

[§] The Doge Enrico Dandolo, who, though blind and bowed with eighty years of war, was the first to plant the banner of Saint Mark on the walls of Constantinople when that city was taken by the Venetians and Crusaders.

The late poems of Aleardi are nearly all in this lyrical form, in which the thought drops and rises with ceaseless change of music, and which wins the reader of many empty Italian canzoni by the mere delight of its movement. It is well adapted to the subjects for which Aleardi has used it; it has a stateliness and strength of its own, and its alternate lapse and ascent give animation to the ever-blending story and aspiration, appeal or reflection. In this measure are written The Three Rivers, The Three Maidens, and The Seven Soldiers. The latter is a poem of some length, in which the poet, figuring himself upon a battle-field on the morrow after a combat between Italians and Austrians, "wanders among the wounded in search of expiated sins and of unknown heroism. He pauses," continues his eloquent biographer in the *Galleria Nazionale,* " to meditate on the death of the Hungarian, Polish, Bohemian, Croatian, Austrian, and Tyrolese soldiers, who personify the nationalities oppressed by the tyranny of the house of Hapsburg. A minister of God, praying beside the corpses of two friends, Pole and Hungarian, hails the dawn of the Magyar resurrection. Then rises the grand figure of Sandor Petöfi, ' the patriotic poet of Hungary,' whose life was a hymn, and whose miraculous re-appearance will, according to popular superstition, take place when Hungary is freed from her chains. The poem closes with a prophecy concerning the destinies of Austria and Italy." Like all the poems of Aleardi, it abounds in striking lines; but the interest, instead of gathering strongly about one central idea, diffuses itself over half-forgotten particulars of revolutionary history, and the sympathy of the reader is fatigued and confused with the variety of the demand upon it.

For this reason, The Three Rivers and The Three Maidens are more artistic poems: in the former, the poet seeks vainly a promise of Italian greatness and unity on the banks of Tiber and of Arno, but finds it by the Po, where the war of 1859 is beginning; in the latter, three maidens recount to the poet stories of the oppression which has imprisoned the father of one, despoiled another's house through the tax-gatherer, and sent the brother of the third to languish, the soldier-slave of his tyrants, in a land where "the wife washes the garments of her husband, yet stained with Italian blood."

A very little book holds all the poems which Aleardi has written, and I have named them nearly all. He has in greater degree than any other Italian poet of this age, or perhaps of any age, those qualities which English taste of this time demands — quickness of feeling and brilliancy of expression. He lacks simplicity of idea, and his style is an opal which takes all lights and hues, rather than the crystal which lets the daylight colorlessly through. He is distinguished no less by the themes he selects than by the expression he gives them. In his poetry there is passion, but his subjects are usually those to which love is accessory rather than essential; and he cares better to sing of universal and national destinies as they concern individuals, than the raptures and anguishes of youthful individuals as they concern mankind. The poet may be wrong in this, but he achieves an undeniable novelty in it, and I confess that I read him willingly on account of it.

In taking leave of him, I feel that I ought to let him have the last word, which is one of self-criticism, and, I think, singularly just. He refers to the fact of his early life, that his father forbade him to be a painter, and says: " Not being allowed to use the pencil, I have used the pen. And precisely on this account my pen resembles too much a pencil; precisely on this account I am too much of a naturalist, and am too fond of losing myself in minute details. I am as one, who, in walking, goes leisurely along, and stops every moment to observe the dash of light that breaks through the trees of the woods, the insect that alights on his hand, the loaf that falls on his head, a cloud, a wave, a streak of smoke; in fine, the thousand accidents that make creation so rich, so various, so poetical, and beyond which we evermore catch glimpses of that grand, mysterious something, eternal, immense, benignant, and never inhuman or cruel, as some would have us believe, which is called God."

GIULIO CARCANO, ARNALDO FUSINATO, AND LUIGI MERCANTINI

I

No one could be more opposed, in spirit and method, to Aleardo Aleardi than Giulio Carcano; but both of these poets betray love and study of English masters. In the former there is something to remind us of Milton, of Ossian, who is still believed a poet in Latin countries, and of Byron; and in the latter, Arnaud notes very obvious resemblances to Gray, Crabbe, and Wordsworth in the simplicity or the proud humility of the theme, and the courage of its treatment. The critic declares the poet's æsthetic creed to be God, the family, and country; and in a beautiful essay on Domestic Poetry, written amidst the universal political discouragement of 1839, Carcano himself declares that in the cultivation of a popular and homelike feeling in literature the hope of Italy no less than of Italian poetry lies. He was ready to respond to the impulses of the nation's heart, which he had felt in his communion with its purest and best life, when, in later years, its expectation gave place to action, and many of his political poems are bold and noble. But his finest poems are those which celebrate the affections of the household, and poetize the pathetic beauty of toil and poverty in city and country. He sings with a tenderness peculiarly winning of the love of mothers and children, and I shall give the best notion of the poet's best in the following beautiful lullaby, premising merely that the title of the poem is the Italian infantile for sleep:

NANNA.

Sleep, sleep, sleep! my little girl:
Mother is near thee. Sleep, unfurl
Thy veil o'er the cradle where baby lies!
Dream, baby, of angels in the skies!
On the sorrowful earth, in hopeless quest,
Passes the exile without rest;
Where'er he goes, in sun or snow,
Trouble and pain beside him go.

But when I look upon thy sleep,
And hear thy breathing soft and deep,
My soul turns with a faith serene
To days of sorrow that have been,
And I feel that of love and happiness
Heaven has given my life excess;
The Lord in his mercy gave me thee,
And thou in truth art part of me!

Thou knowest not, as I bend above thee,
How much I love thee, how much I love thee;
Thou art the very life of my heart,
Thou art my joy, thou art my smart!
Thy day begins uncertain, child:
Thou art a blossom in the wild;
But over thee, with his wings abroad,
Blossom, watches the angel of God.

Ah! wherefore with so sad a face
Must thy father look on thy happiness?
In thy little bed he kissed thee now,
And dropped a tear upon thy brow.
Lord, to this mute and pensive soul
Temper the sharpness of his dole:
Give him peace whose love my life hath kept:
He too has hoped, though he has wept.

And over thee, my own delight,
Watch that sweet Mother, day and night,
To whom the exiles consecrate
Altar and heart in every fate.
By her name I have called my little girl;
But on life's sea, in the tempest's whirl,
Thy helpless mother, my darling, may
Only tremble and only pray!

Sleep, sleep, sleep! my baby dear;
Dream of the light of some sweet star.
Sleep, sleep! and I will keep
Thoughtful vigils above thy sleep.
Oh, in the days that are to come,
With unknown trial and unknown doom,
Thy little heart can ne'er love me
As thy mother loves and shall love thee!

II

ARNALDO FUSINATO of Padua has written for the most part comic poetry, his principal piece of this sort being one in which he celebrates and satirizes the student-life at the University of Padua. He had afterward to make a formal reparation to the students, which he did in a poem singing their many virtues. The original poem of The Student is a rather lively series of pictures, from which we learn that it was once the habit of studious youth at Padua, when freshmen, or *matricolini*, to be terrible dandies, to swear aloud upon the public ways, to pass whole nights at billiards, to be noisy at the theater, to stand treat for the Seniors, joyfully to lend these money, and to acquire knowledge of the world at any cost. Later, they advanced to the dignity of breaking street-lamps and of being arrested by the Austrian garrison, for in Padua the students were under a kind of martial law. Sometimes they were expelled; they lost money at play, and wrote deceitful letters to their parents for more; they shunned labor, and failed to take degrees. But we cannot be interested in traits so foreign to what I understand is our own student-life. Generally, the comic as well as the sentimental poetry of Fusinato deals with incidents of popular life; and, of course, it has hits at the fleeting fashions and passing sensations: for example, Il Bloomismo is satirized.

The poem which I translate, however, is in a different strain from any of these. It will be remembered that when the Austrians returned to take Venice in 1849, after they had been driven out for eighteen months, the city stood a bombardment of many weeks, contesting every inch of the approach with the invaders. But the Venetians were very few in number, and poorly equipped; a famine prevailed among them; the cholera broke out, and raged furiously; the bombs began to drop into the square of St. Mark, and then the Venetians yielded, and ran up the white flag on the dearly contested lagoon bridge, by which the railway traveler enters the city. The poet is imagined in one of the little towns on the nearest main-land.

> The twilight is deepening, still is the wave;
> I sit by the window, mute as by a grave;
> Silent, companionless, secret I pine;
> Through tears where thou liest I look, Venice mine.
>
> On the clouds brokenly strewn through the west
> Dies the last ray of the sun sunk to rest;
> And a sad sibilance under the moon
> Sighs from the broken heart of the lagoon.
>
> Out of the city a boat draweth near:
> "You of the gondola! tell us what cheer!"
> "Bread lacks, the cholera deadlier grows;
> From the lagoon bridge the white banner blows."
>
> No, no, nevermore on so great woe,
> Bright sun of Italy, nevermore glow!
> But o'er Venetian hopes shattered so soon,
> Moan in thy sorrow forever, lagoon!
>
> Venice, to thee comes at last the last hour;
> Martyr illustrious, in thy foe's power;
> Bread lacks, the cholera deadlier grows;
> From the lagoon bridge the white banner blows.

Not all the battle-flames over thee streaming;
Not all the numberless bolts o'er thee screaming;
Not for these terrors thy free days are dead:
Long live Venice! She 's dying for bread!

On thy immortal page, sculpture, O Story,
Others' iniquity, Venice's glory;
And three times infamous ever be he
Who triumphed by famine, O Venice, o'er thee.

Long live Venice! Undaunted she fell;
Bravely she fought for her banner and well;
But bread lacks; the cholera deadlier grows;
From the lagoon bridge the white banner blows.

And now be shivered upon the stone here
Till thou be free again, O lyre I bear.
Unto thee, Venice, shall be my last song,
To thee the last kiss and the last tear belong.

Exiled and lonely, from hence I depart,
But Venice forever shall live in my heart;
In my heart's sacred place Venice shall be
As is the face of my first love to me.

But the wind rises, and over the pale
Face of its waters the deep sends a wail;
Breaking, the chords shriek, and the voice dies.
On the lagoon bridge the white banner flies!

III

Among the later Italian poets is Luigi Mercantini, of Palermo, who has written almost entirely upon political themes — events of the different revolutions and attempts at revolution in which Italian history so abounds. I have not read him so thoroughly as to warrant me in speaking very confidently about him, but from the examination which I have given his poetry, I think that he treats his subjects with as little inflation as possible, and he now and then touches a point of naturalness — the high-water mark of balladry, to which modern poets, with their affected unaffectedness and elaborate simplicity, attain only with the greatest pains and labor. Such a triumph of Mercantini's is this poem which I am about to give. It celebrates the daring and self-sacrifice of three hundred brave young patriots, led by Carlo Pisacane, who landed on the coast of Naples in 1857, for the purpose of exciting a revolution against the Bourbons, and were all killed. In a note the poet reproduces the pledge signed by these young heroes, which is so fine as not to be marred even by their dramatic, almost theatrical, consciousness.

We who are here written down, having all sworn, despising the calumnies of the vulgar, strong in the justice of our cause and the boldness of our spirits, do solemnly declare ourselves the initiators of the Italian revolution. If the country does not respond to our appeal, we, without reproaching it, will know how to die like brave men, following the noble phalanx of Italian martyrs. Let any other nation of the world find men who, like us, shall immolate themselves to liberty, and then only may it compare itself to Italy, though she still be a slave.

Mercantini puts his poem in the mouth of a peasant girl, and calls it

THE GLEANER OF SAPRI.

They were three hundred; they were young and strong,
   And they are dead!
That morning I was going out to glean;
A ship in the middle of the sea was seen;
A barque it was of those that go by steam,
And from its top a tricolor flag did stream.
It anchored off the isle of Ponza; then
It stopped awhile, and then it turned again
Toward this place, and here they came ashore.
They came with arms, but not on us made war.
They were three hundred; they were young and strong,
   And they are dead!

They came in arms, but not on us made war;
But down they stooped until they kissed the shore,
And one by one I looked them in the face,—
A tear and smile in each one I could trace.
They were all thieves and robbers, their foes said.
They never took from us a loaf of bread.
I heard them utter nothing but this cry:
"We have come to die, for our dear land to die."
They were three hundred; they were young and strong,
   And they are dead!

With his blue eyes and with his golden hair
There was a youth that marched before them there,

And I made bold and took him by the hand,
And "Whither goest thou, captain of this band?"
He looked at me and said: "Oh, sister mine,
I 'm going to die for this dear land of thine."
I felt my bosom tremble through and through;
I could not say, "May the Lord help you!"
They were three hundred; they were young and strong,
    And they are dead!

I did forget to glean afield that day,
But after them I wandered on their way.
And twice I saw them fall on the gendarmes,
And both times saw them take away their arms,
But when they came to the Certosa's wall
There rose a sound of horns and drums, and all
Amidst the smoke and shot and darting flame
More than a thousand foemen fell on them.
They were three hundred; they were young and strong,
    And they are dead!

They were three hundred and they would not fly;
They seemed three thousand and they chose to die.
They chose to die with each his sword in hand.
Before them ran their blood upon the land;
I prayed for them while I could see them fight,
But all at once I swooned and lost the sight;
I saw no more with them that captain fair,
With his blue eyes and with his golden hair.
They were three hundred; they were young and strong,
    And they are dead.

CONCLUSION

LITTLE remains to be said in general of poetry whose character and tendency are so single. It is, in a measure, rarely, if ever, known to other literatures, a patriotic expression and aspiration. Under whatever mask or disguise, it hides the same longing for freedom, the same impulse toward unity, toward nationality, toward Italy. It is both voice and force.

It helped incalculably in the accomplishment of what all Italians desired, and, like other things which fulfill their function, it died with the need that created it. No one now writes political poetry in Italy; no one writes poetry at all with so much power as to make himself felt in men's vital hopes and fears. Carducci seems an agnostic flowering of the old romantic stalk; and for the rest, the Italians write realistic novels, as the French do, the Russians, the Spaniards — as every people do who have any literary life in them. In Italy, as elsewhere, realism is the ultimation of romanticism.

Whether poetry will rise again is a question there as it is everywhere else, and there is a good deal of idle prophesying about it. In the mean time it is certain that it shares the universal decay.

Compendio della Storia della Letteratura Italiana. Di Paolo Emiliano-Giudici. Firenze: Poligrafia Italiana, 1851.
Della Letteratura Italiana. Esempj e Giudizi, esposti da Cesare Cantù. A Complemento della sua Storia degli Italiani. Torino: Presso l'Unione Tipografico-Editrice, 1860.
Storia della Letteratura Italiana. Di Francesco de Sanctis. Napoli: Antonio Morano, Editore, 1879.
Saggi Critici. Di Francesco de Sanctis. Napoli: Antonio Morano, Librajo-Editore, 1869.
I Contemporanei Italiani. Galleria Nazionale del Secolo XIX. Torino: Dall'Unione Tipografico-Editrice, 1862.
L'Italie est-elle la Terre des Morts? Par Marc-Monnier. Paris: Hachette & Cie., 1860.
I Poeti Patriottici. Studii di Giuseppe Arnaud. Milano: 1862.
The Tuscan Poet Giuseppe Giusti and his Times. By Susan Horner. London: Macmillan & Co.. 1864.

ERRATA.

For "Rosetti," twice, p. 8, read *Rossetti*.
For "now are seen," line 3, p. 40, read *now is seen*.
For "thou mayst draw," line 20, p. 45, read *else to draw*.
For "Where is he?" line 2, p. 84, read *Where is he now?*
For "Doth not Venice," line 26, p. 148, read *And doth not Venice*.
For "Gonzago," line 15, p. 154, read *Gonzaga*.
Omit "the" in line 18, p. 159.
For "Gemm," line 21, p. 187, read *Gemme*.
Substitute a comma for a period at close of line 30, p. 193.
For "conversation," line 2, p. 200, read *conversion*.
For "aside," line 31, p. 233, read *wide*.
For "loaf," line 19, p. 359, read *leaf*.